THE
WORLDS
OF
Truman
Capote

WILLIAM L. NANCE

STEIN AND DAY/*Publishers*/New York

THE
WORLDS
OF
Truman
Capote

ACKNOWLEDGMENTS

Grateful acknowledgment is extended to Random House, Inc. for use of quotations from the volumes of Truman Capote. Copyright 1945 through © 1960 by Truman Capote.

From *Writers at Work: The Paris Review Interviews, First Series* Copyright © 1956, 1958 by The Paris Review, Inc. Reprinted by permission of The Viking Press, Inc. and Martin Secker & Warburg Ltd.

Passages from "*In Cold Blood* . . . An American Tragedy" are used by permission of Newsweek, Incorporated. Copyright © 1966 by Newsweek, Incorporated.

Passages from "How the 'Smart Rascal' Brought It Off" by Jane Howard are used by permission of *Life*. Copyright © 1966 by *Life*.

Passages from *The Landscape of Nightmare: Studies in the Contemporary American Novel* are used by permission of New York University Press and Peter Owen Ltd., Copyight © 1965 by Jonathan Baumbach.

Passages from "The Author" in *Saturday Review*, January 22, 1966 are used by permission of Haskel Frankel and Saturday Review, Inc. Copyright © 1966 Saturday Review, Inc.

Of the many people who have helped me with this book, I wish in particular to thank Professor Alan W. Friedman, Mr. William Drier, Mrs. Myrna Ford, and especially, my father, Mr. William L. Nance, Jr. I am grateful to the University of Texas at El Paso and the University of Texas at Austin for research grants which aided in the preparation of the manuscript.

—WLN

For Carolyn

CONTENTS

I.	Introductory	9
II.	The Dark Stories	16
III.	*Other Voices, Other Rooms*	40
IV.	The Later Stories	65
V.	*The Grass Harp*	88
VI.	*Breakfast at Tiffany's*	107
VII.	The Artistic Life	125
VIII.	Experiment in Kansas	155
IX.	*In Cold Blood*	186
X.	The Capote Paradox	
	1. Close-up	216
	2. Perspective	229
	Notes	240
	Index	251

Death is the mother of beauty, mystical,
Within whose burning bosom we devise
Our earthly mothers waiting, sleeplessly.

—Wallace Stevens
"Sunday Morning"

Whuen *In Cold Blood*, Truman Capote's "nonfiction novel," began appearing in the *New Yorker* late in 1965, the literary world did a double take. What did this clear-eyed, strong-muscled piece of reporting have to do with the surrealistic introversion of *Other Voices, Other Rooms* (1948), the precocious novel that first brought Capote wide attention—or, for that matter, with the delicate other-worldliness of *The Grass Harp* (1951) or the sophistication of *Breakfast at Tiffany's* (1958)? The Capote most of us remembered was the one who had appeared on the cover of his first novel: a young man of indeterminate age, with soft face and blond bangs, gazing out provocatively as he reclined on a period couch. Now here was this hawk-faced sleuth staring from the covers of the weekly magazines. What were we to make of it? That he had grown up seemed not quite an adequate explanation, though remarkable enough in view of the notorious inability of most American literary *Wunderkinder* to do so. There must be more to this Mr. Capote than had so far met the critical eye.

It was a desire to understand the Capote paradox that led me to undertake this study of his literary career. Having once begun, I was fortunate enough to be granted, in November 1966, a series of interviews with Mr. Capote; the result was another double take, this time my own. At first he seemed a bit vague, gentle in a grandmotherly way, and just generally improbable; almost at once, however, the impression began shifting to one of toughness, effortless intelligence, and—above all—genuine friendliness. As time went on and I read deeper into the available material on Capote (most of it in popular magazines,

9

since he has received surprisingly little attention from scholars and academic critics), I began to notice that almost every record of an encounter with him followed a pattern of which the following reaction of a Kansas man is typical: "We did feel pretty put off by Truman at first, with that funny little voice of his and the way he dressed and all, but after we'd talked to him only for an hour, we just got so we thoroughly enjoyed him." [1]

Among the more unlikely admirers of Capote is Norman Mailer, with whom he once appeared on an "Open End" television discussion. Janet Winn, reviewing the show in the *New Republic* for February 9, 1959, made the following observations:

At first one was somewhat put off by the appearance of both the men. Mr. Mailer, a tall, spare, rather handsome young man, affects a beard—the kind that they're wearing in Cuba these days. Mr. Capote's weird good looks are well enough known to readers of his book-jackets; his voice and inflections are, similarly, a little terrifying. Although one soon ceased to be conscious of any of these trifles, one may well have been struck, at some point or other, by the disparity between what the writers appeared to be and what in fact they *were*. Mr. Capote may *look* effete, but he is not: his mind is vigorous and extremely able. He speaks slowly, often stops to choose his words, and makes every word count. What he says invariably makes excellent sense. His sensibility also proved to be remarkable. He demolished Mr. Mailer's arguments at every turn, but he never "scored." He seemed always keenly aware, as few panelists ever are, that this was a social and public event, as well as a debate, and that accordingly he must see to it that Mr. Mailer not be made to feel uncomfortable or to look like a fool. [2]

A bizarre, somewhat repellent first impression followed by one of clear intelligence and social sensibility has been the impact made not only by Capote himself but also by the sequence of his writing up to the present. His early work, though admittedly skillful, was widely criticized as eccentric, narrowly personal, degenerate, "gothic." *The Grass Harp* was greeted by one relieved reviewer as at least "sunlit gothic," and *Breakfast at Tiffany's* was, most agreed, something else entirely. *In Cold Blood*, of course, was the biggest surprise of all.

Today, while many observers are not entirely pleased with the direction Capote's talents have taken, there are few who do not feel a new respect for him. The remarkable variety in his work, even before *In Cold Blood*, was pointed out by Mark Schorer in his brief but useful introduction to the *Selected Writings* (1963): "Among the surprising qualities of Truman Capote's mercurial talent and a quality that is made very plain by such a selection from the entire body of his work as this is its range, the variety of its development over the nearly twenty years in which the author has been publishing." [3]

It is one of my intentions in this study to show that the changes in Capote's career have not been casual but are the result of a strong and highly conscious effort at growth. From the start he wrote stories which were among the best of their narrow kind, but even then he was trying to make his fiction both a source and an expression of deeper understanding, broader sympathy, greater fidelity to the reality outside his private childhood world. So far has he moved in twenty-three years of publishing that one is tempted to identify at least two distinct Truman Capotes. There is, of course, only one: *In Cold Blood* retains deep traces of the earliest stories, and the intellectual toughness so evident in the nonfiction novel was really there all the time.

We are given a privileged glimpse of the very young Capote by the coincidence that one of his first friends was the novelist Harper Lee. He made her the basis for the character of Idabel Thompkins in *Other Voices, Other Rooms;* she later put him in her novel *To Kill a Mockingbird* as Dill, the strange, brilliant little boy who is "passed around from relative to relative." That novel's young heroine says of her friend, "Beautiful things floated around in his dreamy head. He could read two books to my one, but he preferred the magic of his own inventions. He could add and subtract faster than lightning, but he preferred his own twilight world, a world where babies slept, waiting to be gathered like morning lilies." [4] Miss Lee's thumbnail sketch is excellent, and emphasizes that doubleness in Capote's talents which has recently been astonishing his readers.

Some knowledge of Capote's early life is essential to an

understanding of his work, for that work, even through *In Cold Blood*, bears the clear marks of his childhood. It was, Capote has said, "the most insecure childhood I know of," and his early stories are psychological records of it.[5] His later efforts to see it in more mature perspective are suggested by a remark Holly Golightly makes, in *Breakfast at Tiffany's*, to the narrator who is Capote's counterpart: "But really, darling, you made such a tragedy out of *your* childhood I didn't feel I should compete." [6]

Capote was born Truman Streckfus Persons, on September 30, 1924, in the Touro Infirmary in New Orleans. When he was four years old, his parents were divorced; his mother later married a Spanish Cuban textile manufacturer named Joseph Garcia Capote. After his parents' separation he was raised mostly by elderly aunts and cousins. "I felt isolated from other people," he recalls. "I had few friends my own age—most of them were much older than I." [7] During most of the time until he was ten, he lived in Monroeville, Alabama, with four elderly un-married cousins, three women and one man. The strong attach-ment he formed to one of these women would later be recorded in his story "A Christmas Memory." His first close childhood friends of his own age were his neighbors during these years, Nelle Harper Lee and her brother Edwin. *To Kill a Mocking-bird* contains, Capote says, a very accurate record of this time, even to the episode of the mysterious recluse by whom the chil-dren were fascinated. *Other Voices, Other Rooms* is a dreamlike transmutation of some of the same experiences.

Capote could read before starting school, and he recalls that among his favorite books were the Hardy Boys and Rover Boys series. Not surprisingly, he says that the deepest early impression was made by Poe's tales and that he still remembers "The Tell-Tale Heart" almost verbatim. In a 1958 interview Capote added these notes on his reading:

So far as I consciously know, I've never been aware of direct literary influence, though several critics have informed me that my early works owe a debt to Faulkner and Welty and Mc-Cullers. Possibly. I'm a great admirer of all three; and Katherine Anne Porter, too. Though I don't think, when really examined, that they have much in common with each other, or me, except that we were all born in the South. Between thirteen and sixteen are the ideal if not the only ages for succumbing to Thomas Wolfe—he seemed to me a great genius then, and still does, though I can't read a line of it now. Just as other youthful flames have guttered: Poe, Dickens, Stevenson. I love them in memory, but find them unreadable. These are the enthusiasms that remain constant: Flaubert, Turgenev, Chekhov, Jane Austen, James, E. M. Forster, Maupassant, Rilke, Proust, Shaw, Willa Cather—oh the list is too long, so I'll end with James Agee, a beautiful writer whose death over two years ago was a real loss.[8]

Though there were no writers in his family or, according to Capote, even any readers to speak of, he began writing at the age of nine or ten and seems to have known almost immediately that he had found his vocation. As a partial explanation he suggests, "Growing up in some place like Monroeville, as it surely must have been in similar towns, produced a strange loneliness which added to sensibility, and seemed to increase creativity. In a way, I used up some of my loneliness by writing. The same thing has worked for a great many rural Southern community authors. The geographic isolation tends to sharpen talent." [9]

Capote's first recorded story, written while he was still living in Alabama, was a Monroeville *roman à clef* called "Old Mr. Busybody." He submitted it to a Mobile newspaper contest for schoolchildren, and the first installment was published. The whole town recognized the four characters, Capote recalls, and the resulting furor brought his publishing career to a temporary halt. He continued writing, however, entering a number of newspaper competitions. "I realized that I *wanted* to be a writer," he says. "But I wasn't sure I *would* be until I was fifteen or so. At that time I had immodestly started sending stories to magazines and literary quarterlies. Of course no writer ever forgets his first acceptance; but one fine day when I was seventeen, I had my first, second, and third, all in the same morning's mail. Oh, I'm here to tell you, dizzy with excitement is no mere phrase!" [10]

After leaving Alabama, Capote attended a number of private schools, including Trinity School and St. John's Academy in New York, and spent one year at Greenwich High School in Millbrook, Connecticut. (He also seems to have spent five

13

months, at the age of fifteen, tap-dancing on a Mississippi river-boat.) Capote disliked school and did poorly in his courses, including English. He says he played hooky at least twice a week and often ran away from home—once with an older girl who later became notorious as the Lonely Hearts Killer. Because many of his teachers considered him mentally subnormal, his parents sent him to a psychiatric clinic, where he was, much to his satisfaction, classified as a genius. An English teacher at Greenwich High School, Catherine Wood, is the first person Capote credits with having given him serious help and encouragement in writing. Under her direction he wrote stories and poems for the school paper, the *Green Witch*. He dedicated the 1966 edition of "A Christmas Memory" to her.

At the age of seventeen, Capote moved to New York, where for a time he supported himself by his hobby of painting on glass. Subsequently he went to work for the *New Yorker*, first as an accountant—until it was discovered that he could not add—then as a mail-room clerk, and eventually as a feature writer. He also wrote anecdotes for a digest magazine and read motion picture scripts for a film company. When his short story "Miriam" was published in *Mademoiselle* (it later appeared in the O. Henry Memorial Award volume for 1946), Capote was approached by several publishers. He signed a contract with Random House for a $1,500 advance and, having spent a year in New York, moved to New Orleans and began work on his first novel. With the publication of *Other Voices, Other Rooms* in 1948, followed the next year by *A Tree of Night and Other Stories*, Capote's career was firmly launched. The deliberate care with which he continued to build it will be one of the subjects of this book.

When Capote published *In Cold Blood* and became Literary Man of the Year, he was forty-two years old and stood a reasonably trim five feet, four inches tall. Much was made at the time, even by Capote himself, of his resemblance to Perry Smith, the murderer around whom he built the book—a likeness not only in physical appearance but also in some aspects of character and life history. This resemblance is another example of that paradoxical multiplicity of Capote's that so often provokes double-take reactions. (He has been called a "pocket Hercules," a "cherubic Peter Lorre.") It is also, in relation to his literary career, an extremely significant fact. It is a dramatic reminder that Capote has not only progressed through a steadily broadening, always refreshing variety of achievements; he has also returned full circle to his beginnings—if he ever left them.

The early fiction of Truman Capote is dominated by fear. It descends into a subconscious ruled by the darker archetypes, a childhood haunted by bogeymen, a world of blurred realities whose inhabitants are trapped in unendurable isolation. The stories set in this dark world include "A Tree of Night" (1943), "Miriam" (1944), "The Headless Hawk" (1946), "Shut a Final Door" (1947), and "Master Misery" (1948) (S).[1] Deep below the surface they are really one story, and they have one protagonist. This story will be continued, and its hero will achieve a peculiar liberation in Capote's first novel, *Other Voices, Other Rooms* (1948). The fear and sense of captivity that overshadow these stories result from the individual's inability to accept and respond properly to reality. On the social level this means inability to love other persons. More essentially, it means refusal to accept mysterious and frightening elements within the self, for the persons encountered by the protagonist are most properly viewed as projections of inner personae. One indication of the climate of the protagonist's inner world is the fact that nearly all of these persons are grotesques.

The stories are fundamentally psychic in orientation. In at least two cases—"Miriam" and "Shut a Final Door"—the line between realism and fantasy is definitely crossed: things happen that are literally impossible. Usually, however, the settings seem realistic; we are kept in a world that is conceivably real, though strange, and the effects are wrought through manipulations of the protagonist's consciousness. The characteristic style of the early work is intensely poetic, and the meaning of the stories rests heavily on intricate patterns of symbolism. The most prominent stylistic and symbolic motif in the fiction up to and including *Other Voices, Other Rooms* is that of descent into a state of intensified and distorted consciousness. This happens in each story, the differences being mostly in what might be termed focal length. Sometimes the setting remains normal and the character simply becomes sleepy or drunk, or has a dream. At other times the entire setting takes on dreamlike characteristics, often through weather imagery such as darkness or snow. In the most extreme cases the reader is pulled completely into the illusion by means of apparitions or mysterious voices presented as real. This scale of reader involvement is one of several ways of looking at the stories and not, incidentally, a simple measure of their total effectiveness: Capote handles his various effects always with considerable skill.

Perhaps the most obvious thing to be noted about Capote's early work is its highly personal quality. The stories take place in an inner world almost entirely devoid of social or political concern. Because of this subjective orientation, even the treatment of human relations has about it an air of isolation, of constriction. With this qualification in mind, one may go on to observe that love and the failure of love are of central concern in Capote's fiction. The meaning of love, as it emerges in the early work, would seem to be uncritical acceptance. In each story the protagonist is given an opportunity to accept someone and something strange and disturbing, to push back the frontier of darkness both in the surrounding world and in the soul. Not until Joel works his way through *Other Voices, Other Rooms* does one of them manage to do so. Their characteristic kind of failure appears in simplest form in the tendency to dismiss any challenging new presence as "crazy." Capote's impulse, from "A Tree of Night" to *In Cold Blood*, is to accept and understand the "abnormal" person; it has been, indeed, one of the main purposes of his writing to safeguard the unique individual's freedom from such slighting classifications as "abnormal."

"A Tree of Night," the earliest story included in Capote's *Selected Writings*, sets the pattern of the self-protective hero

17

who lives in fear because of a refusal to accept. Compared to some of the stories which follow, this one is relatively simple. The style is unobtrusive, the symbolic structure modest. Events stay within the bounds of credibility, and yet the reader is chillingly exposed to the grotesque both in the external world and in the semiconscious mind of the young heroine.

Nineteen-year-old Kay, returning to college from her uncle's funeral, is forced to sit in a train compartment opposite two other passengers: a gin-reeking dwarfish woman with a huge head, and a corpselike man. The woman persuades her to drink some gin and goes to get paper cups. Kay is left alone with the man, unable to take her eyes off him, repelled but fascinated, especially by his eyes "like a pair of clouded milky-blue marbles, thickly lashed and oddly beautiful" (S 6).

The movement of this story is Kay's descent into a half-world of subconscious childhood fears. Already begun when she entered the compartment, it accelerates as she waits drowsily for the woman's return. When the man unexpectedly strokes her cheek, she leans forward in confusion and gazes into his eyes. "Suddenly, from some spring of compassion, she felt for him a keen sense of pity; but also, and this she could not suppress, an overpowering disgust, an absolute loathing: something about him, an elusive quality she could not quite put a finger on, reminded her of—of what?" (S 7). When Kay tries to escape, the woman seizes her wrist and shows her a worn handbill describing her companion as "Lazarus, the Man Who Is Buried Alive." She explains that they do a traveling show featuring a mock burial.

The man begins playing obscenely with a peach-seed love charm, insisting that she buy it, and Kay finally runs from the compartment. When she steps out onto the black, freezing observation platform the immediate danger of sleep is removed but her mind begins to slip back toward a ghost-ridden childhood. The area, though new to her, is "strangely familiar." Unable to light a cigarette, she angrily tosses it away and begins "to whimper softly, like an irritable child" (S 14). She longs to go inside and sleep but knows that she is afraid to do so. Suddenly, compulsively, she kneels down and touches the red lantern that hangs in a corner, the one source of warmth and light. A "subtle zero sensation" warns her that the man is behind her, and she finally gathers courage to look up. Seeing his harmless face in the red light, she knows that what she fears is not him but

a memory, a childish memory of terrors that once, long ago, had hovered over her like haunted limbs on a tree of night. Aunts, cooks, strangers—each eager to spin a tale or teach a rhyme of spooks and death, omens, spirits, demons. And always there had been the unfailing threat of the wizard man: stay close to the house, child, else a wizard man'll snatch and eat you alive! He lived everywhere, the wizard man, and everywhere was danger. At night, in bed, hear him tapping at the window? Listen! (S 14–15)

Danger is still everywhere for Kay. Holding onto the railing and "inching upward," she returns from childhood and the deepest part of her mind only to accompany the man back into a coach "numb with sleep." She wants to cry out and waken the other passengers, but the fear of death is too strong: "What if they were not really *asleep?*" (S 15) Tears of frustration in her eyes, she agrees to buy the love charm, "if that's all—just all you want" (S 15). There is no answer, and Kay surrenders to sleep, watching the man's pale face "change form and recede before her like a moon-shaped rock sliding downward under a surface of water" (S 15–16). She is dimly aware when the woman steals her purse and pulls her raincoat "like a shroud above her head" (S 16).

Kay's immersion in the subconscious has not been cathartic. The wizard man she buried alive there as a child has finally come forth like Lazarus, but only to haunt her in an even more insistent shape. She has not eluded him any more than she will elude death. In fact, death seems already on her, short-circuiting her life, as the raincoat-shroud is pulled above her head. But Kay's failure is not simply her mortality. She is like a child living fearfully in the dark because, shutting her eyes against ghosts, she has shut out love and life.

Capote's next story, "Miriam," though its materials are different, follows a pattern essentially the same as that of "A Tree of Night." Like Kay, Mrs. H. T. Miller hides repressed fears beneath a fastidious exterior, the penetration of which provides the main action of the story. A sixty-one-year-old widow, she lives alone and unobtrusively in a modest but immaculate New York apartment. Her life is neither broad nor deep. Her interests are few, and she has almost no friends. Her activities are "seldom spontaneous" (S 17). Snow is falling lightly as she goes out for a movie one night, leaving a light burning because "she found nothing more disturbing than a sensation of darkness" (S 17). She moves along "oblivious as a mole burrowing a blind path," but outside the theater she is agitated by the sight of a little girl with long, silver-white hair. Miriam's intrusion into Mrs. Miller's life begins gently, with a request that she buy her ticket, since children are not admitted alone. On closer examination Mrs. Miller is struck by the girl's large eyes, "hazel, steady, lacking any childlike quality whatsoever" (S 19). As they talk, it emerges that Mrs. Miller's name, until now hidden beneath her late husband's initials, is also Miriam. Disturbed by the girl's coolly self-contained manner, she leaves her and goes in alone.

A week of snow follows, progressively shutting Mrs. Miller off from her familiar world. She loses count of the days. One evening, comfortably settled in bed with hot-water bottle and newspaper, her face masked with cold cream, she is roused by the persistent buzz of the doorbell. She notes that the clock says eleven, though she "was always asleep by ten." Indifferent to the lateness of the hour, Miriam gently forces her way into the apartment. Indifferent also to the season, she wears a white silk dress. The older woman, by now thoroughly frightened, tries to disarm this apparition by recourse to familiar categories: "Your mother must be insane to let a child like you wander around at all hours of the night—and in such ridiculous clothes. She must be out of her mind" (S 21). Miriam continues to study Mrs. Miller, "forcing their eyes to meet" (S 22). In the jewel box she finds a cameo brooch that was a gift from Mr. Miller and insists on having it. Suddenly Mrs. Miller is stunned by the realization that she is, in this "hushed snow-city," alone and helpless. The cameo, now on the girl's breast, emphasizes the identity of the two Miriams, "the blond profile like a trick reflection of its wearer" (S 23).

Miriam leaves and Mrs. Miller spends the next day in bed. When the next morning dawns with unseasonable brilliance, the bad dream seems to be over. Mrs. Miller straightens the apartment and then goes out shopping, this time spontaneously, having "no idea what she wanted or needed" (S 25.) Then, "as if by prearranged plan," she finds herself buying glazed cherries, almond cakes—everything for which Miriam has expressed a desire. Meanwhile the weather suddenly turns colder, clouds cover the sun "like blurred lenses" (S 26), and snow begins to fall. When, later that day, Miriam returns with the intention of staying, Mrs. Miller at first yields with "a curious passivity" (S 27), then begs her to go away, dissolves in tears, and finally runs out the door.

For the next few minutes the story seems to return to the everyday world. Mrs. Miller pounds frantically on the door of the apartment below, is courteously received by a young couple, and incoherently tells them about a little girl who won't go away, and who is about to do "something terrible" (S 28). The man investigates but finds no one, and his wife, "as if delivering a verdict," concludes, "Well, for cryinoutloud . . ." (S 29). Mrs. Miller climbs slowly back to her apartment and finds it as it was before Miriam entered, but also as empty and lifeless "as a funeral parlor" (S 29).

Having lost her bearings now completely, Mrs. Miller is sinking again, this time deeper than ever. "The room was losing shape; it was dark and getting darker and there was nothing to be done about it; she could not lift her hand to light a lamp" (S 29–30). Then, sitting passively, she begins once more to feel that it has all been only a bad dream. "Suddenly, closing her eyes, she felt an upward surge, like a diver emerging from some deeper, greener depth" (S 30). Feeling her mind waiting as though for a "revelation," she begins to reason that Miriam was just an illusion, and that nothing really matters anyway. For all she has lost to Miriam is "her identity," but now she is confident she has again found herself, Mrs. H. T. Miller (S 30). Comforting herself with these thoughts, she becomes aware of the harsh sound of a bureau drawer opening and closing, then the murmur of a silk dress "moving nearer and swelling in intensity till the walls trembled with the vibration and the room was caving under a wave of whispers" (S 30). She opens her eyes to the dull, direct stare of Miriam.

In a 1957 interview for the *Paris Review*, Capote, asked what he thought of his early stories, expressed qualified admiration for *Other Voices, Other Rooms* and added, "I like *The Grass Harp*, too, and several of my short stories, though not 'Miriam,' which is a good stunt but nothing more. No, I prefer 'Children on Their Birthdays' and 'Shut a Final Door,' and oh, some others, especially a story not too many people seemed to care for, 'Master Misery.' " [2]

Capote's judgment on "Miriam," though it tends to ignore the story's close thematic kinship with his others, seems reasonably just. Comparison with "A Tree of Night" can highlight some of the story's limitations. Both have the same underlying theme: subjection to fear because of a failure of acceptance. But while in the earlier story a few simple and believable events are made to evoke bottomless psychological depths, in "Miriam" the machinery becomes an end in itself. The story's haunting effect, which is undeniable, comes from skillful ghost-story manipulation of a too-solid embodiment of the subconscious as alter ego. Miriam reminds one of Poe's William Wilson and Dr. Jekyll's Mr. Hyde. Today's reader wants more subtlety than that.

In the two stories so far examined, the emphasis has fallen more heavily on failure to accept oneself than on failure to love other persons. Kay would not be expected to enter into a much closer relationship with her two traveling companions, and Mrs. Miller's visitor is less a person to be loved than a haunt and a symbol. Capote's next two stories, "The Headless Hawk" and "Shut a Final Door," deal more emphatically with love, and in this way represent at least a partial broadening of scope. Nevertheless there is an essential similarity among all these stories, perhaps most evident in the way they end. Like Kay and Mrs. Miller, Vincent and Walter wind up more conscious than ever that they are trapped.

"The Headless Hawk" begins with an epigraph that could as fittingly be applied to any of the early stories. It is from The Book of Job (24:13, 16–17):

They are of those that rebel against the light; they know not the ways thereof, nor abide in the paths thereof. In the dark they dig through houses, which they had marked for themselves in the daytime: they know not the light. For the morning is to them as the shadow of death: if one know them, they are in the terrors of the shadow of death (S 31).

The story records Vincent's affair with the enigmatic girl, "D.J." Like Mrs. Miller's encounter with Miriam, it is a descent into a dreamlike world of uncertainty, a nonliberating confrontation with subconscious fears. For Vincent this is not the first such experience but the culmination of a long series of failures at love. Corresponding to the extent of his experience is a degree of self-awareness far beyond that of Kay or Mrs. Miller. Vincent knows, as he proceeds through the affair, what its outcome will be. So, in a sense, does the reader, for the story employs a frame chronology in which the central action appears as a flashback. The opening section finds Vincent already nervously resigned to being constantly shadowed by an unnamed, elfin girl; then comes the story of their meeting and eventual breakup, and the brief closing section simply reaffirms the finality of the first part.

As the story opens, Vincent Waters is already down at the "deeper, greener depth" (S 30) from which Mrs. Miller mistakenly thought she was emerging just before Miriam's final appearance. As he closes the art gallery of which he is manager and starts home on a humid afternoon, he feels as though he moves "below the sea. Buses, cruising crosstown through Fifty-seventh Street, seemed like green-bellied fish, and faces loomed and rocked like wave-riding masks" (S 31). He sees the girl, ghostlike in a green transparent raincoat, and she follows him through the streets. Her eyes have a shocked look, "as though, having at one time witnessed a terrible incident, they'd locked wide open" (S 33). Vincent has been oppressed lately by a sense of unreality; voices these days seem to come to him "through layers of wool"

23

(S 32). Entering his basement apartment, he looks back to see the girl standing listlessly on the sidewalk. The rain, threatening all day, still holds back.

Part Two begins abruptly with their first meeting. On an idle winter morning at the gallery she quietly appears before him dressed "like a freak" in masculine odds and ends. She wants to sell a painting, and her few remarks hint that she painted it in an asylum. The institution was apparently presided over by a Mr. Destronelli, whom she mentions as if expecting Vincent to recognize the name. He shakes his head and, making a capsule survey of his life, wonders why eccentricity has such appeal for him. "It was the feeling he'd had as a child toward carnival freaks. And it was true that about those whom he'd loved there was always a little something wrong, broken. Strange, though, that this quality, having stimulated an attraction, should, in his case, regularly end it by destroying it" (S 36). Vincent overcomes "an intense longing to touch her head, finger the boyish hair" (S 36), as she unwraps the picture and places it before him.

A headless figure in a monklike robe reclined complacently on top a tacky vaudeville trunk; in one hand she held a fuming blue candle, in the other a miniature gold cage, and her severed head lay bleeding at her feet: it was the girl's, this head, but here her hair was long, very long, and a snowball kitten with crystal spitfire eyes playfully pawed, as it would a spool of yarn, the sprawling ends. The wings of a hawk, headless, scarlet-breasted, copper-clawed, curtained the background like a nightfall sky (S 36–37).

The picture is crudely done, but to Vincent it seems to reveal "a secret concerning himself" (S 37). He decides to buy it, but before he can write a check the phone rings and the girl vanishes, leaving only the address "D.J.—Y.W.C.A."

Vincent hangs the painting above his mantel and on sleepless nights talks to the hawk, telling it about his life, which he feels has been "without direction, and quite headless" (S 38), a long series of good beginnings and bad endings both in art and in love. He is, he feels, "a victim, born to be murdered, either by himself or another" (S 38). February and March pass but he is

24

unable to find the girl. He becomes more and more disturbed, and friends notice the change in him. On an April evening, wandering the streets slightly drunk, he finds her. At his approach she is terrified, but soon her head relaxes on his chest "like a child's" (S 41) and she agrees to go home with him.

Vincent has lighted his room with candles, and it appears to waver in their "delirious light" (S 41). He himself feels a "drugged drunk sensation" (S 42). On this occasion the girl seems to him more attractive, less abnormal. Unusually relaxed, she talks about her childhood, then about Mr. Destronelli— "Everybody knows him" (S 42). As Vincent embraces her he glances at a mirror where "uncertain light rippled their reflections" (S 43). He asks what "Mr. Whoozits" looks like, then notices that for the first time she is staring at the painting, studying a particular object, but "whether hawk or head he could not say" (S 43). Pressing closer to him, she replies, "Well, he looks like you, like me, like most anybody" (S 43). This rather intricate scene brings together several strands in the story. The initiation of their affair, it takes place in a setting of multiple distortion (Vincent's mind, the candlelit room, the mirror's wavering reflection). The girl sinks into her childhood and emerges with Mr. Destronelli, whom she identifies with both herself and Vincent, staring up at the painting as she speaks so that her words could as easily apply to the figures there, both hawk and human being. Vincent is entering not only into physical union with the girl but into a blurred identification with her, the hawk, and Destronelli. At the same time the latter two remain apart, hovering threateningly over the scene.

Next morning Vincent discovers that the girl has no sense of time and is preoccupied with a mysterious "he" who she thinks brought her here. Vincent declares his love, then remembers numerous others he has loved, female and male, all eccentric and all betrayed by him. But he tells her that there was only one, now dead, and "to his own ears this had a truthful ring" (S 45).

The affair continues for a month and ends on D.J.'s eighteenth birthday. Vincent has kept her a private experience, not mentioning her to any of his friends. He has given her money for clothes, but the things she has spent it on are, like the name

25

D.J., more masculine than feminine. She prepares for the birth-day party "with the messy skill of a six-year-old playing grownup" (S 46). Their celebration consists of dinner at the automat followed by a movie. Both are aware that they are nearing the end, and the impulse to separate comes from the girl as well as from Vincent. As they go to bed, she thanks him for the violets he has given her and adds, "It's a shame they have to die" (S 48).

Meanwhile Vincent has slipped into a dream that seems to compress his life, past and future, into a stagnant present. In an endless hall lit by chandeliers he sees a degenerate old man in a rocking chair. "Vincent recognizes Vincent. Go away, screams Vincent, the young and handsome, but Vincent, the old and horrid, creeps forward on all fours, and climbs spiderlike onto his back" (S 48). Thus laden, he is ashamed to find himself in a throng of elegantly dressed couples, all silent and motionless. Then he recognizes that many of them are similarly burdened, "saddled with malevolent semblances of themselves, outward embodiments of inner decay" (S 48). The host appears, bearing a massive headless hawk on his arm, and orders the guests to dance. Vincent's old lovers one after another glide into his arms, and he hears "a cracked, cruel imitation" (S 49) of his voice speak hypocritically to each. Then D.J. appears, bearing on her back a beautiful child.

"I am heavier than I look," says the child, and a terrible voice retorts, "But I am heaviest of all." The instant their hands meet he begins to feel the weight upon him diminish; the old Vincent is fading. His feet lift off the floor, he floats upward from her embrace. . . .

The host releases his hawk, sends it soaring. Vincent thinks, no matter, it is a blind thing, and the wicked are safe among the blind. But the hawk wheels above him, swoops down, claws foremost; at last he knows there is to be no freedom (S 49).

Beneath the Gothic stage props, the meaning of this dream is reasonably clear. In it, as in the story as a whole, Vincent is burdened with guilt and the expectation of death. With at least a potential sympathy the scope broadens to include others, many of them similarly burdened. The host, no doubt Vincent's image of Mr. Destronelli, carries the headless hawk, the two functioning as a unit like falcon and falconer. The waltz symbolizes the lack of direction in Vincent's life, always circling and changing partners, never progressing. But his affair with D.J. has given him a clearer understanding of himself. Previously he thought it "strange" that the defects in his lovers, after attracting him, destroyed the attraction. Now he blames his own want of love and is overwhelmed by his "wickedness." Presumably it is her complete innocence that drove the lesson home, for she bears on her back a child, the opposite of Vincent's degenerate old man. He has hoped that contact with her would free him, but soon learns that his fate is darker and more inescapable than he thought. For such as Vincent and the girl (and no other kind of person has yet appeared in Capote's fiction) there is no love and no freedom. The hawk that pursues her will get him, too.

The defeat Vincent has dreamed must still be painfully acted out. When he wakes at dawn and reaches out for the "mother-comfort" of the girl's presence, the bed is empty. He finds her in the yard, and as he approaches she whispers, "I saw him. He's here" (S 50). Desperate to free himself of his dreamed guilt, Vincent finds a pretext ready. He knocks her hand away and almost slaps her. " 'Him! Him! Him! What's the matter with you?—' he tried too late to prevent the word—'crazy?' There, the acknowledgment of something he'd known, but had not allowed his conscious mind to crystallize. And he thought: Why should this make a difference? A man cannot be held to account for those he loves" (S 50). It sounds like Mrs. Miller's self-deluded hope that she is rising from the depths and that "like everything else," her meeting with Miriam was "of no importance" (S 30). Vincent, however, has been here before and knows better.

Later in the day Vincent returns from the gallery, violently ill, to learn from the superintendent's wife that D.J. has attacked the gas man with her scissors, calling him "an Eyetalian name" (S 52). Hiding until D.J. goes out, he begins to pack her things. His fever increasing, he falls to the bed and into a surrealistic nightmare in which a butterfly appears and, to his horror, perches like a ribbon bow above the severed head in the painting. He finds the scissors and stabs them at the insect. It escapes and the blades dig into the canvas "like a ravening steel mouth, scraps of picture flaking the floor like cuttings of stiff hair" (S 54). Sitting in terror he recalls things D.J. has told him. In her fantasies Mr. Destronelli has taken many forms, among them those of " a hawk, a child, a butterfly" (S 54). He was in the asylum, and after she ran away she encountered him in other men who mistreated her. One of them was a tattooed Italian; another painted his toenails. She is certain that eventually "he" will murder her. This fantasy of the girl's corresponds to Vincent's dream and knits the story's symbolism into an even more complicated pattern. Its principal function is to emphasize her role as Vincent's alter ego. Like him, she is a traveler in circles and "a victim, born to be murdered," though her victimization has been on a much more concrete and rudimentary level than his. At the same time, Vincent sees even more clearly that as their life-patterns mesh, he is being cast in the role of her destroyer, Destronelli.

The final brief section of the story begins at the moment when D.J. follows Vincent home and stands on the walk outside his apartment. It is July, about two months after their separation. Since then Vincent has been wasted by pneumonia, and his constant haunting by the girl has resulted in a "paralysis of time and identity" (S 56). On this evening he goes out for supper just as the long-threatening rain is about to begin. There is a clap of thunder and, as she joins him in the "complex light" of a street lamp, the sky is like "a thunder-cracked mirror," and the rain falls between them "like a curtain of splintered glass" (S 57).

It can be only a partial justification of the complexity of this story to say that it enmeshes the reader as it does the characters. Capote once said, "All I want to do is to tell the story and sometimes it is best to choose a symbol." [3] For "The Headless Hawk," he chose too many symbols. It is the most complex and involuted of all his short stories, several of which tend toward excess in this respect. Only his first novel, *Other Voices, Other Rooms*, surpasses it in symbolic density, and it is interesting to note that as his career progressed, Capote has moved first to a simpler fictional technique and finally to the "nonfiction novel."

28

The symbolism in "The Headless Hawk," too heavy to be carried naturally by the action, is concentrated principally in three focal points which are themselves intricately and arbitrarily contrived: the painting, Vincent's dream, and the girl's rambling fantasies. All of it is intended to point up meanings already more or less explicit in the dramatic action. These meanings finally come down to one: Vincent himself is the headless hawk. He is both victim and victimizer, and he is directionless and alone. Through a balance brilliantly achieved, whatever else one must say about the story, the girl becomes both a living person and a projection, a delusion of the submerged consciousness (what Miriam is for Mrs. Miller and the wizard man for Kay). At the same time she is a profitless encounter, a test which Vincent fails by rejecting instead of loving. It is this aspect of his theme that Capote emphasizes in his next story.

Walter Ranny of "Shut a Final Door" is in many respects identical with Vincent; certainly the title of his story would fit Vincent's as well. The two stories differ mainly in perspective. Walter is viewed far more objectively than is Vincent, for the story's focus is less on the undulating consciousness than on the external world of persons, places, and events. In this respect it points toward Capote's later work—not the deeply submerged *Other Voices, Other Rooms*, but the later, more social short novels, *The Grass Harp* and *Breakfast at Tiffany's*. Essentially, though, "Shut a Final Door" is part of the dark fiction of fear, failure, and captivity.

The story opens on a sufficiently "social" note: "Walter, listen to me: if everyone dislikes you, works against you, don't believe they do so arbitrarily; you create these situations for yourself" (*S* 58). Anna's remark, for all its glib triteness, is the story of Walter's life. Too insecure for love or even friendship, he is a treacherous coward for whom the reader feels an immediate distaste, only partially removed as the story probes more deeply into his fears.

The conversational tone of the opening is appropriate, for the dominant motif in the story involves malicious and inescapable voices. That, and circles: "He said you said they said we said round and round. Round and round, like the paddle-bladed ceiling-fan wheeling above" (S 59).

The fan is in a drab side-street hotel in New Orleans, where Walter has come with "a feeling of having traveled to the end, the falling off" (S 59). He lies under the fan thinking that his life has been a circle. Trying to find the center, the explanation of it, he rejects as "crazy" Anna's opinion that it was his own doing; he prefers to blame his parents. Still looking for the center, he decides to begin with Irving, the first person he'd known in New York. Like "The Headless Hawk," this story begins at the end, jumps back to the beginning, then progresses to the end again, completing a circle that symbolizes the protagonist's life.

Irving, delicate and boyish, is friendly to Walter during his first lonesome days in New York. He has many friends and introduces Walter to all of them. Among them is Margaret, "more or less Irving's girl friend" (S 60), whom Walter steals, hurting Irving irreparably and establishing the pattern of betrayal that will characterize his own brief social climb. Soon he realizes that he has no friends and tries to analyze his trouble:

He was never certain whether he liked X or not. He needed X's love, but was incapable of loving. He could never be sincere with X, never tell him more than fifty percent of the truth. On the other hand, it was impossible for him to permit X these same imperfections: somewhere along the line Walter was sure he'd be betrayed. He was afraid of X, terrified (S 64).

Walter meets Rosa Cooper, a wealthy heiress, and begins spending most of his weekends at her Long Island home, making valuable contacts. Among these is Anna Stimson, a horsey fashion editor with a highly irregular past. Walter makes her his mother confessor because "there was nothing he could tell her of which she might legitimately disapprove" (S 66). He asks Anna if she loves him.

"Oh," said Anna, "when was anything ever what it seemed to be? Now it's a tadpole now it's a frog. . . . Flying around inside us is something called the Soul, and when you die you're never dead; yes, and when we're alive we're never alive. And so you want to know if I love you? Don't be dumb, Walter, we're not even friends. . . ." (S 66–67).

The theme of deceptiveness is already a familiar one, and will be exploited most fully in *Other Voices, Other Rooms*. Often quite effective when woven into the plot and atmosphere of the stories, it here sounds like shallow cynicism, neither well dramatized nor adequately "distanced" from the author. It is an indication of the way Capote loses power when he tries to philosophize.

When on the same day Walter is fired from his job and dropped by Rosa, he is suddenly flooded with vivid memories of boyhood trips with his father to Saratoga. He has just decided to go there when the telephone rings. It is a long-distance call from a town he doesn't know, and after some rattlings a strange, dry voice says, "Hello, Walter." He hears breathing as clearly as if the person were standing beside him, but when he asks who it is the only answer is, "Oh, you know me, Walter. You've known me a long time" (S 70).

On the train Walter has a dream in which he sees coming toward him a funeral-like procession of cars bearings many of his past and present acquaintances. Feeling naked, he hails the first limousine and sees his father open the door. "Daddy, he yelled, running forward, and the door slammed shut, mashing off his fingers, and his father, with a great belly-laugh, leaned out the window to toss an enormous wreath of roses" (S 71). Walter's problem is basically the same as Vincent's and this dream is reminiscent of his. Both dramatize a fear which is ultimately of death, though Walter's is couched in simpler, more clinical terms: he is a child rejected by his father.

D.J.'s counterpart in this story is the woman Walter finds looking at him when he wakes from this dream. She is a cripple with her left foot encased in a giant shoe. He helps her with her luggage, but it is only that evening, in a hotel bar, that they become acquainted. She explains that she is there because her doctor is going to lecture to a medical convention about her case. Like Walter, she is afraid. She tells him she is a domestic and

31

takes care of a boy named Ronnie: "I'm better to him than his mother, and he loves me more" (S 73). Walter finds her depressing but is too afraid of loneliness to leave her. When the bar closes, the woman asks him, blushing, if he wants to go to her room. He goes, but, seeing her coming out of the bathroom, reeking with dime-store perfume and wearing only "a sleazy flesh-colored kimono and the monstrous black shoe" (S 73), he realizes that he can "never go through with it. And he'd never felt so sorry for himself: not even Anna Stimson would ever have forgiven him this" (S 73–74). When she is ready he comes to the edge of the bed, kisses her cheek, and says, "I think you're so very sweet, but . . ." (S 74). Then the telephone rings.

Walter's search for a mother, as well as his father, is made explicit and becomes one of the principal themes of the closing section. When the phone rings, the woman answers, mistakes "Ranny" for "Ronnie," and is frightened that something has happened to the boy. Then she gets the name correct and begins to hang up, but Walter seizes the phone. The message is the same as before, and after hearing it Walter falls across the woman, crying and begging, "Hold me, please" (S 74). She calls him "Poor little boy," and he goes to sleep in her arms (S 74). The next day he takes the train for New Orleans, "a town of strangers, and a long way off" (S 75). As he lies sweltering in the hotel room, now back at the moment at which the story began, the telephone rings. "So he pushed his face into the pillow, covered his ears with his hands, and thought: think of nothing things, think of wind" (S 75).

Walter's fixation is powerfully, if somewhat crudely, conveyed by the telephone calls, which could have no "natural" explanation. Like Miriam, the bodiless voice is a projection of subconscious fears, and it has the same kind of artificiality that she does. Essentially, of course, they are both related to the more subtle wizard and headless hawk.

The next and final "dark" story, "Master Misery," recalls most strongly the first, "A Tree of Night." The heroines of both are young women, and their fear contains a strong sexual element. More than any of the other stories, "Master Misery" is heavy with suggestions of sleep, dreams, childhood, and the unconscious; and while it differs from "Miriam" and "Shut a Final Door" in containing nothing that is not literally possible, it is perhaps the most bizarre story of all. It is the one that Capote said he liked especially, though hardly anyone else seemed to.

Sylvia is one of a class familiar in American fiction: the young girl from the midwest come to work in New York. She is also a wandering spirit, confirmed in restlessness and unconventionality because she "wants more than is coming to her" (S 109). She is close kin to D.J. of "The Headless Hawk" and also to later heroines, among them Holly Golightly. As the story opens, Sylvia is returning to the apartment she shares with Henry and Estelle, an "excruciatingly married" couple from her Ohio hometown. The day has been unusual, for in a restaurant she overheard a man talking about someone who buys dreams. His companion found this "too crazy" (S 101) for him and left the address lying on the table, where Sylvia later picked it up. Estelle says it is too crazy for her, too, and asks incredulously if Sylvia really went to see "this nut" (S 101).

Though she denies it, Sylvia did; unable to get the idea out of her mind, she had gone to the man, whose name was A. F. Revercomb, and sold a dream for five dollars. He had been pleased with it and asked her to return. Unsettled by the experience, Sylvia speculated that he was mad, but finally left the question open. On the way home she walked through the park and was badly frightened by two boys who began following her. Going to bed at the end of this fateful day, Sylvia feels "a sense of loss, as though she's been the victim of some real or even moral theft, as though, in fact, the boys encountered in the park had snatched (abruptly she switched on the light) her purse" (S 101). She dreams of "cold man-arms" encircling her, and Mr. Revercomb's lips brushing her ear. The day's experiences, especially the selling of her dream, have blended in one overwhelming fear of violation.

A week later she again finds herself near Mr. Revercomb's house. It is the Christmas season, an especially lonely time, and

33

she is drawn to a window display in which a mechanical Santa Claus slaps his stomach and laughs. The figure seems evil to her, and with a shudder she turns away.

Later, as she dozes in Revercomb's waiting room, the quiet is broken by a loud commotion and a "tub-shaped, brick-colored little man" (*S* 104) pushes his way into the parlor, roaring drunkenly, "Oreilly is a gentleman, Oreilly waits his turn" (*S* 104). He is quickly thrown out; when Sylvia emerges a short while later, she sees him, looking "like a lonely city child" (*S* 104) and bouncing a rubber ball. She smiles, for he seems a harmless clown. Oreilly admits that he has made a fool of himself but also accuses Revercomb: "I didn't have an awful lot to begin with, but then he took it every bit, and now I've got *niente*, kid, *niente*" (*S* 105). As to his present occupation he explains, "I watch the sky. There I am with my suitcase traveling through the blue. It's where you travel when you've got no place else to go" (*S* 105). He asks Sylvia for a dollar for whiskey, but she has only seventy cents, for, confronting "the graying invisibility of Mr. Revercomb (impeccable, exact as a scale, surrounded in a cologne of clinical odors; flat gray eyes planted like seed in the anonymity of his face and sealed within steel-dull lenses)" (*S* 106), she had not been able to remember a dream.

She tells Oreilly that she will probably not go back, but he says, "You will. Look at me, even I go back, and he has long since finished with me, Master Misery" (*S* 106). Starting off in the rain, they approach the Santa Claus display and Oreilly, standing with his back to the figure, says,

"I call him Master Misery on account of that's who he is. . . . Only maybe you call him something else; anyway, he is the same fellow, and you must've known him. All mothers tell their kids about him: he lives in hollows of trees, he comes down chimneys late at night, he lurks in graveyards and you can hear his step in the attic. The sonofabitch, he is a thief and a threat; he will take everything you have and end by leaving you nothing, not even a dream. Boo!" he shouted, and laughed louder than Santa Claus. "Now do you know who he is?"

Sylvia nodded. "I know who he is" (*S* 106–107).

In an artificial juxtaposition similar to those in "The Headless Hawk," Oreilly speaks of Revercomb while standing in front of the Santa Claus, emphasizing the growing identification of these two figures and giving the first clear hint that he himself will assume a destructive role toward Sylvia, much as Vincent did toward D.J. In this scene the rain provides the customary atmosphere of distortion and blurred identities.

Sylvia, now living both specifically and generally in a world of dreams, has begun to lose her grip on the world of everyday reality. She has moved to a cheap furnished room and let it become filthy. Fired from her job, she has lived for a month on the income from her dreams. Estelle visits her, scolds her, and insists on knowing whether the decline is because of a man. Sylvia, amused, admits that it is.

"You should have come to me before," Estelle sighed. "I know about men. That is nothing for you to be ashamed of. A man can have a way with a woman that kind of makes her forget everything else. If Henry wasn't the fine upstanding potential lawyer that he is, why, I would still love him, and do things for him that before I knew what it was like to be with a man would have seemed shocking and horrible. But honey, this fellow you're mixed up with, he's taking advantage of you" (S 108–109).

Estelle is the first of Capote's characters to be ridiculed in this way, but she will not be the last. Though satirized here as an embodiment of society's fatuous gentility, she also speaks with its prosaic rightness. Sylvia is, indeed, getting mixed up with a man who will take advantage of her—not only Mr. Revercomb, but that grey eminence's more immediate representative, Oreilly.

Sylvia answers, also more truly than she knows, that the affair she is involved in hasn't "anything to do with love" (S 109). She rejects the suggestion of marriage and reminds Estelle that they're "not children any more; at least, I'm not" (S 110), but her actions when finally left alone seem intended to belie the assertion. First she sucks a piece of sugar, her grandmother's remedy for bad temper, then she pulls from under the bed a musical cigar box made for her by her brother when she was fourteen. The tune it plays is "Oh, How I Hate to Get Up in the Morning." Inside this box of childhood memories she keeps the little book in which she has begun recording her dreams, since they are "endless" now and hard to remember.

Later, hurrying to Mr. Revercomb's she finds the mechanical Santa Claus has been replaced by the equally disturbing display of a plaster girl riding madly on a bicycle that gets nowhere. But Mr. Revercomb likes her dream about the "three blind children" (S 110), and she leaves with an envelope containing ten dollars.

In one of Sylvia's conversations with Oreilly, Master Misery, already linked with the maniacal Santa Claus, is explicitly probed down to his final meaning, death. Oreilly tells her that their vicious circle of dream-selling is "just like life" (S 112), but she disagrees: "It hasn't anything to do with life. It has more to do with being dead. I feel as though everything were being taken from me, as though some thief were stealing me down to the bone" (S 112).

When Oreilly is arrested for stealing a bottle of liquor, Sylvia collapses. For days she lies in her room, hardly eating, drugged with sleep. On the radio she hears a weather report reminiscent of Joyce's "The Dead": "A snowstorm moving across Colorado, across the West, falling upon all the small towns, yellowing every light, filling every footfall, falling now and here" (S 114). Discovering that snow has smothered the city, she opens the window to feed the birds and forgets to close it; snow blows into the room. "Snow-quiet, sleep-silent, . . . Mr. Revercomb, why do you wait upon the threshold? Ah, do come inside, it is so cold out there" (S 115).

The figure she dimly sees at the door just before losing consciousness is not Revercomb's but Oreilly's, and when she wakes he is holding her in his arms and singing, *"cherryberry, moneyberry, happyberry pie, but the best old pie is a loveberry pie . . ."* (S 115). When she asks why he isn't in jail he says he was never there, then quickly changes the subject. With "a sudden feeling of floating" (S 115) she asks how long he has been with her, and he replies that she let him in yesterday—then quickly begins the "wicked" story of how he escaped from the police.

Oreilly stays with her over the weekend, and it is like a beautiful party. They laugh and dance and she feels loved and declares that she will never be afraid again. She decides that she would like to get her dreams back and go home. "And that is a terrible decision, for it would mean giving up most of my other dreams" (S 117). He insists that she go directly to Revercomb with the request; she does, and soon is back in his arms crying, choking, then laughing hysterically. "He said—I couldn't have them back because—because he'd used them all up" (S 118).

As if on a signal, they separate, Sylvia giving Oreilly her last five dollars to buy whiskey for his travels in the blue. Then she starts toward home.

I do not know what I want, and perhaps I shall never know, but my only wish from every star will always be another star; and truly I am not afraid, she thought. Two boys came out of a bar and stared at her; in some park some long time ago she'd seen two boys and they might be the same. Truly I am not afraid, she thought, hearing their snowy footsteps following after her: and anyway, there was nothing left to steal (S 119).

This closing line is delicately ambiguous. Possibly a continuation of Sylvia's thoughts, it is also the last of several hints that her virginity has been lost to Oreilly. This suggested sexual theft is, of course, only a metaphor for the author's real concern: the theft of Sylvia's dreams by Mr. Revercomb. She dreams of Mr. Revercomb as a father-lover, and in her delirium his role is transferred to Oreilly. Sylvia is victimized in much the same way as D.J. was, and both their stories have as a major theme the sad fact that victims who try to be lovers are doomed not only to see themselves reflected in one another but also to advance each other's destruction.

While Capote may be granted his fondness for this story, it is nevertheless weak in several respects. Like "The Headless Hawk," though to a lesser degree, it is a network of meanings too often artificially represented by symbols and only half realized in concrete dramatization. Oreilly in particular is difficult to see as a human being, and the identification of him with Sylvia,

Revercomb, Santa Claus, and the cycling girl is too obviously contrived, as is much of the action.

The principal weakness of the story, however, is at its center, the business of selling dreams. "Dreams" can mean and half-mean many things, and the story contains a vagueness which is less suggestive than confusing. It might, for example, be read with some validity as an attack on psychoanalysis or on the scientific mentality in general—or perhaps an expression of a young writer's fear of exploitation.

While the implications of the story are vague, its overall pattern is clear, and even clearer when it is compared to the stories that preceded it. Like them, it traces the decline into captivity of an individual made vulnerable by refusal or inability to accept reality. But though the pattern is a familiar one, there is a significant change of emphasis: for the first time the victim-heroine is viewed with definite approval. While Capote's early stories are characterized, from a moral standpoint, by a fluctuating and sometimes almost nonexistent narrative point of view, all the earlier protagonists have to some extent been *held responsible*. Even in Kay there was a trace of the victimizer as well as the victim. But Sylvia completely escapes responsibility. She does so by being a childlike, innocent dreamer. The dreamer (almost always feminine), who made her first appearance in D.J. and here becomes the central character of the story, will be the typical protagonist of the stories that follow *Other Voices, Other Rooms*. Because the dreamer is unconventional, whatever moral disapproval enters these stories is reserved for the society from which she deviates.

"Master Misery" completes the first phase of Truman Capote's career as a writer of fiction, the dominant characteristics of which should by now be evident. The protagonist, while varying and developing in ways already discussed, is always and essentially a victim. The central action of each story is not so much his movement into the state of captivity as an immersion in his own deeper being that culminates in a shattering and final revelation of his plight. In each case the dark force that haunts the protagonist is projected outward—through characters of varying degrees of credibility, through images of dream or delirium, through concrete symbols—until it may be said to constitute the very framework and texture of the story.

But in each case it is also focused in one particular manifestation or set of related ones: a wizard man in a tree of night; Miriam; Mr. Destronelli and a headless hawk; a disembodied telephone voice; Mr. Revercomb-Master Misery. That these figures dominate the stories is pointed up by the fact that in every case but one they appear in the title. And Capote's custom of so naming his stories is to continue. It has been noted that the next phase of his career is marked by a new emphasis on the dreamer. The titles of several of the stories express or are related to the dreamer's dream or ideal: "Children on Their Birthdays" and *Breakfast at Tiffany's*, for example. One can see, then, in the very titles of the stories, a progression from fear to fantasy, from captivity to some kind of wistful freedom. Movement from captivity to freedom is also the theme of Capote's next, and longest, piece of fiction—*Other Voices, Other Rooms*.

Truman Capote first achieved wide popularity and critical acclaim in 1948 with the publication of his first novel, *Other Voices, Other Rooms*. It was hailed, and rightly, as a remarkable achievement for an author only twenty-four years old. It is Capote's longest work of fiction to date and was, until *In Cold Blood*, his longest book. In relation to the stories that preceded it, it is in some respects a return to an earlier stage of experience. While the stories are set mostly in the northern locale to which Capote had moved in his late teens, they show an increasing tendency to see experience in terms of mother-figures and father-figures.

Capote has recently said that in his fiction up to the time of *In Cold Blood* he seemed to be stuck about ten years back in terms of the psychic experience he could encompass artistically.[1] In *Other Voices, Other Rooms*, he seems for the first time to have acknowledged his growing awareness of this fact by returning to his earlier years for the material of the novel. To escape from the closed, neurotic world the stories represent, he would have to come to terms with his childhood.

Biographical data seem to support this view. After moving to New York at the age of seventeen and remaining there for a year, writing short stories and working for the *New Yorker*, Capote returned to New Orleans, took an apartment at 811 Royal Street, and started a novel. After finishing three-fourths of this first attempt he destroyed it, then moved to "a remote rural farm in Alabama" and started *Other Voices, Other Rooms*, which, he says, is "made of all sorts of things from my childhood." [2] Here for the first time we find the Southern setting and the young boy whom we think of as *the* Capote character. This boy will appear at an even earlier age in that deeper return to childhood, "A Christmas Memory," but the main line of development which begins here will be continued in *The Grass Harp* and *Breakfast at Tiffany's*.

In the closing line of *Other Voices, Other Rooms*, its young hero turns to look back, symbolically, "at the boy he had left behind" (OV 127).[3] The novel is an account of Joel's growth from childhood to maturity. He achieves this growth by learning, with the help of a series of lessons and ordeals, to accept wholeheartedly—that is, to love—the life that awaits him, however disappointing and mysterious it may seem. He finds and accepts "his proper place" and in so doing gains the freedom that goes with the achievement of a sense of identity.

Described in these general terms, the novel might seem to depict the initiation of any young man into full stature in his society, but it does not. It might be better described as an initiation out of society; for in *Other Voices, Other Rooms*, as in the stories that preceded it, the world the hero is asked to accept is a world whose norm is abnormality. It is a world that begins where daylight merges into shadow—a refuge from society for the maimed in body and spirit. Though unconventional in this sense, it is nevertheless a place of trial where one achieves freedom by understanding and acceptance. Joel does what his older counterparts failed to do: he outfaces the monsters of his childhood, sees them in truer perspective and with proper detachment, and exposes them for what they are.

As the story opens, Joel Harrison Knox, aged thirteen, is on his way from New Orleans to Skully's Landing, just outside Noon City, a small town somewhere in the deep South, to find his father. He does not know his father, for his parents were divorced when he was very young. His mother, whose surname he bears, has recently died, and Joel has been living uneasily with his Aunt Ellen and her family. His father's name is Edward R. Sansom, and it is a quaintly worded letter bearing this name and expressing a desire to "again assume my parental duties" (OV 7) that has brought Joel on this journey. A delicate boy with large brown eyes of a "girlish tenderness" (OV 6), he is entering a strange and somewhat forbidding world; and, as the name Noon City suggests, he and the reader are entering a complex network of symbolism. One of the principal symbolic patterns in the novel, as in the earlier stories, is that of a descent into a world of partial and distorted consciousness in which images from the subconscious have free play and external objects take on portentous meanings. Noon City is isolated and to be reached only by way of "swamplike hollows" where "luminous green logs . . . shine under the dark marsh water like drowned corpses" (OV 5). The letter speaks of a beautiful home and a cultured atmosphere, but Joel's questions about his father and the Landing elicit vaguely disturbing reactions and practically no information.

Joel had not been very surprised at the arrival of his father's letter, for he had been leading a vivid fantasy life which featured the eventual appearance of some beneficent figure patterned in part on "Mr. Mystery, the vaudeville hypnotist, and Lucky Rogers, the movie star" (OV 35). These fantasy figures usually appeared against the backdrop of "a hushed frozen white wasteland" (OV 35) of snow (something Joel dreams of seeing in real life), and snow was also associated in his mind with the death of his mother. With a parallel ambivalence, Joel's hope of rescue by a father-figure is mixed with fear of the unknown. The father who dominates Joel's thoughts at the beginning of the story usually takes an appealing form but sometimes a threatening one; above all he is mysterious.

He is also, it should now be clear, identical with the figure who loomed over the dark stories. In them he lacked almost completely the benign qualities; he was the father as bogeyman. Only as Mr. Revercomb (Reverend-Coxcomb) did he begin to display some of the ambivalence he now assumes. Most important, he was overwhelming, never reduced to a tolerable perspective. No matter how fully understood, he always retained enough dark power to keep his child-victim frozen in fear. His real place of residence was the individual's mind, and in each story he confronted that individual at the bottom of a descent into the subconscious. Furthermore—and this is a clue to his status as a psychological symbol and to the possible manner of his exorcism—he appeared always in conjunction with a person or situation that called for acceptance, an acceptance which the individual was never able to give. Of Joel he will also demand acceptance.

Joel arrives at Noon City "crazy with questions he wanted answered" (OV 12), but learns little except that at the Landing there is also a cousin who seems to be "a private joke too secret for sharing" (OV 12). As he enters the dusty main street he notices a rough, boyish, red-haired girl of about his own age prancing up and down. She is Idabel Thompkins. He hears an irate woman call her a "freak" and declare that she "oughta be in the penitentiary" (OV 15). The opinion seems to be shared by the entire town, including Idabel's parents and her "sweet" sister Florabel.

At dusk Joel finds the wagon which has been sent for him, driven by Jesus Fever, an ancient Negro. Moving slowly through the dark, they are joined by Idabel and her sister. Idabel refuses to ride and regards Joel with a hostile stare. Later he notices that she has dropped back and is running like a "pale animal" (OV 23) through the dark. A cloud comes over the moon and the girls leave, inviting Joel to visit them. Soon he is asleep. When they arrive, Joel is "scowling at a dream demon" (OV 25). It is as if his visit to the Landing were to be itself a dream.

The first person Joel meets at the Landing is Miss Amy, his father's second wife, a small, fussy, simpering woman with "the vague suggestion of a mustache fuzzing her upper lip" (OV 28). She speaks with constant reference to someone named Randolph, who is apparently the genius of the place. The house itself— musty, and lit only by lamps and candles—seems to have died years ago. Amy tells Joel that Randolph was born in the bed he has just slept in and that Randolph's mother, a Memphis belle named Angela Lee, died there. From the window he sees a garden which will play an important part in the story, and which casts its spell over the Landing and the entire book. Lying "under a fiery surface of sun waves," it is "a jumbled wreckage of zebrawood and lilac, elephant-ear plant and weeping willow. . . . Massive chinaberry and waterbay formed a rigidly enclosing wall." At the far end, "like a set of fingers, a row of five white fluted columns lent the garden the primitive, haunted look of a lost ruin" (OV 29–30). The pillars are the relics of a mysterious fire that struck one December when Amy was a child, and the garden is the space once occupied by the burned portion of the house. Joel notes there are four doors opening on the upstairs hall and wonders which one might belong to his father. He asks Amy about his father but she does not answer.

In the front entrance chamber there is a tall mirror "like the comedy mirrors in carnival houses; he swayed shapelessly in its distorted depth" (OV 31). This is the first of many references to mirrors, their principal function being to reflect the gradual change in Joel's image of his own identity. A moment after passing this one, sitting alone in the kitchen, he is suddenly taken with the terrible thought that his father might be watching him even now, deciding that "that runt is an imposter; my son would be taller and stronger and handsomer and smarter-looking. Suppose he'd told Miss Amy: give the little faker something to eat and send him on his way. And dear sweet Lord, where would he go?" (OV 32).

The second person Joel meets at the Landing is Missouri Fever, called Zoo, the Negro maid-of-all-work and the granddaughter of Jesus Fever. To some extent a figure familiar from the work of such Southern writers as Carson McCullers and Harper Lee, she is also, like everyone at the Landing—and like most Capote characters—a grotesque. Tall and graceful, "slant-eyed, and darker than the charred stove," she boasts a neck so long as to make her "almost a freak, a human giraffe" (OV 33). The bandana around her neck hides a hideous scar left by the razor of Keg Brown, now on the chain gang because he cut her throat shortly after marrying her at the age of fourteen. The kitchen becomes Joel's only refuge during his first days at the Landing, and Zoo to some extent his confidante. She provides a refreshing center of relative naturalness and common sense in the midst of strangeness. For Joel she is a mother-replacement but also a part of his ordeal, furnishing him one more opportunity for acceptance or rejection, mature or childish response. Almost the first thing Zoo says to him is, "We countin' on you, young fella" (OV 32).

Drawn again to the garden, Joel can hardly raise his eyes, for the sky is "pure blue fire" (OV 39). He discovers an old bell,

44

mildewed green and with a small green lizard hidden inside it. Next he glances up at the windows, wondering which belongs to his father and which to Randolph. It is at this point that he sees "the queer lady":

She was holding aside the curtains of the left corner window, and smiling and nodding at him, as if in greeting or approval; but she was no one Joel had ever known: the hazy substance of her face, the suffused marshmallow features, brought to mind his own vaporish reflection in the wavy chamber mirror. And her white hair was like the wig of a character from history: a towering pale pompadour with fat dribbling curls (OV 40).

Joel is entranced, but when the curtain falls closed he instinctively takes a backward step, stumbling against the bell, whose raucous note signals his retreat.

This scene climaxes the first stage of the novel and completes Joel's introduction to Skully's Landing. It haunts his progress through the rest of the story, and will be echoed and completed by the book's closing scene. As his recollection of the mirror image suggests, this vision in the window is intimately related to the question of Joel's own identity.

For the moment he feels "without identity" (OV 42), certain, like Walter Ranny, that he has "locked the door and thrown away the key: there was a conspiracy abroad, even his father had a grudge against him, even God" (OV 42). He is capable of the beginnings of sympathy for Zoo, wondering if "she was like him, and the world had a grudge against her, too" (OV 43), but his dominant feeling is fear. Still, he has left the door open slightly, praying, at Zoo's private prayer meeting, "God let me be loved" (OV 44).

By suppertime Joel has met Randolph, who is older than he expected and skillful at putting a young boy at ease. Made bold by the sherry which his host languidly pours for him, Joel mentions the lady in the window. Randolph suggests that she was a hallucination caused by the heat. Joel is puzzled by Randolph's face, which seems composed of nothing but circles: "though not

45

fat, it was round as a coin, smooth and hairless; two discs of rough pink colored his cheeks, and his nose had a broken look, as if once punched by a strong angry fist; curly, very blond, his fine hair fell in childish yellow ringlets across his forehead, and his wide-set, womanly eyes were like sky-blue marbles" (OV 46). His conversation, too, is strange, like a tale in some foreign language that excludes the boy.

Randolph revives the subject of the lady in the window, this time with amusement, seeming "to have advance knowledge of the facts" (OV 48). Amy's reaction is even more revealing. When Joel describes the apparition, she starts to speak, but Randolph gives her foot a sharp kick and, when she wails hysterically, slaps her across the mouth.

Joel's inclination is to run; unable to, he mentally elaborates on his vision of the lady, beginning to associate her with one of his personal bogeys—the Snow Queen in whose palace little boys' hearts are turned to ice (OV 10). More afraid, he tries to make use of a familiar escape mechanism, one which has become increasingly difficult in recent months. Gazing at the window, he tries to find his "far-away room" and at last succeeds. In it are Mr. Mystery and another frequent visitor, who "came in various costumes and disguises, sometimes as a circus strong-man, sometimes as a big swell millionaire, but always his name was Edward R. Sansom" (OV 49).

Joel is shaken out of this reverie when Randolph moves closer to him on the loveseat and takes his hand. "A charming boy, little Joel, dear Joel," he whispers. "Try to be happy here, try a little to like me, will you?" (OV 50). Like the Snow Queen in the window, Randolph is beckoning. This time Joel reacts differently. Hesitant at first, he looks into Randolph's eyes only to see "his own boy-face focused as in double camera lenses" (OV 50). Deciding the plea is "in earnest," he responds, "I like you already" (OV 51). Much about Randolph is obscure to Joel, but the boy does understand sincerity and need love. In responding to this offer of affection, he makes his first important step toward acceptance of his new surroundings. Another point here is significant: when Joel saw the lady in the window, the hazy quality of her face "brought to mind his own vaporish reflection in the wavy chamber mirror" (OV 40); now he sees himself in Randolph's eyes, linking all these visions and reflections together.

Hardly has Joel passed one test when an even stranger one presents itself. The conversation is suddenly interrupted by a queer sound, and into the room, which seems to the inebriated Joel to have "a bent tilted look," a red tennis ball comes bouncing. Amy rushes out, and Randolph is nervously evasive; Joel does not know how to react. Feeling cheated at not being allowed to see his father, he asks to know at least whether the lady in the window was "real." Randolph answers, "A matter of viewpoint, I suppose. I know her fairly well, and to me she is a ghost" (OV 52).

Joel can only retreat from so much mystery, and the next morning he writes a desperate letter to his Aunt Ellen asking her to rescue him from the Landing and send him to military school. Cheered by this progress, he next decides to visit Idabel and Florabel. Stopping at the mailbox, he finds Zoo talking to Little Sunshine, the hermit. Sunshine is a friend of Randolph's, and Joel has heard them drinking and carousing together far into the night. He observes that the old man "had a blue cataract on one eye, hardly a tooth in his head, and smelled bad" (OV 55), yet Zoo says he has "more purentee sense 'n most anybody" (OV 55) and that if she had sense enough she would marry him. Joel decides he is not afraid of Little Sunshine "even though he was a kind of hermit, and everybody knows hermits are evil crazy folks" (OV 55).

Once again he has managed to accept the strange and unpleasant rather than reject it as "crazy," as Capote's earlier protagonists were wont to do. His acceptance of Little Sunshine will pay rich dividends later. At present Joel only asks him for a protective charm of the kind he had just given Zoo. Sunshine says he must come and get it, adding that "the devilman" (OV 57) will guide his feet past Drownin Pond to the Cloud Hotel.

He explains that the place was once an exclusive resort until a boy of Joel's age dived into Cloud Lake and crushed his head between two sunken logs. This 1893 tragedy led to the decline of the resort and the suicide of its owner, Mrs. Cloud. Other drownings are rumored, but none of the bodies was ever found. The lake turned an "evil color," the chimneys "sank low in the swampy earth" (OV 58), and the hotel decayed. Little Sunshine, the stable boy, who had often lain awake at night listening to "the furry blend of voices" (OV 57), stayed on because it was his "rightful home," and "if he went away, as he had once upon a time, other voices, other rooms, voices lost and clouded, strummed his dreams" (OV 58).

This story of Little Sunshine's contains one of Joel's most important lessons, and its point will gradually be driven home through the rest of the story. For Joel, as for Little Sunshine, home is a decayed and forbidding place, but it must be accepted, even if it should prove to be presided over by the devilman. The "other voices, other rooms" of Little Sunshine's dreams and of the novel's title refer, then, to one's "rightful home," one's fate, one's identity.

Moving outward from the shadowy world of the Landing and the Cloud Hotel, Joel encounters Idabel Thompkins. Himself something of a misfit, he is fascinated by her unconventionality; she in turn, according to her sister, has a crush on him. His second encounter with her, however, is discouraging. Repelled by the violence she displays in a quarrel with Florabel, and offended when she calls him "sissy-britches" (OV 62), he concludes that, like every other tomboy, she is just "gut-mean" (OV 63). Turning dejectedly back toward the Landing, he notices the mailbox and feels renewed hope of getting back to a place where "everybody was like everybody else" (OV 63). It is too early for the mailman, but when Joel peeks into the box, his letter is gone.

Part two, the second half of the novel, finds Joel that evening, after a bowl haircut from Zoo, watching his face in the darkened window "reflected transparently, changed and mingled with moth-moving lamp yellow; he saw himself, and through himself, and beyond" (OV 65). Several things are suggested here. First of all, some change is beginning to register in Joel's appearance. Also, where formerly he saw only a shapeless face, he now has a vision of self and beyond self, into the future and the alien, dark though it is. The use of a window for a mirror continues the series of reflection-vision images which link together Joel, Randolph, and the mysterious lady. In a manner corresponding to the changes in his mirror image, Joel is undergoing an inner change. At the beginning his theme was simply "Let me be loved." Now, after a momentary tiff with Zoo, he urges, "I love you because you've got to love me because you've got to" (OV 66).

Randolph tells Joel that the house is sinking at the rate of four inches a year, and the boy elaborates this bit of information into a long reverie.

It was drowning in the earth, this house, and they, all of them, were submerging with it; Joel . . . imagined moles tracing silver tunnels down eclipsed halls. . . . Go away, he said, for his imagination was too tricky and terrible. But was it possible for a whole house to disappear? . . . That was what had happened to his father. . . . He took steps slowly, awake but dreaming, and in the dream he saw the Cloud Hotel . . . this was the place folks came when they went off the face of the earth, when they died but were not dead. . . . He walked in the dark . . . listening for a name, his own, but even here no father claimed him. The shadow of a grand piano spotted the vaulted ceiling like a luna moth wing, and at the keyboard, her eyes soaked white with moonlight, her wig of cold white curls askew, sat the Lady (OV 66–67).

This meditation, which occurs at the middle of the book, just before Joel's first meeting with his father, is a capsule summary of the story on both dramatic and symbolic levels. Like the novel as a whole, it records Joel's halting but continued progress from the attitude of frightened rejection—"Go away!"—to one of sensitive, questioning openness to revelation. The passage moves through a series of variations on the theme of disappearance, suggesting that as Joel moves toward his new life, much of the old has to die. (In a few moments he will meet Edward Sansom and learn that the ideal father is gone, never to be recovered.) His thoughts next lead him, as events later will, to the Cloud Hotel, which is a more remote, dreamlike symbolic version of Skully's Landing and has already drowned into the earth. Looking for his father and his own identity in this place of decay, he finds only the mysterious snow lady and further mystery. With a precision that can be fully appreciated only later, this passage summarizes the novel, yet preserves the note of uncertainty that characterizes Joel at his present stage of awareness.

Joel's meditation is interrupted by the red tennis ball bouncing down the stairs into the mirrored chamber and striking his knee. Randolph, apparently drunk, emerges from an upper room and tells him to bring a glass of water. Joel stands a long while unable to move, listening to the "voices in the walls" (OV 68)— the sounds of the drowning house. When he finally enters the bedroom he feels like an intruder, yet is unable to withdraw. On a table near the bed stands a "milk-glass nude suspending a tiny silver mirror" (OV 68). Reflected in this mirror he sees a pair of eyes and instantly forgets everything else. A "teary grey," they watch him dumbly.

Informed that the invalid in the bed is Mr. Sansom, Joel protests that they never told him. Randolph leaps up, his kimono swinging out and revealing "pink substantial thighs, hairless legs" (OV 69), then stoops drunkenly down to Joel's size and whispers, "Tell you what, baby?" (OV 69). The eyes appear in the glass again, and "a hand trimmed with wedding gold" (OV 69) drops a red ball. It is "like a cue, a challenge, and Joel, ignoring Randolph, went briskly forward to meet it" (OV 69).

At last he has found his father, but it is almost as if he had not. This man can do little more than demand loyalty and love. But Joel, loyal by nature and learning how to love, meets the challenge. While this is a big step forward, it should be kept in mind that the situation confronting him here is at least relatively clear-cut in its demands. Significantly, the much more complex challenge presented by Randolph is for the moment set aside.

That Joel's acceptance still has its limits is made clear by the next scene. Having already sent a second letter to Ellen, he goes fishing with Idabel. One reason he accepts this invitation is to avoid the new chore of reading to his father, who is paralyzed and can speak only a few words ("boy, why, kind, bad, ball, ship"). He communicates almost exclusively with his eyes, which, "like windows in summer, were seldom shut, always open and staring, even in sleep" (OV 70). Now Joel frees himself of this burden, but only to feel like the "captive" (OV 71) of Idabel as she leads him through the woods. Their partial reversal of masculine and feminine roles is one instance of a rather general confusion of sexes in *Other Voices, Other Rooms*. Confusion of sexes, while an important element in itself, is part of the larger theme of deceptiveness which Capote first enunciated explicitly in "Shut a Final Door," but which has been present throughout his work up to this time, especially in the imagery of submersion which has appeared in each story. Distortion and uncertainty mark the worlds into which all of his protagonists have penetrated, and Joel will go deepest of all.

When Joel tells Idabel that his life at the Landing is like a bad dream, she advises him to wake up. But, herself something of a dreamer, she also lends him her toy colored glasses to wear. She won them at the "travelin-show" (OV 72) and wears them constantly. Joel would like some, too, he thinks, as the "white face of afternoon" takes shape overhead. For "his enemy . . . was there, just behind those glasslike, smokelike clouds; whoever, whatever this enemy was, his was the face imaged there brightly blank" (OV 73). Again the window-mirror pattern is enlarged, this time to include the sun, now hidden behind "glasslike" clouds. A series which began with Joel's seeing just his own blurred identity in a wavering mirror now reaches, in a sense, its full symbolic extension. The mysterious figure which has dominated his life now hangs gigantically over him. And now, after finding that the heroic father-image he has been pursuing will never be fulfilled, he begins to think of this obscure figure as "the enemy." The father is being displaced by the wizard man.

When Joel recounts one of Zoo's stories, Idabel dismisses it in a familiar way: "Oh, shoot! Everybody knows Zoo's crazy for true" (OV 73). Here Idabel illustrates the fluidity of Capote's thematic patterns, for she is using against Zoo the very weapon that is used against her by Noon City society. In dismissing Zoo as one who "sees things," she is also, of course, rejecting Joel. Now he in turn reacts in the same way, thinking, "What a mean liar she was. Zoo was not crazy. She was not" (OV 74). It seems

51

to be one guarantee of Joel's salvation that he tends habitually to side with the less conventional, the less "normal." To add to the confusion, Idabel shocks him by suggesting, with casual innocence, that they strip and bathe. When he points out that she's a girl, she counters, "Son, what you've got in your britches is no news to me, and no concern of mine: hell, I've fooled around with nobody but boys since first grade. I never think like I'm a girl; you've got to remember that, or we can't never be friends" (OV 74).

Later, as they lie on the grass in easy friendliness, Joel wishes he could tell her of his affection; but when he delicately kisses her cheek she explodes in fury. They wrestle, Joel now filled with a "puzzled rage" (OV 76), and the glasses break and cut his buttocks. "Idabel was astride him, and her strong hands locked his wrists to the ground. She brought her red, angry face close to his: 'Give up?'" (OV 76). Joel can only say, "I'm bleeding."

Neither of them understands why they fought, and soon it seems as if nothing had happened. But this bitter love-making has had its effect on Joel. More clearly than before he sees that Idabel is no way out for him—and, by extension, that no woman is. Some of the anxiety that this episode sets up in him will be removed by a later encounter with sexual love, but other effects will remain, pushing him more and more toward a feminine role. While Joel is still being formed, Idabel is already confirmed in her identity, and the present experience simply manifests it. The dark glasses which symbolize her efforts to adapt to the flaw in her nature have, in wounding Joel, also revealed their pathetic inadequacy. He is sorry for her, and the experience leaves them still friends, sadly resigned to the way things are.

Joel returns to the Landing, where he presently is admitted for the first time to Randolph's room. Crowded with bizarre ornament, it is, Randolph tells him, a "gaudy grave" in which he lies "dead drunk and curled, as in my mother's womb, in the warm blood of darkness" (OV 77–78). Joel is posing for a portrait, for Randolph is a painter. Not surprisingly, he tells Joel that his work suffers from a tendency toward distortion. Completely closed off from the reality around him, Randolph himself seems unreal. In the mirror he sees not a consistent self but "whatever personality imagination desired him to resemble (OV 78). Each of us, he tells Joel, is entirely isolated, each a Narcissus seeking his identity in mirrors and finding only there "the one beautiful comrade, the only inseparable love" (OV 78).

While these words link Randolph to Joel as a searcher-in-mirrors, they do more to show the difference between the two. Randolph is resigned to existence at the far extreme of narcissistic womb-life, a point from which Joel has been steadily moving away during the course of the story. Yet it is the novel's central paradox that this movement is carrying him closer to Randolph.

One of the items in the room is a snapshot of three men and a girl. Joel recognizes one of the men as a younger Randolph, and one seems vaguely to resemble his father. With the picture as a starting point, Randolph tells him the long and fantastic story of his acquaintance with Edward Sansom and the events that led Joel himself to the Landing. Randolph had once lived with the girl in the photo, but she had fallen in love with a prizefighter named Pepe Alvarez, whose manager was Ed Sansom. Randolph soon realized that his jealousy derived from a love of Pepe rather than of the girl. In defense of this he tells Joel that "any love is natural and beautiful that lies within a person's nature: only hypocrites would hold a man responsible for what he loves" (OV 82). The four lived together like "grotesque quadruplets" and attended a Mardi Gras ball to which Randolph wore the costume of a silver-haired French countess. Later, Pepe and the girl ran away and Randolph, by mistake, shot Sansom. Lying delirious, Sansom called for his wife and Joel, so Randolph took him to the Landing, acquired Amy as Sansom's nurse-wife, and sent for his son.

This narrative is an important stage of Joel's development, for it shows him clearly how tenuous is his connection with Randolph and the Landing—how little, in any ordinary sense, he owes them. Whatever commitment he makes to them will not be of an ordinary kind.

Zoo's dream has always been to go north and see snow, and

with the death of Jesus Fever she departs. One by one Joel's props seem to be falling away. Now he is ready to imitate Zoo's flight, and he soon gets a chance. Reading to his father a few days later, he hears Idabel's whistle below in the garden and hurries out the door with Sansom's judgment hissing in his ears: "Bad, boy bad bad!" (OV 95). Idabel seems unsure of herself, and for once he feels stronger than she. She has finally run away from her "old bastard daddy," an escape that seems more successful than Joel's, for even as they talk he feels Sansom's eyes watching him. The "travelin-show" is in town, and Idabel suggests that they first stop there, then run off together and "just walk around outside till we come on a nice place" (OV 97). Joel assumes this includes marriage, but she insists they must live like "brothers." He has never picked up the charm he asked Little Sunshine for, so he proposes that they go first to the Cloud Hotel.

They reach a creek that has to be crossed on a wooden beam, and Joel insists on going first, carrying Jesus Fever's old sword, which Zoo has given him. Half way across he begins to feel that he will never reach the other side, will always be balanced here "suspended between land, and in the dark, and alone" (OV 100). This feeling of suspended movement, which corresponds to his present position in life, is intensified in the next instant by the sight of a thick cottonmouth piled at the far end of the beam. Idabel, peering over his shoulder, breathes, "Jesus, oh Jesus" (OV 100). Joel wonders, "How did Mr. Sansom's eyes come to be in a moccasin's head?" (OV 199), and freezes in a whirling vision of the Cloud Hotel, Randolph, Jesus Fever, Zoo, snow, and Mr. Sansom's eyes—each in some way a facet of death. Idabel unceremoniously spins him around, takes his sword, and thrusts at the snake jeering, "Big grand-daddy bastard" (OV 100). As the snake strikes she swings the sword blindly, killing it. She urges Joel on across, but he refuses, for "what use could there be now in finding Little Sunshine? His danger had already been, and he did not need a charm" (OV 100).

Another of the novel's symbolic focal points, this episode again demonstrates to Joel that both masculinity and Idabel are for him dead-end streets. When the time comes he will visit the Cloud Hotel, but it will be in the company of Randolph. The snake that bars his way now is one more embodiment of the father as bogeyman—in Idabel's words, "Big granddaddy bastard." She, already certain of the enemy and of herself, is capable of action; Joel, on the other hand, is not yet ready. So far he understands only that his immersion in the element that can either save or destroy him has already taken place.

Joel's escape with Idabel, frustrated in one direction, will be interrupted only a short while before proceeding in another; he returns for a typically unpleasant supper with Amy and Randolph, but by prearrangement Idabel is waiting for him in the garden. During this intervening time he takes another important step. Sent to Randolph's room for a bottle of sherry, he there makes the climactic discovery that the letter which brought him to the landing, purportedly his father's, was really in Randolph's hand. At just that moment Mr. Sansom's door is blown open, and Joel sees his father's eyes and smile reflected in the bedside mirror. He enters and kneels by the bed, holding Sansom's hand to his cheek until there is "warmth between them." Then

he kissed the dry fingers, and the wedding ring whose gold had been meant to encircle them both. "I'm leaving, Father," he said, and it was, in a sense, the first time he'd acknowledged their blood; slowly he rose up and pressed his palms on either side of Mr. Sansom's face and brought their lips together: "My only father," he whispered, turning, and, descending the stairs, he said it again, but this time all to himself (OV 103).

In one action Joel finds his father, abandons him, and embarks on an attempted escape from the Landing.

The contradictions here are only apparent, and the scene once again drives home the fact that the novel's real meaning is a symbolic one. On this level one always finds his father only to leave him, aware at last that he is not the embodiment of all hopes and all fears. (The name seems to be a reversal of Samson, the strong man who became weak—and also to suggest "sun.") Joel here shows that he has come far enough to accept the fact of his father's mortality and to do so with love, thus fulfilling his debt to Edward Sansom. Joel's subsequent escape is not primarily from this man, who now has no terrors for him, but rather from the Landing and his fate—a fate from which, he now realizes, Edward Sansom cannot protect him. Joel is, in other words, still motivated mostly by fear. This fear is directed toward all the elements in his present world which remain unpleasant and mysterious to him, and it still finds its dominant symbol in the infantile image of the father as evil. Sansom's eyes still pursue him as he runs.

The exhilaration of escape is mixed, this time more than ever, with erotic excitement. Idabel has hung a rose awkwardly in her hair, and she tells him that only today has she really come to like him. Then another sound begins to blend with their own, and they almost stumble upon two Negroes making love in a clearing of the woods. They watch as the love-making moves to a climax and the spent lovers form "on the bloom of moss a black fallen star" (OV 104). The two children react quite differently to this revelation. Joel notices that it leaves Idabel looking "mean and angry and scared" (OV 104). He, on the other hand, is elated, knowing now that "it was not a giggle or a sudden white-hot word; only two people with each other in withness, and it was as though a tide had receded leaving him dry on a beach white as bone, and it was good at last to have come from so grey so cold a sea" (OV 104). Joel has passed another barrier, gaining more ground against fear.

Though they will stay together for a few more hours, this third and final failure has ended his relationship with Idabel. As he comes to understand more fully that love is essentially the joining of complementary units into a perfect whole, he realizes that his destined complement is not this girl. Because for a while she provided an escape from a more difficult acceptance, he accepted her. But, as with Edward Sansom, whom he has also finally accepted, the relationship reaches a necessary limit and can only end in pity.

At the traveling-show their favorite entertainer is the golden-haired Miss Wisteria, who looks like a little girl but claims to be twenty-five years old. Slowly it comes over Joel that Idabel is "in

56

love." First she, then he rides on the Ferris wheel with the blonde
midget, who tells Joel her pathetic story and then, looking down
at Idabel waiting below, says, "Poor child, is it that she believes
she is a freak too?" (OV 108). As she talks, her hand moves
as though independently up Joel's thigh and between his legs.
He is disturbed, but knows now that he does not want to hurt
anyone—neither Idabel nor Miss Wisteria—and he wishes he
could say, "It doesn't matter, I love you, I love your hand" (OV
108). He knows the world is a frightening place, full of change
and deception, but is coming to believe that there is an answer:
love, which "vanquishes the Snow Queen"; for "its presence finds
the name, be it Rumpelstiltskin or merely Joel Knox: that is
constant" (OV 108).

A rainstorm shorts out the carnival lights and Joel, looking
for Idabel, runs to an old "haunted" house. A large, wind-blown
poster enfolds and frightens him, but seeing that it blows away
the moment he stops struggling, he applies the lesson to Randolph (whose face he thinks he saw just before the lights went
out). He tells himself that there is nothing to fear in Randolph,
who is obviously "only a messenger for a pair of telescopic eyes"
(OV 109). Yet, still fearful that he cannot appease the nameless
"fury" Randolph represents, he goes on seeking Idabel in the
dark house, only to find Miss Wisteria trailing after him. He remains hidden but pities her, for he at least "owned a room, he
had a bed" (OV 110). He falls asleep wishing for his mother
and hearing the wind "opening doors, closing them" (OV 109).

Part Three, the final short section of the novel, finds Joel back
at the Landing seriously ill. The depth of his illness is represented by a long dream sequence in which he first finds himself
"guilty" and executes sentence with a bullet through the head
that causes only "a tickling" (OV 112). Next he is in his secret
hideaway room with Mr. Mystery, but suddenly he loses "his
powers to direct adventures" there (OV 112) and drops into the
parlor of the Landing. Present are all the people he has met or
even heard of in the course of the story, most in black formal
attire and all moving in procession, to the solemn music of a
pianola, around a flower-decked box in which lies Joel himself,

dressed in white, "his face powdered and rouged, his goldbrown hair arranged in damp ringlets" (OV 113). Each of them drops in an offering—"Idabel her dark glasses, . . . Mr. Sansom his tennis balls, Little Sunshine a magic charm, and so on" (OV 112). The room starts to vibrate and the house sinks "down into the earth, down down, past Indian tombs, past the deepest root, the coldest stream, down, down, into the furry arms of horned children whose bumblebee eyes withstand forests of flame" (OV 113).

Joel is now ready to abandon the juvenile escapism represented by the secret hideaway room. A new world has engulfed him, and he has gained enough strength by this time to accept it almost completely. Like similar dreams in "The Headless Hawk" and "Shut a Final Door," this one deals with death and surveys the life of the protagonist. It is also reminiscent of Joel's earlier meditation on disappearance, and it amplifies that earlier realization with a vivid description of the sinking not only of the house but of Joel's entire past. He sinks, too, in the spiritual death that traditionally precedes rebirth, taking with him mementos of all his acquaintances, symbolic of the various lessons he has learned from them.

Joel slowly regains consciousness to find himself under the motherly care of Randolph and content to stay that way indefinitely. Studying his face in a hand mirror, he is disappointed at the scant signs of emerging manhood, though he does note that "babyfat has given way to a true shape, the softness of his eyes had hardened: it was a face with a look of innocence but none of its charm, an alarming face, really, too shrewd for a child, too beautiful for a boy. It would be difficult to say how old he was" (OV 114–115). Joel now identifies with Randolph more closely than ever and feels that he understands him "absolutely" (OV 115). He would gladly be rid of the "old Joel" but "not quite yet, he somehow needed him still" (OV 114).

Joel's unreadiness to accept Randolph completely is evident when the latter proposes to dress up in a costume, insisting, "You mustn't laugh" (OV 115), and Joel can't help laughing. Still too fearful to declare his love, he reasons that loving Randolph would be problematical anyway, for what was he? "Faceted as

58

a fly's eye, being neither man nor woman, and one whose every identity cancelled the other, a grab-bag of disguises . . . X, an outline in which with crayon you color in the character, the ideal hero" (OV 117). Joel has come a long way in his understanding of Randolph, who, Capote here makes clear, is meant to function not primarily as a sexual deviate but as a generalized symbol of all humanity in its need for love—an ideal object for the complete, undiscriminating commitment of which Joel is now almost, but not quite, capable.

The idyllic time does finally end, for external reasons which are not immediately clear. One day Randolph, obviously disturbed, tells Joel that they have been invited to the Cloud Hotel. Joel now learns that Zoo is back, her attempted escape having failed as completely as his. After one day's walking she was stopped by three men and raped. Joel asks her if she saw snow and she tells him, "There ain't none. Hit's all a lotta foolery, snow and such: that sun! it's everywhere." "Like Mr. Sansom's eyes" (OV 118), thinks Joel.

Early one morning he and Randolph hastily depart for the Cloud Hotel, the latter wobbling helplessly on the old mule. At noon they stop for lunch and Joel "cuddles up" to watch an ant crawling into Randolph's ear. After a while he becomes aware of "silence, and the tense prolonged asking of Randolph's eyes," and feels himself "prickle mysteriously" (OV 121). When he explains about the ant Randolph's face sinks into "sugary folds of resignation" (OV 121). Joel, though he feels that he now understands Randolph's nature, does not yet know all its implications for himself.

Their slow trip through autumn woods toward the Cloud Hotel is a death-haunted journey into the past. The hermit is angry at first, obviously not expecting company, but then recognizes and welcomes them. Crossing the "waltz-waved" ballroom floor, they pass a fallen chandelier, a spider-webbed piano and a clock stopped forty years before. But the heart of the house contains a surprise: "Beyond the ballroom, and in what had once been Mrs. Cloud's private apartment, were two simply furnished spacious rooms, both beautifully clean, and this was where Little Sunshine lived: the evident pride he took in these quarters in-

59

creased the charm of their surprise, and when he closed the door he made nonexistent the ruin surrounding them" (OV 122). Joel's introduction into these beautiful rooms of Little Sunshine's is the climax of one of the novel's symbolic patterns and leads directly to the approaching final revelation. He is learning that by accepting his "proper place," even though it be in the midst of corruption, he can make it a private world of order and beauty. These rooms are the rooms of the novel's title, from which "other voices" call to the wanderer who has strayed.

While Randolph and Little Sunshine begin one of their whiskey-inspired conversations, Joel lies by the fire and soon sees there the "embryo" shape of a "painted, disembodied head." He searches for the features of his destined lover, yet fears, too, because "If he recognized the figure in the fire, then what ever would he find to take its place?" (OV 123). A violent clanging rouses Joel and the others, and they realize it is the mule dragging his spittoon-anchor up the stairs and across the upper floor. Little Sunshine goes after the animal with a flashlight; Randolph is too drunk to move, but Joel follows "bravely," advancing through a thicket of familiar Capote imagery: "Around the torch swooped white choirs of singing wings which made to leap and sway all within range of the furious light: humped greyhounds hurtled through the hall, their silent shadow-feet trampling flowerbeds of spiders, and in the lobby lizards loomed like dinosaurs; the coral-tongued cuckoo bird, forever stilled at three o'clock, spread wings hawk-like, falcon-fierce" (OV 124). The mule lunges from the balcony, but the expected crash doesn't come; when Joel opens his eyes, he sees it hanging by the twisted reins, its "lamplike eyes . . . golden with death's impossible face, the figure in the fire" (OV 124). The mad John Brown has died to free a slave, for Joel has finally found what he was both seeking and fleeing from. Advancing bravely beyond his last hesitation, he becomes worthy to see the vision of death.

In the morning they leave, and the day is like "a slate clean for any future" (OV 125). Joel, caught by a "crazy elation," runs and leaps and, "folding a turban of moss about his head," asks Randolph, "Look, who am I?" (OV 125). When no answer comes from Randolph, lurching along grim-mouthed and oblivious, Joel supplies it himself: "I am me. . . . I am Joel, we are the same people" (OV 125). He looks for a tree, intending to climb to the top and claim the world. When, halfway up, he looks down to see Randolph walking blindly in a circle, he is puzzled at first, then suddenly realizes the truth about his friend: "More paralyzed than Mr. Sansom, more child-like than Miss Wisteria, what else could he do, once outside and alone, but describe a circle, the zero of his nothingness?" (OV 125).

Joel leads Randolph home, and there he learns that the cause of his forced march to the Cloud Hotel was a visit from Aunt Ellen, made in response to his second letter. Following Randolph's directions, Amy has told her that Joel and his father were away on a hunting trip.

Quickly deciding he has no further need of Ellen, Joel turns to Zoo, only to find that she has disappeared through the hedge. Joel is left alone in the silent garden. Clouds come over the sun and he waits for them to pass, expecting some miracle such as his sudden translation back to New Orleans. The clouds become darker, become "John Brown and . . . the Cloud Hotel" (OV 127), and "when they were gone, Mr. Sansom was the sun" (OV 127).

Nothing has happened, but he feels that something will, so he waits while two hours pass. Deciding the moment has come, he raises his eyes to the Landing's windows, now gold with the mirrored October sunset. Beyond one of them someone is watching him, and it is Randolph's window.

Gradually the blinding sunset drained from the glass, darkened, and it was as if snow were falling there, flakes shaping snow-eyes, hair: a face trembled like a white beautiful moth, smiled. She beckoned to him, shining and silver, and he knew he must go: unafraid, not hesitating, he paused only at the garden's edge where, as though he'd forgotten something, he stopped and looked back at the bloomless, descending blue, at the boy he'd left behind (OV 127).

Earlier in the novel, during one of Joel's conversations with Idabel, there appeared this cryptic observation: "Now at thirteen Joel was nearer a knowledge of death than in any year to come: a flower was blooming inside him, and soon, when all tight leaves unfurled, when the noon of youth burned whitest, he would turn and look, as others had, for the opening of another door" (OV 71). Now he has finally come through, and he brings Kay and Walter and all the others with him. Standing in this sunken garden, he looks up not into a tree of night and the eyes of a wizard man, not into dark clouds that hide the face of "the enemy," but into a noonday sky and the face of his father. And, as he moves with full acceptance toward Randolph, he also seems to see in him the mother he had left behind in the ambivalent snow. He has looked into the face of death that hid behind his childhood fears and seen through it into the world of maturity, which, in a way he could never have imagined, is a fulfillment of his childhood dreams.

This closing scene of the novel is not only a culmination but also a summary. It opens at noon, and finds Joel still lonely and preoccupied with thoughts of a magical escape from Skully's Landing. Then come the clouds, ominous with remembered images of decay and death. Penetrating them, as he penetrated the Cloud Hotel, he sees the face in the fire—that face which, when one dares look at it directly, loses its threatening aspect. He has found his father just as he found Edward Sansom at the middle of the novel. But there is another aspect to his search: he must find his proper place and his identity: "Numb with apprehension" (OV 127), he must wait with complete openness for the final revelation.

While the first phase led Joel toward Sansom, the second leads him toward Randolph. All he is free or required to do is remain open to the impressions that come, and this he does. His acceptance of Randolph has been prepared for by all that went before, but particularly important are two lessons learned on the hectic night when he tried to escape. It was while riding on the Ferris wheel with Miss Wisteria that he realized that the one important thing is love, which alone can vanquish the Snow Queen. Earlier, seeing the two Negroes embracing in the woods, he had learned that the essence of love was "withness"; with Miss Wisteria he goes on to learn that the nature of the parts makes no difference so long as they join in a harmonious whole. For the world is, after all, just a blur of deception and change: not even the sexes are distinct or stable. Everything is "changing, changing, like the cars on the Ferris wheel," and "while the old man grows spinsterish, his wife assumes a mustache" (OV 108).

The other lesson of that night he learned from the flying poster: that only by ceasing to struggle against the enveloping darkness can one become free. Joel continues to hold back somewhat, but his thoughts on the carnival night had laid the theoretical foundation, and after the maturing experience at the Cloud Hotel and the vision in the noonday garden he is ready to accept Randolph actively and completely as the object of his love. And, as anticipated in a long series of symbols, in "seeing through" to this friend he also discovers himself.

Other Voices, Other Rooms is an almost unbelievably intricate novel—a fact not surprising if one has read the earlier stories, particularly "The Headless Hawk" and "Master Misery." In all of them, the symbolic patterns lead toward an ultimate complex oneness, an overlapping and merging of symbols. *Other Voices, Other Rooms* in particular might be compared to a closed sphere of interwoven endless circles, or even of one endless strand. The novel's question is: Who is Joel? His answer—"I am me. . . . I am Joel, we are the same people"—completes a circle. Furthermore, his "we" includes almost everyone and everything in the book. His identity is his father, whom he came to find, but also Randolph, whom he found. His father is the sun, and also Little Sunshine, who is also the Cloud Hotel and Drownin Pond and the sinking Landing. The Landing is Skully's, or death's, and so is the snake, which is also Mr. Sansom, as well as Idabel's father and Zoo's grandfather and all fathers. And so on. It is a remarkable achievement, if somewhat like a maze with no exit. This maze entangles the reader in a poetic experience which has the irrational power of childhood itself: it must be grown out of, but, like childhood, it continues to haunt the memory. Capote was completely right when he remarked of the book, eight years after finishing it, "Despite awkwardness, it has an amazing intensity, a real voltage." [4]

Viewed as a liberation, the story is markedly ambivalent. Its explicit meaning is that Joel has broken out of his childhood prison and achieved maturity, yet the way in which he does it, and the symbolic pattern surrounding the action, suggest a narcissistic confinement. This contradiction is presumably intended to function as a vital paradox; still, one feels uneasily that Joel and Capote have not made quite as clean a break with childhood as they think, though they are moving in the right direction. In *In Cold Blood*, as we shall see, Capote attempts a somewhat comparable liberation; there, too, his success is something less than complete. In each case the intention is clear, however, the personal effort admirable, and the artistic achievement worthy of respect. That *Other Voices, Other Rooms* marks a significant change in Capote's writing will be evident when we turn to the stories that follow it.

• IV. THE LATER STORIES •

The year 1948 saw the publication not only of "Master Misery" and *Other Voices, Other Rooms*, but also of a story which seems at first glance to have little in common with them—"Children on Their Birthdays." If Capote's early stories are about captivity and *Other Voices, Other Rooms* is about liberation, the later stories—though some of their characters are quite literally imprisoned—have about them an air of limitless vistas. Among the other works of this later period are "A Diamond Guitar" (1950), "House of Flowers" (1951), "A Christmas Memory" (1956), and "Among the Paths to Eden" (1960) (S).[1]

The typical protagonist of these stories—as of the two longer works written during the same years, *The Grass Harp* and *Breakfast at Tiffany's*—is an unattached, unconventional wanderer, usually a girl or a childlike woman, whose life is a pursuit of some ideal of happiness. Holly Golightly's aim is to have breakfast at Tiffany's; Miss Lily Jane Bobbit from Memphis, Tennessee, puts it this way: "Not that I live here, not exactly. I think always about somewhere else, somewhere else where everything is dancing, like people dancing in the streets, and everything is pretty, like children on their birthdays" (S 86). Miss Bobbit and her counterparts are usually viewed through the eyes of a male narrator who regards them from a distance with a whimsical admiration that is sometimes very much like love.

This feeling is evident in the opening lines of "Children on Their Birthdays":

Yesterday afternoon the six-o'clock bus ran over Miss Bobbit. I'm not sure what there is to be said about it; after all, she was only ten years old, still I know no one of us in this town will forget her. For one thing, nothing she ever did was ordinary, not from the first time that we saw her, and that was a year ago (S 76).

The speaker of these words is a boy somewhat older than Miss Bobbit's ten years, and little more than that is known about him.

The opening lines of the story quickly establish its chronology, revealing that it will follow a circular pattern similar to those of "The Headless Hawk" and "Shut a Final Door." But those stories moved in circles to emphasize the constriction of the protagonist's world and the finality of his fate; because the element of narrative distance was vague or nonexistent, the reader felt enclosed with Vincent and Walter in their dark prisons. "Children On Their Birthdays," on the other hand, is a charmed circle enclosing a memory like a dream. For Miss Bobbit was not quite real, and the fact that the six-o'clock bus that brought her also takes her away somehow emphasizes this fact. Like Capote's later heroines, she is not so much a person as a charming experience that leaves a poignant memory.

Miss Bobbit arrives on a birthday—that of Billy Bob, the narrator's cousin—and most of the children in town are eating ice cream on his porch when the bus from Mobile swings around Deadman's Curve to deposit her and her gaunt, silent mother in the road. A wiry little girl in a yellow dress, she walks with a "grown-up mince" (S 76) and, like that other child-woman, Miss Wisteria, she inspires general astonishment. Resplendent with orange lipstick and penciled eyes, she combines the "skinny dignity" of a lady with a gaze of "manlike directness" (S 77). She asks directions in a carefully cultivated voice, declines an invitation to ice cream, and goes on her way. The girls immediately begin picking at their new rival, but the more mature thirteen-year-olds, Billy Bob and Preacher Star, watch the house across the street, where she is boarding, "with misty, ambitious faces" (S 79). After a while Miss Bobbit reappears in a skirt "like a powderpuff" (S 79), sets a victrola on the sundial in the yard and starts it playing. Seeming to contain her own illumination against the growing darkness, she begins to dance. And when the moon came rolling down the ridge, and the last supper bell had sounded, and all the children had gone home, and night iris was beginning to bloom, Miss Bobbit was still there in the dark turning like a top (S 79).

Miss Bobbit is not seen again for some time, but the land-lady spreads the news that her father, "the dearest daddy and the sweetest singing man in the whole of Tennessee" (S 80), is in the penitentiary; that her mother is a complete recluse; and that Miss Bobbit herself has been in bed for several days with a fever. That afternoon Aunt El discovers that her prize roses are missing, and "naturally" she gets "a little hysterical" (S 81). Learning that Billy Bob has taken them to Miss Bobbit, she gives him a severe whipping. Billy Bob, unregenerate, later confides to the young narrator, "She's . . . the cutest dickens I ever saw, gee, to hell with it, I don't care, I'd pick all the roses in China" (S 82).

When, one day, Preacher and Billy Bob torment a chubby little colored girl in front of Miss Bobbit's house, they find her coming at them like an angry school teacher. Wagging her finger and stamping her foot, she scolds, "A pretty pass, a fine situation when a lady can't walk safely in the public daylight" (S 83–84). She dusts off the girl and takes her up on the porch, and for the rest of the year she is seldom far from "this baby elephant" (S 84), whose name is Rosalba Cat. At first the landlady objects, but "Miss Bobbit had a certain magic, whatever she did she did it with completeness, and so directly, so solemnly, that there was nothing to do but accept it" (S 84). Even the trades-people in town call her "Miss Bobbit" and give her stiff little bows as she passes. Her claim that Rosalba is her sister causes jokes at first, but eventually even that begins to seem natural.

One Sunday, when the family is at church and the narrator is home alone, Miss Bobbit pays him a call. Sitting primly, she comments that she finds the odors of a church offensive, then hastens to explain her religious beliefs more fully. Far from being a "heathen," she believes in both God and the Devil, but she insists the way to "tame" the latter is not just to listen to sermons against him. "No, love the Devil like you love Jesus:

because he is a powerful man, and will do you a good turn if he knows you trust him" (S 85). Her way of disarming society's bogeyman seems to work, for the Devil has done her several favors in the past. At present she is calling on him to help her get out of this town, which she has chosen simply as a way-station on her journey to the place where "everything is pretty, like children on their birthdays." Miss Bobbit's philosophy is as unconventional as her behavior, and the narrator Mr. C. seems to regard both with complete approval.

The practical means she has chosen to get out of town is the sale of magazine subscriptions, and she has come to ask if he doesn't think Billy Bob and Preacher would be willing assistants. They are, of course, and wear themselves out helping her. So hard do they work, in fact, that Aunt El finally insists that Billy Bob quit. He protests violently and finally tries to kill himself, using what he has heard is a sure-fire formula: "a mess of collards all slopped over with molasses" (S 86).

Miss Bobbit is called to his bedside and, in her businesslike manner, does something "that shocked Aunt El very much" (S 87): stripping the covers off Billy Bob, she rubs him down from head to toe with alcohol. To his mother's objections she replies, "I don't know whether it's nice or not, but it's certainly very refreshing" (S 87). Her nursing is as shocking as her theology and equally successful, silencing criticism. It should be noted, incidentally, that in once more defying accepted standards she is also making light of sexual distinctions and mores much as Idabel did, and eventually Joel, too, in *Other Voices, Other Rooms*.

The adults yield to Miss Bobbit also in letting the boys continue in her service. Finally, though, their rivalry for her affection brings them to blows and separation. For months the two friends remain apart but keep a close watch on each other. At Christmas, Preacher sends Billy Bob a book with the inscription, "Friends Like Ivy On the Wall Must Fall" (S 89). Billy Bob says that it's corny and Preacher is a dope, but then he climbs up into the pecan tree and stays there all afternoon "in the blue December branches" (S 89). But most of the time he is happy, for Miss Bobbit and Sister Rosalba "treated him like a man;

that is to say, they allowed him to do everything for them" (S 89).

Miss Bobbit once again triumphs over society by successfully opposing the efforts of the principal, the newspaper editor, and the whole town to make her go to school. Billy Bob, who does have to go to school, spends much of his time there fighting for Miss Bobbit. She expresses her appreciation but tells him not to worry about the insults: "It's a compliment, kind of. Because deep down they think I'm absolutely wonderful" (S 90). If the narrator's agreement was not already clear, he now makes it explicit: "And she was right: if you are not admired no one will take the trouble to disapprove" (S 90). The logic is questionable, but the sentiment is becoming a familiar one.

The big event of Miss Bobbit's year in the town is the amateur show organized by Manny Fox, a stranger who appears one day and begins a gaudy promotion campaign. The prize offered is a Hollywood screen test. (Fox also runs an employment agency, offering, for a large cash payment, jobs on fruit ships out of New Orleans.) Almost everyone in town pays his dollar to attend the show. Miss Bobbit has practiced secretly for the contest, and her appearance near the end of the program is a last-minute surprise. The narrator can tell right away that it isn't going to be "one of her classical numbers" (S 92), for she taps across the stage in a cloud-blue skirt, "tossing her hips, her curls, rolling her eyes" (S 92), and at one point makes a whistle-provoking display of blue-lace underwear. She sings a racy song in a "rowdy sandpaper voice" (S 92) and winds up doing a full split, holding a lighted Roman candle and singing "The Star-Spangled Banner"—which Aunt El declares to be "one of the most gorgeous things she'd ever seen on the American stage" (S 93).

Miss Bobbit wins the contest, but Manny Fox skips town the next day, advising everyone to watch the mails—which they do, with growing despair. After two weeks Miss Bobbit organizes the Manny Fox Hangman's Club, begins writing letters to editors, and sends over three hundred descriptions of Fox to sheriffs throughout the South. When he is arrested and the boys get their money back, Miss Bobbit suggests that they finance her trip to Hollywood. They, in return, are to get ten per cent of her life's earnings, which will doubtless soon make them all rich. No one likes the idea, "but when Miss Bobbit looked at you, what was there to say?" (S 94).

The last part of the story is told in a style appropriate to the end of a dream. It is a time of "buoyant summer rain shot through with sun" (S 94) and of dark, restless nights. For Billy Bob it is a difficult time for Miss Bobbit has meant more to him than a thirteen-year-old's crush. She was "the queer things in him, like the pecan tree and liking books and caring enough about people to let them hurt him. She was the things he was afraid to show anyone else" (S 95). Before leaving, she assures Billy Bob that she is "not going to die" (S 95), and that someday he will live with her and Sister Rosalba high on a mountain.

There was, the narrator recalls, a "strange smile" about yesterday, the day she was to leave. The sun came out, and Miss Bobbit sat on the porch all afternoon surrounded by well-wishers. Aunt El, in a "wonderful" gesture, told Billy Bob to pick the Lady Anne roses for her. The only sour note was Preacher Star, hanging around down at the corner. About twenty minutes before bus time he approached Billy Bob, who had picked enough roses "for a bonfire" (S 96), and they silently divided them into two giant bouquets. Rain began, "fine as sea spray and colored by a rainbow" (S 96). When Miss Bobbit saw them across the street, "two boys whose flower-masked faces were like yellow moons" (S 96), she ran toward them, her arms outstretched. The watchers called out, their voices "like lightning in the rain," but Miss Bobbit did not seem to hear. "That is when the six-o'clock bus ran over her" (S 96).

Capote says that this story developed out of an adolescent crush on a real girl named June Bug Johnson. Miss Johnson was only one of a number of women, all possessing similar traits, who have appealed so strongly to him that he has built stories around them. An early instance of this is Idabel Thompkins of *Other Voices, Other Rooms*, whose character was based on one of Capote's earliest friends, the novelist Harper Lee. But the

Capote heroine first assumes her definitive shape and central position in Miss Bobbit. The significance she has for Billy Bob gives a clue to her significance for Capote. She is the dreamer in him, the child, the delicate spirit wandering in search of ideal happiness. She is "the queer things in him," and also, perhaps, the things he has been too wise an artist to show anyone else. One of the most important results of the liberation he achieved at the time of *Other Voices, Other Rooms* was the ability to place his alter ego in perspective by somehow managing to find it embodied in real persons he has known, thus freeing himself from it while at the same time continuing to possess it lovingly. Though still narcissistic in its deeper levels, his later fiction has a new air of turning outward, of freshness and sunlight. There is a new sadness in it, too, for the break with childhood is not made without pain. Miss Bobbit and her later counterparts exist finally not as real persons but as bittersweet memories.

One sign of new vigor in Capote's grasp of reality, and evidence of the tougher side of his nature, is the very real strength these heroines possess during their brief hour. Their confident pursuit of an ideal gives them the power to beat society at its own game and to compel its grudging admiration. Like Capote himself, they know how to get what they want. This was not the case with their predecessors, all of whom were directionless and fated to destruction. Randolph was the epitome of this type. Utterly helpless, almost a nonentity, he was a suitable object for Joel's absolute dedication but an artistic dead end for Capote. Eight years after the publication of *Other Voices, Other Rooms*, Capote told an interviewer that it already seemed to him like something written by a stranger. "I am," he said, "very pleased I was able to write the book when I did, otherwise it would never have been written." [2]

Aside from the other difficulties he presented, Randolph was too much a part of the novel's Gothic symbolic structure to continue to serve an author bent on increased contact with the real world. Randolph is an artist, but, as he tells Joel, "I could scarcely be called an artist; not, that is, if you define *artist* as one who sees, takes and purely transmits: always for me there is the problem of distortion" (OV 76). Completely turned in on himself, he seems to be Capote's object lesson in what not to become—a scapegoat bearing the least wholesome qualities of the childish dreamer and asking, not to be cast out into the wilderness, since he had wandered into his own wilderness, but to be transcended by acceptance and love. It was not Randolph but Idabel, the representative of the real world outside Skully's Landing, whom Capote found feasible as a character to be retained and embodied in new shapes. These shapes are not always feminine; in fact, the sexlessness embodied so grossly in Randolph continues to appear, much more subtly, in the later Capote protagonists. In them, however, it is a part of their strength rather than their weakness.

The story "Jug of Silver," which Capote included in *"The Grass Harp" and "A Tree of Night" and Other Stories* (1956) but excluded from his *Selected Writings*, seems to be an attempt at something he did much better in "Children on Their Birthdays," but it provides an interesting sidelight on the development of his protagonist. The story is narrated by a young man comparable to "Mr. C.," and the central character is a sort of male Miss Bobbit. He is a poor country boy named Appleseed who comes to town determined to win the jug of nickels and dimes exhibited at the drugstore by guessing the amount of its contents exactly. He has a sister, a thin, quiet girl, and his aim in seeking the prize is to have false teeth made for her so she can go to Hollywood for a screen test. Appleseed and his sister form a composite person: "Middy didn't always tag along with her brother. On those occasions when she didn't come, Appleseed wasn't himself; he acted shy and left soon." [3] The boy has absolute confidence in his dream—"A lady in Louisiana told me I could see things other folks couldn't see 'cause I was born with a caul on my head" [4]—and the main point of the story is the power which this confidence gives him. To everyone's astonishment, he guesses the contents of the jug to the last penny. Eventually he moves away, but his legend flourishes in the minds of the townspeople. It would be nice, the narrator concludes, to add that his sister became a movie star, "but that's not what happened, so why should you lie?" [5]

Capote's next two stories, taken together, constitute a foray into the romantic tropics. "A Diamond Guitar" is set in the familiar South of pine trees, red dirt, and prison farms but also contains something of the exotic, in this way anticipating "House of Flowers." And, though set in a different key, it has much in common with "Children on Their Birthdays." Though the story does not employ the dramatized first-person narrator, it has much of the impersonality that characterized the portrayal of Miss Bobbit; like her, Tico Feo is primarily an impression made on someone else, and that someone, Mr. Schaeffer, shares the experience of Billy Bob, Preacher Star, and Mr. C.

Mr. Schaeffer is one of the older inmates of a Southern prison farm. A lanky, faded-looking man, he is respected but has no friends among the convicts. Once, however, he did have a friend: the main action of the story is presented as a long-finished episode that began with the arrival of a blond-haired Cuban boy of eighteen, sentenced to two years for knifing two sailors in a brawl. His name is musical, Tico Feo, and he carries a guitar studded with glass diamonds. He is brought to Mr. Schaeffer and advised to imitate him, and his blue eyes and fun-loving face make the shy older man think of "holidays and good times" (S 122). Much like William Faulkner's Tall Convict in "Old Man," Mr. Schaeffer is essentially innocent, having been sentenced to ninety-nine years for the "one really bad thing" he did in his life: killing a man who "deserved to die" (S 123). Over the years he has let the memory of his previous life become "like a house where no one lives and where the furniture has rotted away" (S 123), but now he feels "as if the lamps had been lighted through all the gloomy dead rooms" (S 123).

Tico Feo and his happy-sad music are popular in the bunkhouse, though some of the prisoners, from jealousy or for "more subtle reasons" (S 125), tell ugly stories about him. He becomes Mr. Schaeffer's inseparable friend and is given a cot near his, and "except that they did not combine their bodies or think to do so, though such things were not unknown at the farm, they were as lovers" (S 125). One source of uneasiness for the older man is the boy's wanderlust. One of his few possessions, prized even more highly than the guitar, is a Rand McNally map of the world on which he shows his friend the many places he has been and the many others, such as Madrid and the North Pole, where he wants to go.

Spring comes and Tico Feo plans to escape, inviting Mr. Schaeffer to go with him. The older man is afraid, but the "knowledge of age churning like nausea inside him" (S 127) weakens his resistance to the boy's lure of "the world, *el mundo*, my friend" (S 127). On the chosen day Mr. Schaeffer feels close to panic, but when the boy's hand closes on his "with a tender pressure" (S 130), he slips with him into the creek and runs. He trips on a log and falls on his back, his legs still running, and as he lies there waiting to be captured he sees a vision of his friend's face suspended above him like "part of the white winter sky—it was so distant, judging. It hung there but an instant, like a hummingbird, yet in that time he'd seen that Tico Feo had not wanted him to make it, had never thought he would, and he remembered once thinking it would be a long time before his friend was a grown man" (S 130). The other prisoners know the truth, but the Captain announces that Mr. Schaeffer broke his ankle in an attempt to capture the escaping boy.

The passing of three long, cold winters brings the story back to the time it opened. Little has changed except that there is "a thicker frost of white" (S 131) in Mr. Schaeffer's hair and a limp in his walk. Undisputed owner of the diamond guitar, he once let a new prisoner try to play it, but the tunes came out sour. He keeps the instrument under his cot and "in the night his hand sometimes searches it out, and his fingers drift across the strings: then, the world" (S 131).

Capote's dreamers are always victims and prisoners, though nowhere else so literally as here. In the starkness of his captivity, in his contemplation of the ambivalent face of his dream hovering over him, Mr. Schaeffer is a reversion to such earlier protagonists as Sylvia and the immature Joel. The story is a rather explicit rejection of the homosexual option that Joel accepted in *Other Voices, Other Rooms*, and this is probably one reason why Capote handles the emotional action at a greater distance from himself than before—always for him a cause of diminished power. No longer sharing the dark intensity of the early stories, "A Diamond Guitar" falls short of the poignant charm of the later ones. Our inability to believe very fully in Mr. Schaeffer or to regard Tico Feo as much more than a rather unpleasant oddity can help us to understand why Capote achieved greater success in some of his other treatments of the same general theme. The mood such a theme seeks to convey is most appropriately embodied in a feminine character, most acceptably set in a frankly childlike world, and most intensely transmitted through an involved narrator closely identifiable with the author himself. "Children on Their Birthdays" has these qualities, and the later story "A Christmas Memory" will be an even purer embodiment of them.

In "House of Flowers" Capote moved in a very different direction. The romantic, tropical world that Tico Feo brought into the prison with his diamond guitar becomes the actual setting of this story, a product of Capote's 1948-1949 vacation in Haiti. He published the story in 1951 and three years later collaborated with Harold Arlen in its production as a musical play. Unlike any of his other stories, it was apparently written as a preparatory exercise for a stage version. As this would suggest, it is the most exotic of all Capote's stories, told in a whimsical, playful tone that seems to place it even further from his personal world of experience and imagination than "A Diamond Guitar." It was, in fact, based on stories he heard, as Capote himself has explained. During his stay in Port-au-Prince, he found that the most pleasant place to take his evening drink was on the porches of the bordellos, beautiful old houses that lined a road outside of town, facing the sea. "I learned about everything that happened in Port-au-Prince—but absolutely everything, no matter how low—and everybody wondered how I knew so much about what was going on." [6] Later he wrote a magazine article about Haiti, then decided to work toward a musical, in the process writing the story (which won an O. Henry

Award). Though remote from his other work in many ways, it is still about a girl who is a prisoner and a dreamer. This time, however, he decided to let the dream come true.

Ottilie is a beautiful young prostitute who, as her friend Baby says, should have been the happiest girl in Port-au-Prince. She has lots of steady customers, five silk dresses, and three gold teeth worth thirty thousand francs. She works with seven other "ladies," under the sharp eye of a spinsterish madam, in a rickety old house "frosted with fragile, bougainvillaea-vined balconies" (S 133). Only seventeen, she seems "a delightful dreaming child surrounded by older, uglier sisters" (S 133). Her native mother is dead, and her father, a planter, has returned to France. She was raised by a peasant family whose sons introduced her to sex at an early age, and at fourteen she was befriended by a "jolly nice man" who brought her to this house. Only rarely does she feel nostalgia for the mountains.

In spite of her good fortune, Ottilie is strangely discontented, and the cause of her discontent is love: when her friends describe its bliss, she grows sulky, for she has never felt that way about any man. Finally she goes to see a *Hougan*, who tells her that when she holds a wild bee in her hand without being stung, she will know she has found love. She thinks of Mr. Jamison, a middle-aged American who has given her many gifts, and wonders if she is in love with him. In a honeysuckle vine she finds some black bees and catches one. "Its stab was like a blow that knocked her to her knees" (S 134).

In March, with carnival approaching, Ottilie refuses to join in the preparations. Her friends persuade her to accompany them to a cockfight, and there Baby calls her attention to the admiring stare of a handsome, ginger-colored young man who looks as arrogant as the cock he is holding. His name is Royal Bonaparte; after dancing with her, he asks her to come with him to his house in the mountains. Teasing him, she runs through the trees and into a "veil of rainbow fern" (S 137) where he catches her. After an hour, as Royal lies asleep, she sees some bees and tries the test again. This time it works. Two days later she becomes Royal's bride and leaves with him, in spite of the pleas and tears of her friends. At first they think she will return after a few weeks, but after six months the proprietress decides she is dead.

Royal's house is "like a house of flowers" (S 138), and its one room, dark and cool and lined with rustling pink and green newspapers, contains a stove, a table and mirror, and a large brass bed. This bed belongs to Royal's grandmother, Old Bonaparte, a "charred, lumpy creature, bowlegged as a dwarf and bald as a buzzard" (S 139), who is widely respected and feared as a maker of spells. Each night they wait for her to go to sleep before making love, yet sometimes Ottilie sees "a gummy, starstruck eye shining in the dark" (S 139). Because of her love for Royal, she does not complain, and for a long time she does not even miss her former life. Still she keeps the silk dresses and stockings in good repair.

Royal's gradual return to some of his bachelor ways saddens her, but the real torment is Old Bonaparte, who watches her malevolently and has a habit of sneaking up from behind and giving her vicious pinches. When the girl seriously threatens to cut out her heart, she stops this practice but continues thinking up new ways to be annoying. She begins to put things in Ottilie's sewing basket to curse her—a cat's head, a green snake, spiders, a lizard, a buzzard's breast—and the girl quietly cooks each day's find into the old lady's supper. For a time she seems to thrive on the diet, but when Ottilie reveals her secret Old Bonaparte rises from her chair "with swelling veins and a stricken, powerless tongue" (S 142) and crashes across the table. In a few hours she is dead.

With the house to herself, Ottilie has more time to feel bored and to recall her pleasant life in Port-au-Prince. Then Old Bonaparte's spirit begins to haunt her. Waking in the night, she sees an eye watching her and screams. She confesses to Royal how she killed the old woman; he is sure that, whatever the morality of the deed, she must be punished if she is to be freed from the haunt. He decides, accordingly, to leave her tied to a tree all day without food or water. She struggles, but he leaves her firmly tied and cursing him with all her might. When the goat and the chickens gather to watch her, she sticks out her tongue at them.

77

After a while Ottilie dozes, and she thinks it is a dream when Baby and Rosita appear, sent by Mr. Jamison to try to bring her back. She proudly shows them her house and refuses to go with them; when they begin packing her things, she unpacks them just as fast. Baby remarks that she is "crazy," but finally they realize she is in love and decide to report her dead. Ottilie agrees and asks them to tie her up again: "That way no bee is ever going to sting me" (S 146). She cries when her friends leave, but before they have disappeared down the hill she has forgotten them completely. Twilight approaches and birds sail into their trees. When she hears Royal on the path she lets her neck go limp and rolls back her eyes, thinking happily, as his footsteps quicken to a run, "This will give him a good scare" (S 147).

In finding her dream come true, Ottilie moves into a world of romance in which nothing, not even death, need be taken seriously. Capote has sometimes been called a fantasist and has indignantly denied it. Taken as a charge of irresponsibility, the designation would be better applied to "House of Flowers" than to the earlier, more apparently fantastic, stories, which, as Capote insists, are serious examinations of real states of mind.[7] The story of Ottilie has a fundamental unseriousness which Capote has, fortunately, seldom put into his fiction. And, where it deviates from romantic cliché, the story has something rather chilling about it. Though Old Bonaparte somewhat resembles the archetypal bogeys of the dark fiction, the atmosphere of the story does not sustain that kind of reading, and Ottilie's murderous innocence seems an extreme case of the chill exclusiveness that tends to mar Capote's dreamers.

"A Christmas Memory" is Truman Capote's nonfiction short story. In 1956, the year it was published, Capote was in the midst of a major change in literary direction. Five years had passed since his short fiction had drifted into the shallows of "House of Flowers," and his vital fictional development had shifted to the short novel. During the next three years he made disappointing experiments with drama (*The Grass Harp*) and musical comedy (*House of Flowers*), and went on a cine-

78

matic lark (*Beat the Devil*) in Italy. Then, deciding that he had been wasting his time, he began preparing seriously for the nonfiction novel with some "finger exercises," the most important of which was *The Muses Are Heard* (1956), his report on the Russian tour of an all-Negro production of *Porgy and Bess*. In the same year he returned to the very roots of his own experience in "A Christmas Memory," a frank memoir which, while generally accepted as one of his finest and most charming short stories, has become his own avowed favorite among his shorter works because it is "true." In 1966, riding the tidal wave of popularity whipped up by *In Cold Blood*, Capote arranged for a pre-Christmas publication of the story in a slim, boxed volume bearing a reproduction of an actual snapshot of himself, a smiling little boy, with the elderly cousin with whom he spent much of his childhood.

The story is his idealized recollection of his relationship with this woman. As such it has a unique importance among his works, for it embodies the archetype of an emotional pattern which underlies all his later fiction and even exerts a subtle influence on *In Cold Blood*. Asexual admiration of a childlike dreamer-heroine is the usual attitude of the Capote narrator. The pastness of the experience is also essential; Capote's is a fiction of nostalgia. "A Christmas Memory" is one of his best and most satisfying works because it places the feelings he can dramatize most powerfully in the setting which is best suited to them—which, as Henry James would say, artistically does most for them.

Capote begins by asking the reader to remember a November morning more than twenty years ago and the kitchen of a country house. A little old woman with a craggy but delicate face and eyes "sherry-colored and timid" (*S* 148) is standing at the window. Suddenly she exclaims, "Oh my, it's fruitcake weather!" The narrator explains:

The person to whom she is speaking is myself. I am seven; she is sixty-something. We are cousins, very distant ones, and we have lived together—well, as long as I can remember. Other people inhabit the house, relatives; and though they have power

79

over us, and frequently make us cry, we are not, on the whole, too much aware of them. We are each other's best friend. She calls me Buddy, in memory of a boy who was formerly her best friend. The other Buddy died in the 1880's when she was still a child. She is still a child (S 148–149).

Their annual ritual, the baking of thirty fruitcakes, begins with a trip to gather pecans, followed by an evening spent cracking them: "Caaarackle! A cheery crunch, scraps of miniature thunder sound as the shells collapse and the golden mound of sweet oily ivory meat mounts in the milk-glass bowl" (S 149–150). The second day is to be spent buying the many ingredients, but first there is the problem of money. During the year, they have supplemented the "skinflint sums" given them by the family by selling handpicked fruit and preserves, holding rummage sales and backyard entertainments—once by winning seventy-ninth prize in a national football contest. The slowly accumulated Fruitcake Fund is tapped only for a weekly dime to permit Buddy to go to the picture show. His friend has never seen one and doesn't intend to. Her life has, in fact, been extremely circumscribed; yet she has numerous accomplishments, among them the ability to tame hummingbirds, tell ghost stories, and concoct old-time Indian cures. She is superstitious and always spends the thirteenth of the month in her bed, which is painted rose pink, her favorite color.

To get whiskey, the most expensive of the fruitcake ingredients, the two friends pay an apprehensive visit to Mr. Haha Jones, proprietor of "a 'sinful' (to quote public opinion) fishfry and dancing cafe down by the river" (S 152). Mr. Jones, a sort of benevolent bogeyman with razor scars across his face, decides to charge them one fruitcake rather than the usual two dollars. Buddy's friend later remarks, "Well, there's a lovely man. We'll put an extra cup of raisins in *his* cake" (S 153).

Then comes the baking. "The black stove, stoked with coal and firewood, glows like a lighted pumpkin. Eggbeaters whirl, spoons spin round in bowls of butter and sugar, vanilla sweetens the air, ginger spices it; melting, nose-tingling odors saturate the kitchen, suffuse the house, drift out to the world on puffs of chimney smoke" (S 153).

80

In four days the cakes are finished. They are intended for "friends," most of them met only once or not at all—people who have struck their fancy. Among them are President Roosevelt, a Baptist missionary couple, a knife grinder, the driver of the six-o'clock bus from Mobile (perhaps the same who unwittingly ended the life of Miss Bobbit), and a young couple who chatted with them one day and took the only snapshot they ever had taken. Buddy decides it is because his friend is shy with everyone *except* strangers that these acquaintances seem their truest friends. Besides, the thank-you notes make them feel "connected to eventful worlds beyond the kitchen with its view of a sky that stops" (S 154).

Mailing the cakes takes the last of their money, and they return home to celebrate by drinking up the last two inches of whiskey in Mr. Jones's bottle. After a while they begin singing two songs at once and dancing, she with "the hem of her poor calico skirt pinched between her fingers as though it were a party dress: *Show me the way to go home*, she sings, her tennis shoes squeaking on the floor" (S 155).

Suddenly two relatives enter, very angry. They tell Buddy's friend she "must be a loony" to give whiskey to a child of seven, and exhort her to "kneel, pray, beg the Lord!" (S 155). She runs to her room and cries into her pillow because she is "old and funny," but Buddy insists that she is fun—"More fun than anybody" (S 155).

The next day they go to the woods for a Christmas tree. Decorations, made from colored paper and Hershey-bar tin foil, are attached to the tree with safety pins. The two friends make gifts for the family, then separate to prepare each other's. Unable to buy the bicycle and the chocolate-covered cherries which each knows to be the other's true heart's desire, they make each other kites, as they did last year and the year before.

On Christmas morning they are awake long before dawn and rouse the rest of the family by dropping a kettle and tap-dancing in the hall. The others finally appear, "looking as though they'd like to kill us both" (S 159), and after breakfast the presents are opened. Except for the kite, Buddy is disappointed. "Who wouldn't be? With socks, a Sunday school shirt, some handkerchiefs, a hand-me-down sweater and a year's subscription to a religious magazine for children. *The Little Shepherd*. It makes me boil. It really does" (S 159).

This hostility toward those outside the magic circle is another reminder of the social alienation of Capote's dream world. Always inclined toward this kind of exclusiveness, he has tried to counteract it in various ways, especially in the non-fiction novel. Here, at a distance of over twenty years, he allows it free rein.

Buddy and his friend spend Christmas day not with their relatives but out in the fields flying their kites. She, growing meditative, tells Buddy she has always believed that the Lord's coming would be "like looking at the Baptist window: pretty as colored glass with the sun pouring through, such a shine you don't know it's getting dark. And it's been a comfort: to think of that shine taking away all the spooky feeling" (S 160). Now, however, she decides that probably the Lord shows himself even in this world: " 'That things as they are'—her hand circles in a gesture that gathers clouds and kites and grass and Queenie pawing earth over her bone—'just what they've always been, was seeing Him. As for me, I could leave the world with today in my eyes' " (S 160). This dreamer, because she is a Bible-reading Christian, thinks not of children on their birthdays but of a more conventional heaven. In this Christmas meditation she almost succeeds in grasping it immediately, transcending death.

And here Capote, through memory, comes closer to sharing it than anywhere else in his fiction. Buddy's own particular dream of starring in the movies links him to Miss Bobbit and Appleseed, reminding us that they and he and his elderly friend are all essentially the same dreamer.

Death intrudes, however: Buddy is sent to military school and moves to a new home. "But it doesn't count. Home is where my friend is, and there I never go" (S 161). For several years she writes, but gradually she begins to confuse him with the Buddy who died in the 1880's. One November morning she cannot rouse herself to welcome fruitcake weather.

And when that happens, I know it. A message saying so merely confirms a piece of news some secret vein had already received, severing from me an irreplaceable part of myself, letting it loose like a kite on a broken string. That is why, walking across a school campus on this particular December morning, I keep searching the sky. As if I expected to see, rather like hearts, a lost pair of kites hurrying toward heaven (S 161).

The part of himself that Capote identifies with his child-hood friend did not escape him at her death. Or, if something was cut away, it has continued to pulse like a severed arm. Repeatedly he has felt a need to project the emotional pattern of this early friendship into other relationships, in most respects very unlike that first one, and to build stories around them. "A Christmas Memory" is in a sense continued in *The Grass Harp*, which was published five years earlier. There the boy is about ten years older, and it is the death of his friend, there named Dolly Talbo, and his own entry into the adult world that bring the story to a close. *Breakfast at Tiffany's* picks up his career in New York a few years later and presents, in Holly Golightly, another version of his childhood friend. In "Among the Paths to Eden," Capote's last short story to date, he portrays another of her counterparts.

"Among the Paths to Eden," published at about the time Capote began his Kansas research for *In Cold Blood*, shows signs of the new strength and freedom he feels he derived from his work on the nonfiction novel. One of his principal aims in that project was to enlarge the range of characters he could portray sympathetically. In this story he does precisely that.

"Among the Paths to Eden" resembles earlier works in depicting a non-sexual encounter between a male observer and a wistful dreamer-heroine, but its spirit is new. The story is told in the third person in a playful comic tone that places the author at a slight, good-natured distance from the hero, Mr. Ivor Belli—who in turn views his brief acquaintance, Miss Mary O'Meaghan, in much the same way. The setting is a very real, undreamlike New York, and the time—virtually the first instance of it in Capote's fiction—is the present.

Specifically, the setting is a large, rather forbidding cemetery in Queens where Mr. Belli has come on a March day to place jonquils on the grave of his recently departed wife. His motive is exercise and fresh air, not sentiment, for Sarah "had been a woman of many natures, most of them trying: he had no desire to renew so unsoothing an acquaintance, even in spirit" (S 238). His two daughters are well married and he, at fifty five, has settled comfortably back into single life, almost but not quite dismissing the possibility of remarriage. On the present occasion his spirits are reasonably high, but the surroundings quickly begin to depress him. He hastily jams the flowers into a rock urn on his wife's headstone, but the thought that her scolding tongue is silent fails to rekindle "the suddenly snuffed-out sense of immortality, of glad-to-be-aliveness" (S 239). He notices the wind is chillier and turns to leave, but a woman stands in his way.

In Mary O'Meaghan, the childlike simplicity of the Capote heroine takes the form of simple-mindedness. Her dream is to find a husband, and so, following the advice of a friend, she reads the obituary column and haunts the cemetery in search of a widower hungry for domesticity. This pathetic shrewdness has not been successful, though to Mr. Belli her tall but rather heavy figure, her kitchen hands, "the clean shine of her Scandinavian skin . . . the blueness of her genial eyes," add up to "a very decent-looking person whose looks he liked" (S 241). He decides that here is someone you can trust, and is immediately reminded of another trustworthy friend, his secretary, Esther Jackson—or Esther "(as he'd lately, absentmindedly, called her)." He estimates that both women are "rather on the right side of forty" (S 241).

Miss O'Meaghan, aware that her most powerful lure is her cooking, begins to bait the trap by offering him peanuts— explaining meanwhile how she misses her own cooking since her father died, since "it's no pleasure cooking just for yourself" (S 241). Mr. Belli accepts with pleasure and invites her to sit with him on his wife's tombstone, "both awed and amused" at the thought of what Sarah, "that vivacious scene-maker, that energetic searcher for lipstick traces and stray blonde strands, would say if she could see him shelling peanuts on her tomb with a woman not entirely unattractive" (S 242).

When she sits primly down, he notices that her left leg is stiff. She explains that as a child she fell from a roller coaster at Coney Island, miraculously escaping with only this injury. Thinking he is Italian, she invites him to a spaghetti dinner. When he tells her he is a Russian Jew, she shifts to "Red cab-bage soup—hot or cold—with sour cream," and adds. "Poor fellow. How you must miss your wife's cooking" (S 243). This starts Mr. Belli on a new train of thought about his wife, who was indeed an excellent cook and also had, he now recalls, several other admirable qualities. "He felt, was all at once happy to feel, mournful, sorry he had not been sorry sooner; but, though he did genuinely value Sarah suddenly, he could not pretend regret that their life together had terminated, for the current arrangement was, on the whole, preferable by far" (S 244). Miss O'Meaghan's professed amazement that he is a grandfather starts another train of thought, and in a moment, "perhaps" because the wind has stopped and the sun is warmer, he finds that "his expectations had re-ignited, he was again immortal, a man planning ahead" (S 245).

Miss O'Meaghan wins new admiration from Mr. Belli by hitting on a mutual love for parades and music. With perfect instinct she mentions Helen Morgan, and the effect is powerful. " 'Jesus Christ,' he whispered. Ruby Keeler, Jean Harlow: those had been keen but curable infatuations; but Helen Morgan, albino-pale, a sequinned wraith shimmering beyond Ziegfeld footlights—truly, truly he had loved her" (S 246). Miss O'Meaghan asks if he will listen to her imitation, shyly advising him to imagine that "everything's soft and smoky" and she's sitting on a piano. When she lets her head droop back in a romantic posture Mr. Belli is embarrassed, for "it was a tactless visit that glamour made on Mary O'Meaghan's filled-out and rosy face; a visit that should not have been paid at all; it was the wrong address" (S 247). She waits, as though for music, and then sings, "*Don't ever leave me, now that you're here! Here is where you belong. Everything seems so right when you're near. When you're away it's all wrong"* (*S* 247). Mr. Belli is shocked, for what he hears is "exactly Helen Morgan's voice, and the voice, with its vulnerable sweetness, refinement, its tender quaver toppling high notes, seemed not to be borrowed, but Mary O'Meaghan's own, a natural expression of some secluded identity" (*S* 247).

She sings on, and then, too late, they see a funeral procession, "a black caterpillar composed of sedate Negroes" (*S* 247), passing near them in shocked surprise. Miss O'Meaghan stops in embarrassment, but when Mr. Belli kindly asks for an encore, it is "as if she were a child to whom he'd handed a balloon, a unique balloon that kept swelling until it swept her upward, danced her along with just her toes now and then touching ground" (*S* 248).

Mary O'Meaghan, as the embodiment of romantic yearning, is endowed with some of the airy lightness of earlier Capote dreamers who "traveled in the blue" and "lived in the sky." And her dream is unfulfilled as theirs. When she declines to sing again at present but renews the invitation to dinner, she again becomes for Mr. Belli the ominous husband-hunter who must be escaped. Her fate is to be a transparent medium of romance, the reviver in Mr. Belli's heart of the zest for life and love but not the beneficiary of those feelings. When he rises to go she firmly asks if he has considered marrying again. He answers that twenty-seven years is enough "for any lifetime";

but as he said it, he realized that, in just this moment, he had come to a decision, which was: he *would* ask Esther to dinner, he would take her bowling and buy her an orchid, a gala purple one with a lavender-ribbon bow. And where, he wondered, do couples honeymoon in April? At the latest May. Miami? Bermuda? Bermuda! "No, I've never considered it. Marrying again" (*S* 249–250).

As he speaks, the color drains from Miss O'Meaghan's face. She walks toward the gate with him, however, and they even share a laugh about her husband-hunting technique. She still insists that it is practical, and Mr. Belli says, "One day. With a livelier fellow" (S 252). Just then they see "an alive little man spouting cheery whistlings and with plenty of snap to his walk" (S 252), and Mr. Belli adds, "Good luck, Miss O'Meaghan. Thanks for the peanuts" (S 252).

We have seen that Capote's discovery and repeated use of the dreamer-heroine played an important part in his artistic and personal development. In this story he seems to be genially acknowledging the gift. Mary O'Meaghan jogs Mr. Belli's memory and give him a transfusion of life, yet can have no real personal relationship with him because she is already essentially a part of him, almost nonexistent as a distinct person. She has an early counterpart in the motherly woman with a clubfoot who offers herself to Walter Ranny in "Shut a Final Door." Walter was unable to respond except as a child, or to profit in any usable way from her benevolence. Mr. Belli, on the other hand, is certain of his identity and can see his companion in perspective. He knows that her place is not in Eden (as Miss Bobbit's is not in Hollywood) but somewhere among the criss-cross paths that such men as he traverse on their way there.

· V. THE GRASS HARP ·

Three years after *Other Voices, Other Rooms*, Truman Capote published his next major work, the short novel *The Grass Harp* (1951). The story opens on a note of reminiscence: "When was it that first I heard of the grass harp? Long before the autumn we lived in the china tree; an earlier autumn, then; and of course it was Dolly who told me, no one else would have known to call it that, a grass harp" (G 9).[1]

Like the opening lines of "Children on Their Birthdays," these establish much of the story's basic pattern: the first-person narrator recalls a past episode and a heroine who had a special meaning for him. The present narrator, Collin Fenwick, could be a slightly older Joel Knox, but his most obvious antecedent is the young hero of "A Christmas Memory," whose elderly "friend" corresponds to Dolly Talbo.

In his 1958 *Paris Review* interview, Capote, asked how much of his writing was autobiographical, replied, "Very little, really. A little is *suggested* by real incidents or personages, although everything a writer writes is in some way autobiographical." [2]

Today Capote readily acknowledges that he identified with Buddy, Joel, and Collin, though he points out that *Other Voices, Other Rooms*, a blend of many elements from his childhood, corresponds to reality only as a dream might.[3] In contrast, *The Grass Harp* gives the impression of being set in the world of real people, thus firmly establishing a movement from the subjective toward the objective which will be carried much further in Capote's subsequent works.

The grass harp is a field of Indian grass between River Woods and the hilltop cemetery outside a small Southern town.

In autumn the wind turns it into a "harp of voices" that tells the story of all the people buried on the hill, "of all the people who ever lived" (G 9). Dolly Talbo, who explains this to Joel, is his father's cousin. Since the age of eleven, when his mother died, he has lived with her and her sister Verena, both of them unmarried. Verena is a businessswoman and the richest person in town. After his mother's death she had come for him, "a whip-thin, handsome woman with shingled peppersalt hair, black, rather virile eyebrows and a dainty cheekmole" (G 10). Collin was terrified of her and also too afraid of his father—who had become violent after his wife's death—to return his farewell hug. He soon regretted this, for a few days later his father was killed when his car skidded off a cliff.

It is a while before Collin notices the timid Dolly, but when he does he is captivated. Her presence is "a delicate happening" (G 11) and, though older than her sister, she seems to Collin like another of Verena's adopted children.

Collin learns that he can peer through cracks in the attic floor into almost any room in the house. In this way he first sees Dolly's room, nunlike in its austerity except that the walls and even the floor are painted pink. Verena's room looks like an office, and she works at her desk, wearing a green eyeshade, far into the night. Though active in business she has no close friends. Once she had been "greatly attached to" a jolly girl named Maudie Laura Murphy, and she was bitter when Maudie Laura decided to marry and leave. Occasionally she receives snapshots, and on these evenings she paces her room with the lights off, and one can sometimes hear a "hurt rusty crying sound as though she'd tripped and fallen in the dark" (G 12).

The center of life is the kitchen, presided over by Dolly's friend Catherine Creek, a lifelong servant of the family. Dark as a Negro, she claims to be an Indian and wears a string of turquoise beads. She packs her almost toothless gums with cotton wadding, with the effect that no one can understand her except Dolly; this suits them both since "everything they had to say they said to each other" (G 13). She calls her friend Dollyheart but refers to Verena as That One. She and Dolly quickly admit Collin to their private world.

Five years pass, and in summing them up Collin sounds like

a Joel Knox who has learned the questionable lesson of Little Sunshine—that acceptance precludes judgment: "I know: Dolly, they said, was Verena's cross, and said, too, that more went on in the house on Talbo Lane than a body cared to think about. Maybe so. But those were the lovely years" (G 13). He never brought friends to the house and never wanted to. Once he took a girl to the movies, but when he afterwards refused to let her inside to spy, she taunted, "All the world knows Dolly Talbo's gone and you're gone, too" (G 14). Though he liked the girl "well enough," he gave her a shove, and "she said her brother would fix my wagon, which he did: right here at the corner of my mouth I've still got a scar where he hit me with a Coca-Cola bottle" (G 14). The line of alienation separating Capote's chosen few from the rest of the world—a line first drawn in "Master Misery" and taken for granted in *Other Voices, Other Rooms*—is, in *The Grass Harp*, drawn more distinctly than ever. It is, in fact, the backbone of the story's plot.

Life in the Talbo house has some of the bizarre qualities that it had at Skully's Landing, but its isolation from the outer world is less complete. Collin, for example, goes to school. Still, the part of his life that seems real is that lived in the company of Dolly, mostly in the kitchen. The one serious note of sadness in the house is Verena. She would like, Collin thinks, to join them, "but she was too like a lone man in a house full of women and children, and the only way she could make contact with us was through assertive outbursts" (G 15).

Once a week the three friends go festively to River Woods to gather herbs, leaves, and strange roots for Dolly's highly reputed dropsy cure. An instinctive naturalist, "she could tell you of a storm a day in advance, predict the fruit of the fig tree, lead you to mushrooms and wild honey, a hidden nest of guinea hen eggs. She looked around her, and felt what she saw" (G 14). Where the field of Indian grass joins the woods there is a double-trunked China tree that holds an ancient tree house, as easy to reach as climbing stairs. Dolly tells Collin it is a ship that sails "along the cloudy coastline of every dream" (G 16). Storing their provisions in the tree house, they fan out in search of the ingredients of Dolly's medicine. She alone knows the formula, which she says was given to her by gypsies. Together they brew and bottle the medicine, and together they spend the modest profits, mostly on things advertised in magazines: "Take Up Woodcarving, Parcheesi: the game for young and old, Anyone Can Play a Bazooka" (G 17–18).

Verena, aside from worrying that someone might die from the cure and sue them, does not show much interest in it until the year the profits are high enough to pay income tax on. Then she begins asking questions, but Dolly is evasive. Verena lets the matter ride for a time, but the following summer, when Collin is sixteen, she makes her move. Returning from her regular August buying trip to Chicago, she brings a man called Dr. Morris Ritz. "He wore bow ties and sharp jazzy suits; his lips were blue and he had gaudy small swerving eyes; altogether, he looked like a mean mouse" (G 18). Everyone wonders about Verena's carryings-on with the little Jew from Chicago. He lives in the best room at the Lola Hotel but makes no friends in town, and Verena never mentions him at home. The two of them show a great interest in the deserted canning factory, and one day the newspaper carries the information that Verena has bought it. Shortly after this, she announces that Dr. Ritz is coming to Sunday dinner. Dolly, frightened to death, insists that she will eat in the kitchen with Catherine, and at the last moment she collapses on her bed and has to be brought to the table by force.

The purpose of the occasion is the announcement of Verena's plan. Ritz produces some cheap gummed labels advertising "Gypsy Queen Dropsy Cure," and Verena explains that they are going to apply for a patent if Dolly will only tell them the formula. Dolly tremulously but firmly refuses: "It won't do: because you haven't any right, Verena. Nor you, sir" (G 21). Later in the evening Collin watches from the attic as Verena continues trying to force her will. Dolly begs to be allowed to keep the one thing that has ever been hers, but Verena replies bitterly that she has given her and the others "everything" and been rewarded with a house that she is ashamed to invite friends to.

I could hear the breath go out of Dolly. "I'm sorry," she said faintly. "I am truly. I'd always thought there was a place for us here, that you needed us somehow. But it's going to be all right now, Verena. We'll go away."

Verena sighed. "Poor Dolly. Poor poor thing. Wherever would you go?" The answer, a little while in coming, was fragile as the flight of a moth: "I know a place" (G 23).

In this rather classic confrontation between the strong and the weak of this world, the realist and the dreamer, there is at least a partial balance of sympathy: Verena has some room for complaint. But her point of view cannot, finally, be accepted. The lines of battle have been drawn, and the next move is Dolly's. She makes it, with a calm decisiveness that surprises Collin, by gathering up a few belongings and a protesting Catherine Creek and moving early the next morning into the tree house. It is to be a temporary move, "Until we know better what our plans will be" (G 24). Collin, at his own insistence, goes along.

The first person to discover the tree-dwellers is eighteen-year-old Riley Henderson. As they eat their breakfast of leftovers they hear his gun, and soon he appears, garlanded with bleeding squirrels. He immediately declares himself their friend, offering them two squirrels and climbing, against Dolly's protestations, into the tree house with them.

Collin is thrilled when Riley casually addresses him by his first name, for the young man is something of a local hero, though he remains aloof and will not "let us love him, be his friend" (G 26). Riley's father died when he was a child and his mother was institutionalized after trying to drown his two younger sisters in the bathtub. Since the age of fifteen he has been his own boss, wild in his ways but a stern guardian of his pretty sisters. With an independence worthy of Miss Bobbit he quit school to hunt and fish, and he became a good carpenter and mechanic. In the tree house Riley seems to relax, losing the "tense, trigger-tempered" expression he usually wore in town. And Dolly seems to enjoy his company. "Certainly she was not afraid of him: perhaps it was because we were in the tree house, and the tree house was her own" (G 28–29). At last Dolly has become a mother, and her family is growing.

It is Riley who spreads the word of their whereabouts through the town. Verena, informed by Dolly's brief note that they were leaving, has already contacted the sheriff and instituted a search. The telegram sent to neighboring authorities describes Dolly as *"probably insane but not likely to be dangerous"* and adds, *"post description bakeries as she is a cake eater"* (G 29).

This desperate character is, meanwhile, settling down to a routine of simple domesticity. Even while washing in the creek she wears a veil, and when Collin asks her why, she replies, "But isn't it proper for ladies to wear veils when they go traveling?" (G 30). One of numerous similarities between Dolly and her several counterparts in Capote's writing, especially Holly Golightly of *Breakfast at Tiffany's*, is that she sees herself as a traveler. The direction of her travel is always *away*, and the destination vague. Dolly sees her residence in the tree as the first leg in an indefinite journey, and the tree house itself as a symbolic escape-raft like Huckleberry Finn's. In Dolly's case the escape is primarily a spiritual one, for her tastes are domestic and her range is limited by the need to have available the ingredients for the dropsy cure. As Collin and Catherine discuss where they might go on their forty-seven dollars, she says, "To tell you the truth, I think we should set up right here in River Woods" (G 30).

The quiet of the woods is soon interrupted by the approach of a small group of eminent citizens stalking "solemnly, stiffly" toward the tree. First comes Sheriff Junius Candle in high-laced boots and with a pistol on his hip; with him are Judge Cool, the Reverend and Mrs. Buster, and Mrs. Macy Wheeler. Mrs. Wheeler, out of place in her "starched town clothes," screeches when a vine brushes her leg, and Collin laughs. The townspeople look up, "an expression of perplexed horror collecting on some of their faces: it was as though they were visitors at a zoo who had wandered accidentally into one of the cages" (G 31). The sheriff puts his hand on his gun, and the minister begins an exhortation, rubbing his hands together "like the dry scraping feelers of an insect" (G 31).

The Grass Harp contains Capote's fullest expression of antagonism between his chosen dreamers and the rest of society. The Capote characters we have met don't fit in, and, since Joel

93

Knox, they don't seem to want to. They are innocent pilgrims wandering in search of some better place. Society for its part considers them "crazy" and tries to put them into its prisons and its starchy straitjackets. But, as Miss Bobbit divined, beneath its hostility lies envy. On the present occasion the representatives of society stand below Dolly and her crew "like dogs gathered around a tree of trapped possums" (G 32). Catherine shouts down a threat, but fortunately no one can understand her; "if they had, the sheriff might have shot her through the head: no exaggeration; and many of the white people in town would have said he did right" (G 32).

Not everyone in the posse is an enemy, it seems. When Mrs. Buster calls Dolly a "poor mad woman," Judge Cool rebukes her, and he challenges the Reverend's certainty of the Lord's will: "Perhaps the Lord told these people to go live in a tree; you'll admit, at least, that He never told you to drag them out —unless, of course, Verena Talbo is the Lord, a theory several of you give credence to, eh Sheriff?" (G 32).

Judge Cool embodies another kind of progression in the development of Capote's themes. Though his dreamers may easily be dismissed by society as of no value, the same cannot be said of Dolly's new recruit. In him, society is condemned by someone right out of its highest ranks, a man whose profession gives him a special claim to wisdom. A broadening of the social base has already been evident, of course, in the selection of Capote code heroes. Miss Bobbit beat the town at its own materialistic game. Her later counterpart, Holly Golightly, will receive an even greater tribute of admiration from her peculiar world.

In the present scene, whatever its ultimate significance may be, Capote does a rather delightful job of demolishing his villains. Judge Cool advises them that they have no legal right to interfere with Dolly, and when the sheriff starts to climb, the judge advises those above to kick him in the head if he gets too close. Then (in a rather blatantly contrived scene) he leaps and grabs the sheriff's leg as the latter seizes Joel's. Dolly pours orangeade down the sheriff's neck, and he falls on top of the judge and the Reverend Buster.

94

The forces of conventionality retreat, but the judge stays, as seems only natural. "He might have been put together from parts of the tree, for his nose was like a wooden peg, his legs were strong as old roots, and his eyebrows were thick, tough as strips of bark" (G 35). Judge Charlie Cool is a simple country man, though he is a Harvard graduate, has twice traveled in Europe, reads a page of Greek every morning before breakfast, and wears flowers in his buttonhole. Almost seventy, he has been forced into early retirement by political enemies. His wife is dead and his sons, "prissy-mouthed, prudent men," have divided his house into two apartments and shunt him back and forth between their two families. At ease now in the tree house, he hangs his gold watch on a twig. Collin notices an "emotional, feminine tremor" in Dolly's voice when she speaks to the judge.

Dolly is puzzled by the hostility of the townspeople, and the judge tells her, "It may be that there is no place for any of us. Except we know there is, somewhere; and if we found it, but lived there only a moment, we could count ourselves blessed. This could be your place. . . . And mine" (G 37–38). Judge Cool, speaking with an authority apparently delegated to him by Capote, expresses a new view of the dream—one that corresponds to this book's advance from involvement in childhood toward a new involvement in a realistic world. Sadly, he concedes that the dream may be unattainable and that the problem is, in Robert Frost's words, "what to make of a diminished thing." Perhaps the best the dreamer can do is to grasp the dream and, by a sort of spiritual civil disobedience, assert its reality in the face of an unbelieving society.

Judge Cool becomes the father of the family—"a man again, more than that, a protector" (G 38). That night Riley returns with news of plans for their arrest, and tells the judge that his own sons feel he has "brought it on himself." Dolly weeps, and her tears set off "silent explosions of love that, running the full circle round, bound us each to the other" (G 39).

The judge announces that they must be prepared, and begins a systematic statement of their "position" that is more philosophical than military. He says that Dolly and all of them are

95

"pagans," or to put it less shockingly, "spirits." "Spirits are ac-
cepters of life, they grant its differences—and consequently are
always in trouble" (G 40). Only by accepting the differences can
one hope to find "the one person in the world" whom each
seeks—the one person "to whom everything can be said" (G 41).
The judge had given up hope of finding that person—had expected to go on living like most people do, hiding from others,
afraid of being identified.

But here we are, identified: five fools in a tree. A great piece
of luck provided we know how to use it; no longer any need
to worry about the picture we present—free to find out who we
truly are. If we know that no one can dislodge us; it's the uncertainty concerning themselves that makes our friends conspire
to deny the differences (G 41).

The judge says he has surrendered himself "by scraps and
bits" to many people who, put together, might have made "the
one person in the world." Now he feels, "This is my chance to
find that man—you are him, Miss Dolly, Riley, all of you"
(G 41).

Capote has made Judge Cool his foremost spokesman, and
this passage is the author's fullest statement of the values that
underlie his fiction and perhaps all his writing. The judge is
describing the Capote hero, the dreamer-victim. Everyone we
have met in his stories is included here. Here are the early
sufferers, prisoners even in their hearts because even in their
hearts they were afraid to accept the differences, to recognize
the bogeymen who were part of themselves.

The fiction turned from dark to light when, in Joel Knox,
they jumped to inner freedom by accepting their identity. Joel
found his "one person in the world" in Randolph, and with him
retreated into his private rooms, moving almost completely out
of the social world. Most of his later counterparts are involved
to some extent in that social world but with the full realization
that even if they themselves accept the differences, the world
of convention and law does not. Consequently they remain victims, but defiant ones. What each of them longs for is a friend—
someone who will accept him completely as he has accepted him-

self—someone who is, in fact, the self. Even a passing encounter with such a one may be all that can be hoped for.

To set the tone of mutual trust, Judge Cool tells one of his own innocent secrets. Riley then confides his fear that he will never amount to anything or learn how to love. He, too, would like to find the "one person in the world." "Maybe, if I could care for somebody that way, I'd make plans and carry them out: buy that stretch of land past Parson's Place and build houses on it if I got quiet" (G 44). Gently the judge tells him, "Son, I'd say you were going at it the wrong end first. . . . How could you care about one girl? Have you ever cared about one leaf?" He explains, "First, a leaf, a fall of rain, then someone to receive what a leaf has taught you, what a fall of rain has ripened. No easy process, understand . . . I've never mastered it—I only know how true it is: that love is a chain of love, as nature is a chain of life" (G 44).

Judge Cool's definition of love is quite similar to Randolph's in *Other Voices, Other Rooms.* He told Joel that

happiness in love is not the absolute focusing of all emotion in another: one has always to love a good many things which the beloved must come only to symbolize; the true beloveds of this world are in their lover's eyes lilac opening, ship lights, school bells, a landscape, remembered conversations, friends, a child's Sunday, lost voices, one's favorite suit, autumn and all seasons, memory, yes, it being the earth and water of existence, memory (OV 79).

This kind of love obviously tends away from the personal, and above all from the sexual. One is reminded of what finally touched Miss Bobbit's heart (and also brought about her death): the sight of two boys coming toward her with "flower-masked faces . . . like yellow moons." As Judge Cool has divined, Dolly is an epitome of this kind of love. She confesses that, by these standards, she has been in love all her life. She has never loved "a gentleman"—except her Papa—but she has loved "everything else" (G 45).

That Capote is beginning to take a broader view, seeing some of the defects as well as the virtues of this philosophy of childhood innocence, is evident in his use of varying moral points of view in *The Grass Harp*. One is that of Dolly's friend, Catherine Creek. Neither very appealing nor even very believable as a character, she does provide occasional comic and common-sense relief. She follows up Dolly's disquisition on love with this observation: "I've got a bowl of goldfish, just 'cause I like them don't make me love the world. . . . People ought to keep more things to themselves" (G 45). Earlier, Catherine had told the group that she had received one letter in her life, a puzzling one that said only, "Hello Catherine, come on to Miami and marry me, love Bill." Now, in the silence, she suddenly stiffens and says, "It's just come to me who it was sent my letter: Bill Nobody. That One, that's who. Sure as my name's Catherine Creek she got some nigger in Miami to mail me a letter, thinking I'd scoot off there never to be heard from again" (G 46). Dolly sleepily tells her there's nothing to be afraid of. The friends huddle together under the quilt, and the last thing Collin sees is the judge taking Dolly's hand. On this last peaceful night in the tree, all hearts have been opened, and the little group of dreamers have perhaps come as close to perfect happiness as they ever will.

Early the next morning Collin and Riley leave the tree and go for a leisurely swim, not realizing that at the same time the sheriff has come to the woods with deputies and a warrant of arrest. When the boys come back they hear shouts, and on the edge of the grass field Collin sees Catherine being dragged and beaten by three local bullies. Wishing he could kill them, he joins in her spirited defense. At Catherine's suggestion, he kicks one of them in the "booboos," but finally has to hide in the grass and watch as they drag her toward the cemetery. Collin finds the tree house apparently deserted, but then he hears Dolly calling his name and spies her and the judge, "like gulls resting on a ship's mast" (G 50), high in the tree. The judge had seen the sheriff approaching in time for them to take refuge there. Learning that Catherine had gone to look for him, he tells them what happened to her "in the field of grass" (G 50). Dolly, unwilling to believe, asks, "Collin, what do you think: is it that after all the world is a bad place?" (G 50) He knows how he must answer, for "no matter what passions compose them, all private worlds are good, they are never vulgar places: Dolly had been made too civilized by her own, the one she shared with Catherine and me, to feel the winds of wickedness that circulate elsewhere: No, Dolly, the world is not a bad place" (G 51).[4]

Riley, who has been gathering provisions and spying in town, describes Catherine's dignified conduct as she was taken to jail, then tells them a startling piece of news: Dr. Morris Ritz has stolen a large amount of money from Verena's safe and skipped town. Dolly's face reveals a rising urge to go to Verena, but "some sense of self, a deeper will" holds her back. Sadly, she tells Collin, "It's better you know it now . . . you shouldn't have to wait until you're as old as I am: the world is a bad place" (G 56). The judge looks "autumnal, bare, as though he believed that Dolly, by accepting wickedness, had forsaken him. But I knew she had not: he'd called her a spirit, she was really a woman" (G 56).

The next day, the first of October, is one Collin says he will never forget. They all wake early, and Riley, taking him along, leaves for town to buy coffee and to scout around. Hiding in Riley's car behind the bakery, Collin is discovered by its proprietor, Mr. County, and invited inside for breakfast. As he talks to the motherly Mrs. County, his feelings give way. "So little, once it has changed, changes back: the world knew us: we would never be warm again: I let go, saw winter coming toward a cold tree, cried, cried, came apart like a rain-rotted rag" (G 60). Collin observes that Mr. County, "for manly reasons," was embarrassed at the scene, but that he himself felt "no shame" (G 60).

Collin is suffering social growing pains much as Joel Knox suffered personal ones. He must accept not only his own eccentricity but also the awareness that society will not accept it. And, more cogently and authoritatively than Catherine Creek, Mrs. County expresses society's view of eccentricity. She tells Collin that she understands Dolly has broken up housekeeping because of some disagreement with Verena, and while he wants to explain that the situation is more complicated than that, he wonders if it really is.

"Now," she continued thoughtfully, "it may sound as though I'm talking against Dolly: I'm not. But this is what I feel—you people should go home, Dolly ought to make her peace with Verena: that's what she's always done, and you can't turn around at her time of life. Also, it sets a poor example for the town, two sisters quarreling, one of them setting in a tree; and Judge Charlie Cool, for the first time in my life I feel sorry for those sons of his. Leading citizens have to behave themselves; otherwise the entire place goes to pieces" (G 60–61).

It is with an increased social consciousness that Collin will move on through the events of this climactic day—many of them related to the next piece of news Collin receives from Mrs. County. Citing another example of eccentricity, she tells him about a wagonload of evangelists just arrived in town, and says that rumor somehow links them with Dolly.

In the square Collin sees an old truck decorated to look like a covered wagon and bearing the sign, "Let Little Homer Honey Lasso Your Soul For The Lord." Later, on the road outside town, they encounter the wagon again and discover that its driver is a woman. Though not young, she has "very red lips," a "dragging slow-fuse voice," and legs that it seems a shame to hide beneath a fringed chamois skirt and knee-high cowboy boots. As she asks how to find Dolly Talbo, what looks like "an entire orphanage" empties out of the truck. Fifteen in number, they range from infants to near-adults, most of them wearing some item of cowboy attire. "But they were a discouraged-looking lot, and sickly too, as though they'd lived years off boiled potatoes and onions" (G 65). The woman introduces herself as Sister Ida and acknowledges the children as hers, adding, "Some of their daddies are dead; I guess the rest are living—one way or another: either case it's no concern of ours" (G 65). Little Homer Honey is about twelve, with tiny steel-rimmed glasses and a ten-gallon hat that makes him look like "a walking mushroom." In their revival meetings he dances and twirls a rope while the other children haul in "God's Washline," a rope with clothespins for contributions.

Riley has learned that last night's meeting was disrupted by the Reverend Buster, who incited the sheriff and Verena and demanded all the proceeds. Hearing all this, Collin is surprised when Riley tells him soberly that "a loose woman like that was no one to associate with Dolly" (G 67). Riley has not yet learned something that should be clear by now to the reader of Capote: conventional morality, particularly with regard to sex, has no significance for free spirits.

Dolly, full of pity for Verena and worried about Catherine, asks Collin whether she should give up. With her eyes "tilted toward the heights of the tree, searching, it seemed, a passage through the braided leaves," she says that what she has wanted is the freedom to choose, to have her own life. Then, taking Collin's hand, she tells him something at which his "heart reeled" and "the tree closed inward like a folding umbrella" (G 68): Judge Cool has asked her to marry him. Looking at her face, Collin realizes that there has been a profound change— that "whatever else, she could never again be a shadow in the corner" (G 68). Resentful at seeing her "moving forward into the future, while I, unable to follow, was left with my sameness" (G 68), he is somewhat reassured to learn that she hasn't accepted the proposal yet. She explains that she has not yet earned the privilege of making up her own mind.

When Dolly learns about Sister Ida, she takes Collin and sets out in search of her. The two women embrace like old friends, and Dolly invites the troupe to dinner. Their coming sets off an exhilarated flurry of preparations, centered around a stew into which they throw just about everything. Sister Ida supervises a family bath in the creek, and Collin complacently watches "girls old enough to be married . . . trotting around and not a stitch on; boys, too, big and little all in there together naked as jaybirds" (G 71–72). Ida tells Collin and Riley her story, a sad one of poverty, troubled love affairs, and a rampant maternal instinct: "Seems somehow I can't get on without another life kicking under my heart: feel so sluggish otherwise" (G 76). The sympathy between Ida and Dolly is not surprising:

101

though extremely different on the surface, they are equally innocent at heart.

Dolly and the judge give Ida their forty-seven dollars and the judge's gold watch. "It's wrong," Ida says. "But I thank you" (G 77). Just then thunder rolls, and two of the boys come running with the news that the sheriff and a group of men are coming, armed with guns. The judge, rising to the occasion, takes command and deploys his army. "The women, you little kids, get up in the tree house. Riley, see that the rest of you scatter out, shinny up those other trees and take a load of rocks" (G 77). He alone remains on the ground, "guarding the tense twilighted silence like a captain who will not abandon his drowning ship" (G 77).

The sheriff comes swinging up the path followed by twenty men, most of whom Collin knows for bullies and fools. The judge stands toe-to-toe with the sheriff, as if daring him to cross a line. At this crucial moment Little Homer slowly begins lowering his lasso. "It crawled, dangled like a snake, the wide noose open as a pair of jaws, then fell, with an expert snap, around the neck of Reverend Buster, whose strangling outcry Little Homer stifled by giving the rope a mighty tug" (G 79). This launches a mock-epic battle that rages wildly but lasts only a few moments.

Suddenly a shot slams "like an iron door," and Riley falls slowly from his tree to land in a bloody heap. In the sudden silence all eyes turn on Big Eddie Stover, but Dolly, her absorbed gaze on Verena, says, "Responsible? No one is that; except ourselves" (G 80). Riley, wounded in the shoulder, is carried away, and the crowd begins to disperse. A light rain is starting to fall as Ida and the children bid a loving farewell to Dolly and Judge Cool.

Verena, finding in Dolly a new defiance, says, "You're not yourself." "You'd best look again," Dolly replies. "I am myself" (G 81). Dolly has followed her heart and found her love returned—has stuck to her dream but also, finally, faced the fact of its tragic incompatibility with the way things are. Now, having found her identity as Joel Knox found his, she is immediately faced, as Joel was, with the need to accept, love, and protect someone weaker.

Realizing that Verena is seriously ill, she asks Collin and the judge to help her sister into the dry, "raftlike" tree house. Verena frankly blames the judge for supporting Dolly's recent "tommyrot." When he reveals his proposal of marriage, Verena half suspects she is dreaming. "Except I never have dreams, or perhaps I only forget them. This one I suggest we all forget" (G 83). The judge replies, "I'll own up: I think it is a dream, Miss Verena. But a man who doesn't dream is like a man who doesn't sweat: he stores up a lot of poison" (G 83). Verena, ignoring the judge and concentrating on Dolly, soon feels she has divined the answer: "I see. You've accepted him, have you?"

The rain had thickened, fish could have swum through the air; like a deepening scale of piano notes, it struck its blackest chord, and drummed into a downpour that, though it threatened, did not at once reach us: drippings leaked through the leaves, but the tree house stayed a dry seed in a soaking plant. The Judge put a protective hand over the candle; he waited as anxiously as Verena for Dolly's reply. My impatience equaled theirs, yet I felt exiled from the scene, again a spy peering from the attic, and my sympathies, curiously, were nowhere; or rather, everywhere: a tenderness for all three ran together like raindrops. I could not separate them, they expanded into a human oneness (G 83).

This moment represents a turning point for Collin. Aware for some time that his idyllic life with Dolly is nearing an end, he has felt "left behind" in his isolation. Now that the moment seems to be at hand, he suddenly seems able to bear it. Retaining the sense of exile, he nevertheless finds an emotional solution in a transcendent sympathy which not only maintains in some way his connection with Dolly but also joins him with his new rival, his old enemy, and—potentially at least—all mankind. The gift for loving acceptance that liberated Joel Knox is here exercised on a much larger scale. Clearly, the movement toward ever more universal tenderness is one Capote has found rewarding. Collin's attitude of detached observation combined with universal sympathy is, we shall see, remarkably close to that assumed by Capote in the nonfiction novel. And it is Dolly Talbo, more than anyone else, who has taught Collin this tender but strangely impersonal love—just as her counterparts, including Randolph and Miss Bobbit, teach it to Capote's other representatives. It is for such gifts as this, I have suggested, that the mature Capote is expressing his gratitude in "Among the Paths to Eden."

For the moment, Collin's inability to take sides is shared by Dolly. Verena tells her, "We have had our lives," but the judge counters that she and he, at least, have not. Verena, looking "woebegone, wasted," confesses that she had envied Dolly her pink room: "I've only knocked at the doors of such rooms, not often—enough to know that now there is no one but you to let me in" (G 84). She acknowledges that their home is really Dolly's, and begs, "Only don't leave me, let me live with you. I'm feeling old, I want my sister" (G 84). The rain is a "transparent wall" through which the judge sees Dolly recede, just as Collin had seen her recede a few moments before. Their tree-house dream is vanishing too, "like the doomed houses rivers in flood float away" (G 84). Near midnight the rain stops and they know it is time to leave. "We took nothing with us: left the quilt to rot, spoons to rust; and the tree house, the woods we left to winter" (G 84).

The stay in the tree house becomes for the friends "a monument and a signpost" (G 85), and the final section of the story is a return from dream to reality. Collin and Verena come down with colds, and Dolly nurses them devotedly. When it is discovered that she herself has pneumonia, Catherine takes over, refusing to let the ambulance Verena has hired take Dolly to the hospital sixty miles away. The judge pays daily visits which Catherine chaperones superfluously. "If in other ways he was a disappointed man, it was not because of Dolly, for I believe she became what he'd wanted, the one person in the world—to whom, as he'd described it, everything can be said. But when everything can be said perhaps there is nothing more to say" (G 87).

Collin's participation in the general movement toward equilibrium is evident not just in the final tree-house episode, but also in a subplot that deals with his infatuation with his schoolmate Maude Riordan—a sentiment more "normal" than his attachment to Dolly, if not nearly so convincing. Here, too, he swings from emotional involvement to a detached and generalized sympathy. When he peers through a window into the room where Maude is caring for the injured Riley Henderson, thus verifying his suspicion that Riley is Maude's true love, he at first wishes he were a giant and could tear down the house and "denounce them both" (G 90). But then he reminds himself that he has no real cause to accuse Maude of betrayal. Returning home, he begins an indignant letter to Riley, only to find himself after a few minutes "telling him he was my best friend, my brother" (G 91). Once again Collin finds himself unable to condemn; once again his sympathies are "nowhere; or rather, everywhere." And, having accepted the role of observer, he next accepts the role of storyteller: earlier, Maude had shyly invited him to come to her Halloween party in a skeleton suit and tell fortunes, since he was so good at "fibbing" (G 54). He had determined to refuse, but now, as his resentment and self-pity subside, he changes his mind.

Dolly and Catherine take on the skeleton suit project with abundant good will, if few other qualifications, and later, against the doctor's orders, Dolly gets out of bed to accompany Collin to the attic in search of silver paint. It is ten-thirty, "a dark hour in a town where respectable doors are locked at nine" (G 92). The paint they find is not silver but gold, which Dolly declares is even better. Dolly tells Collin that she disapproved of his being sent to live with a houseful of women, but that nevertheless "it was done; and somehow I'm not worried about it now: you'll make your mark, you'll get on" (G 92). She reminds him of Judge Cool's lesson that love is "a chain of love," and says she hopes he understands it. She paints golden bones all over him and, when they laughingly realize he is trapped like a man painted into a corner, she advises, "You have to whirl. Whirling will dry you" (G 93). She begins blissfully whirling in ungainly circles, but suddenly stops: "It was as though she had collided with another dancer: she stumbled, a hand on her forehead, a hand on her heart" (G 93). Collin puts his arms around her, "the paint bleeding its pattern against her," and calls for help —but Dolly whispers, "Hush now, hush" (G 93). Dancing like a little girl into the arms of a benevolent death, she has suffered a stroke. Sitting near the hat tree in the hall at sunrise, Collin sees the veil on her velvet hat quiver in the breeze and knows that she is gone. "Some moments past she'd gone by unseen; and in my imagination I followed her. She had crossed the square, had come to the church, now she'd reached the hill. The Indian grass gleamed below her, she had that far to go" (G 94).

Finished with his story, Collin meditates on himself. He has read, he says, that "past and future are a spiral," but his own life seems to him "more a series of closed circles, rings that do not evolve with the freedom of a spiral: for me to get from one to the other has meant a leap, not a glide. What weakens me is the lull between, the wait before I know where to jump. After Dolly died I was a long while dangling" (G 94).

Riley marries Maude Riordan in June with Collin as usher and Judge Cool as best man. Walking home with Verena in the shimmering heat, the coming year lengthening before him not as a spiral but as a closed circle, he daringly makes the leap and informs Verena that he wants to go away. He decides to go to law school, and by the following September is ready to set out for a northern city "where in my honor pennants flurried" (G 97). After saying goodbye to other friends, he seeks out Judge Cool among the old men in the square. They stroll out along the River Woods road, Collin trying to memorize the details of the scene—"for I did not believe I would return, did not foresee that I would travel the road and dream the tree until they had drawn me back" (G 97).

Without intending it they find themselves on the cemetery hill, and descend to "the summer-burned, September-burnished field. A waterfall of color flowed across the dry and strumming leaves; and I wanted then for the Judge to hear what Dolly had told me: that it was a grass harp, gathering, telling, a harp of voices remembering a story. We listened" (G 97).

*B**reakfast at Tiffany's* almost
completes the movement in Truman Capote's fiction from the
submerged world of childhood to the real world of people and
events. It employs the same New York setting as "The Headless
Hawk" and "Shut a Final Door," but there the resemblance
ends. Between those stories and this one, Capote the writer has
grown up. The early stories were inward-turning, conscious of
the outside world only as a symbolic extension of inner fears.
Breakfast at Tiffany's, on the other hand, is as topical as
Winchell's column, as cool and sophisticated as the tough, eccentric society it talks about. Its unnamed narrator, an aspiring
writer who might well be Capote himself during his first months
in New York, is an older Collin Fenwick who has set his own
affairs in order and begun to look around him at the world. He
observes it more objectively than before, but once again his
attention is focused on a dreamer-heroine whose prototype is
the elderly friend of "A Christmas Memory." This story, too, is
a memory.

   I am always drawn back to places where I have lived, the
houses and their neighborhoods. For instance, there is a brownstone in the East Seventies where, during the early years of the
war, I had my first New York apartment . . . a place of my
own, the first, and my books were there, and jars of pencils to
sharpen, everything I needed, so I felt, to become the writer
I wanted to be (*S* 162).[1]

The tone suggests that nothing is to be taken too seriously, and
nothing is.

The narrator explains that he would probably never have thought of writing about Holly Golightly except for a conversation with Joe Bell, a bartender and mutual friend, that "set the whole memory of her in motion again" (S 163). In a now familiar pattern, the frame is set up to enclose a dreamlike past experience that still leaves its glow. Holly had been a tenant on the floor below, and this was "a long time ago." But it was just the previous Tuesday that Joe Bell called, "a croak of excitement in his froggy voice," and asked him to hurry over.

Bell has just had a visit from a photographer who also once lived in the brownstone and who, according to Winchell's column, has just spent two years in Africa. He has left some photographs of a Negro man proudly displaying a wood carving of "a head, a girl's, her hair sleek and short as a young man's, her smooth wood eyes too large and tilted in the tapering face, her mouth wide, overdrawn, not unlike clown-lips" (S 164). It is simultaneously a typical primitive carving and "the spit-image of Holly Golightly" (S 165), and the story is that the girl passed through the village with two white men, both sick with fever, and for a time "shared the woodcarver's mat" (S 166).

Holly's two former friends make what they can of this clue, so slight and so long-awaited. Bell admits that he was in love with her, though he never wanted "to touch her. . . . You can love somebody without it being like that. You keep them a stranger, a stranger who's a friend" (S 167). The narrator leaves and, let down and lonely, wanders by the brownstone and looks at the mailboxes where he first saw her card: "*Miss Holiday Golightly*; and, underneath, in the corner, *Traveling*" (S 168).

The narrator catches his first sight of Holly by leaning over the bannister, "just enough to see without being seen" (S 169). Her custom is to ring other tenants' bells, since she keeps losing her own keys, and it is the dismayed protesting of the photographer on the top floor that attracts the new resident's attention. From his point of vantage he notices first the "ragbag colors" of Holly's "boy's hair," then observes that in spite of her black evening dress and chic thinness she has "an almost breakfast-cereal air of health" (S 169). Dark glasses hide her eyes, giving latitude to his speculation about her age: "It was a face beyond childhood, yet this side of belonging to a woman. I thought her anywhere between sixteen and thirty; as it turned out, she was shy two months of her nineteenth birthday" (S 169). Though the setting could hardly be more different, here is a young observer peering down, like Collin from the attic, at a childlike heroine who has much more in common with Dolly Talbo than the sound of her name. Holly is, at the moment, giving the brush-off to an oily, thick-lipped man, punctuating his angry dash down the stairs with the advice, "The next time a girl wants a little powder-room change, take my advice, darling: *don't* give her twenty cents!" (S 170).

During the next few days, Holly begins calling on her new neighbor for door-opening chores. He wonders whether she is a model or a young actress but decides that she hasn't time for either. He sees her at a wide variety of places with an equally wide variety of men, and carries on further research by examining the contents of her trash can. In this manner he learns that her reading is confined to tabloids, travel folders, and astrological charts, and that she receives V-mail letters "by the bale" (S 171). He observes that she has a cat, and that she plays the guitar and occasionally sings, "in the hoarse, breaking tones of a boy's adolescent voice" (S 171). Her usual repertoire of Broadway show tunes is occasionally varied with others that "smacked of pineywoods and prairie." The one that seems to be her favorite goes: "*Don't wanna sleep, Don't wanna die, Just wanna go a-travelin' through the pastures of the sky*" (S 172).

The narrator's relationship with Holly Golightly moves along in this private-eye fashion until, one night in September, she turns the tables by appearing on the fire escape and tapping at his window as he lies reading in bed. Wearing only a bathrobe, she explains that she is escaping a drunken "beast." She says she particularly loathes "men who bite," and loosens the robe from her shoulder to show him the mark. She apologizes for intruding but explains that he looked "so cozy. Like my brother Fred. We used to sleep four in a bed, and he was the only one that ever let me hug him on a cold night. By the way, do you mind if I call you Fred?" (S 173). After a moment she adds, "I suppose you think I'm very brazen. Or *tres fou*. Or something." When he denies it she seems disappointed: "Yes, you do. Everybody does. I don't mind. It's useful" (S 173). She tells him that except for his size he looks like Fred, who was six-feet-two. "My other brothers were more your size, runts. It was the peanut butter that made Fred so tall. Everybody thought it was dotty, the way he gorged himself on peanut butter; he didn't care about anything in this world except horses and peanut butter" (S 174). She insists he "wasn't dotty, just sweet and vague and terribly slow; he'd been in the eighth grade three years when I ran away" (S 174). Fred's defining characteristic seems to be that he is odd, that people call him crazy. Holly accepts him without reserve, just as she accepts the oddities in herself and even takes pride in them. Joel Knox and Miss Bobbit achieved their strength and freedom by the same kind of acceptance.

The narrator tells Holly he is a writer, and she asks him to tell her "the story part" of something he's written. When he explains that they're "not the kind of stories you can tell" (S 174), she asks him to read her one. He nervously reads one he has just finished, about two women who live together, one of whom prevents the marriage of the other by anonymously spreading scandal. His listener's apparent boredom chills him, and at the end she asks, "if it's not about a couple of old bull-dykes, what the hell *is* it about?" (S 175). By now he is "in no mood to compound the mistake of having read the story with the further embarrassment of explaining it" (S 175). Holly goes on to assure him she has nothing against Lesbians, and even to ask if he knows a nice one she might get as a roommate. She had one in Hollywood, she explains, and found her an excellent homemaker. "Of course people couldn't help but think I must be a bit of a dyke myself. And of course I am. Everyone is: a bit. So what? That never discouraged a man yet, in fact it seems to goad them on" (S 176).

Holly talks on, half-revealing another strange facet of her life. Reminded that it is Thursday, she mentions that she pays weekly visits to a man in Sing Sing, a notorious criminal named Sally Tomato who used to frequent Joe Bell's bar. One day she was contacted by a "lawyer" who asked if she wanted to "cheer up a lonely old man" and make a hundred dollars a week, and she found the offer too "romantic" to turn down. Pretending to be his niece, she takes messages from the lawyer such as, "It's snowing in Palermo," or "There's a hurricane in Cuba." She describes visiting days at the prison in terms reminiscent of "Children on Their Birthdays": the occasions are "sweet as hell," the wives dressed in their finery and the children shining as if they were going to get ice cream. It's like "a party," and because there is no grille, "all you have to do to kiss somebody is lean across" (S 177). When the narrator expresses concern at all this, she says, "Don't worry, darling. I've taken care of myself a long time" (S 179).

She pulls the covers up to his chin and lies down beside him, looking "like a transparent child" (S 179). He pretends to sleep, and after a long time feels her delicate touch on his arm, feels her tears against his shoulder, and hears her whisper, "Where are you, Fred? Because it's cold. There's snow in the wind" (S 179). He asks why she is crying and she jumps up, says she hates "snoops," and climbs back out the window.

Holly's closest relative among the Capote heroines is Miss Bobbit; all her asserted exploits notwithstanding, she is just as child-wise and sexless as that little girl. She has, however, been pursuing her dream much longer than Miss Bobbit has and knows much more about sadness. Her companion's warning about the Tomato affair seems to have made her feel the chilliness of her isolation, the vulnerability beneath her hard shell. The narrator himself feels lonelier than usual during the next few weeks, but finally he receives a note inviting him for drinks. He is admitted that evening by a gnomelike man who informs him that Holly is in the shower. The room is bare except for suitcases and unpacked crates, one of which serves as a table for martini mixings, another for a lamp and phone. He warms to the room immediately, liking its "fly-by-night look" (S 181). The little man, speaking in "a jerky metallic rhythm, like a teletype," abruptly demands of the newcomer:

"So what do you think: is she or ain't she?"
"Ain't she what?"

"A phony."

"I wouldn't have thought so."

"You're wrong. She is a phony. But on the other hand you're right. She isn't a phony because she's a *real* phony. She believes all this crap she believes. You can't talk her out of it. . . . Benny Polan, respected everywhere, Benny Polan tried. Benny had it on his mind to marry her, she don't go for it, Benny spent maybe thousands sending her to headshrinkers. Even the famous one, the one can only speak German, boy, did he throw in the towel. . . . She's strictly a girl you'll read where she ends up at the bottom of a bottle of Seconals. I've seen it happen more times than you've got toes: and those kids, they weren't even nuts. She's nuts" (S 181–182).

Holly Golightly, a remote descendant of the heroine of "Master Misery," has not let the psychiatrists steal her dreams. She belongs to a later generation of Capote heroines who have learned to preserve their integrity by safeguarding their uniqueness. Society helplessly admires her and considers her crazy at the same time, but Capote and his narrator have only admiration for her.

The little man identifies himself as O. J. Berman, a Hollywood actor's agent. He discovered Holly living with a jockey at Santa Anita at the age of fifteen and arranged a minor part in a movie, only to have her turn it down at the last moment. He describes her as a "goddamn liar," but his disapproval is only superficial, as his presence on this occasion suggests. Within a half hour the apartment is crowded with prosperous looking middle-aged men, each apparently surprised not to be the only guest. Holly floats among them carrying her cat.

Eventually she joins the narrator, and stays long enough to give him a considerable new insight into her thinking. She explains that she didn't want to be a movie star because it requires the sacrifice of one's ego, and "I want to still be me when I wake up one fine morning and have breakfast at Tiffany's" (S 187). Holly's life of traveling is really a search for a home, a place "where me and things belong together" (S 187). She hasn't found the place yet, but she knows it will make her feel like Tiffany's does, with the sense of security, the "quietness and proud look of it" (S 188).

She asks the narrator if he knows what the "mean reds" are, and distinguishes them from the blues, which only make you sad. "But the mean reds are horrible. You're afraid and you sweat like hell, but you don't know what you're afraid of. Except something bad is going to happen, only you don't know what it is" (S 188). He confesses that he knows the feeling and says some people call it *angst*. He suggests that a drink can help, but Holly says she's already tried that, and also aspirin and marijuana. What does her the most good is going to Tiffany's: "It calms me down right away; . . . nothing very bad could happen to you there, not with those kind men in their nice suits, and that lovely smell of silver and alligator wallets" (S 188). Unable to make a home of the near-at-hand paradise, she dreams of settling down with Fred after the war in a more distant one. "I went to Mexico once. It's wonderful country for raising horses. I saw one place near the sea. Fred's good with horses" (S 188).

The character of Holly Golightly was, Capote says, inspired by a real girl who told him many of the things Holly tells the narrator in the story.[2] If the above reflections were among these, this anonymous young lady may deserve considerable credit for helping to shape his literary career. Whether or not this is the case, her technique for handling the "mean reds" seems to be Capote's own. His early stories were all about the "mean reds," and the antidote he found was the dream. Joel Knox made the transition by finding his "proper place," but had to retire from the real world to do it. His later counterparts, because they try to live in the world, must consequently be travelers. Holly, realizing as Miss Bobbit did that "the next best thing is very often the best," makes do for the time being with the artificial peace of Tiffany's.

Holly's immediate plan is to finance the next leg of her journey by marrying a wealthy "middle-aged child" (S 185) named Rusty Trawler. Meanwhile she acquires a roommate, a grotesquely tall, horsey fashion model named Mag Wildwood, and, learning that Mag is engaged to a Brazilian with presidential aspirations, begins laying plans to snare him for herself. The narrator has encountered this man, named José, in the apartment and is "charmed" by his physical perfection and bash-ful manner.

Not long after the party in Holly's apartment, the narrator has his first story accepted by a small university review. Elated, he pounds on Holly's door and shows her the letter. At first she objects to his not being paid, but then, realizing that he wants congratulations rather than advice, she offers to take him to lunch. He waits in her bedroom, which has the same "camping-out atmosphere" as her parlor except that it houses an extrava-gant double bed. Finally dressed, she cups her hand under his chin and says, "Listen, I'm glad about the story. Really I am" (S 197).

It is a Monday in October, 1943, and a beautiful day. They have a drink at Joe Bell's and watch a parade on Fifth Avenue. "Afterwards, avoiding the zoo (Holly said she couldn't bear to see anything in a cage), we giggled, ran, sang along the paths toward the old wooden boathouse, now gone" (S 198). Holly puzzles him by describing, in vague, impressionistic terms, a childhood which seems "happy in a way that she was not, and never, certainly, the background of a child who had run away" (S 198). When he finally gets her to admit that she has been on her own since she was fourteen, and that the pretty recol-lection isn't true, she explains, "But really, darling, you made such a tragedy out of your childhood I didn't feel I should com-pete" (S 198).

He spends a number of "hither and yonning days" with Holly, but after a time he gets a nine-to-five job which makes their meetings rare. Now and then he sees her, usually with Rusty, Mag, and the Brazilian. Late in the winter, Holly gives him an account of a trip to South America. Leaving Mag and Rusty along the way, she had gone to Havana with José and had a wonderful time. To convince Mag that she hadn't "spent the whole time sleeping with José," she claimed to be a dyke. "Leave it to me: I'm always top banana in the shock depart-ment. Be a darling, darling, rub some oil on my back" (S 203).

While he does so she tells him she has shown his story, now published, to Berman and that he is impressed. Berman agrees, however, that he's on the wrong track: "Brats and niggers.

Trembling leaves. *Description.* It doesn't *mean* anything" (*S* 203). Tempted to bring his hand down hard on her bare buttocks, he asks her to give an example of "something that means something." When she mentions *Wuthering Heights*, he objects that she's referring to "a work of genius"; then, learning that she knows only the movie, he annoys her with his disdain.

"Everybody has to feel superior to somebody," she said. "But it's customary to present a little proof before you take the privilege."
"I don't compare myself to you. Or Berman. Therefore I can't feel superior. We want different things."
"Don't you want to make money?"
"I haven't planned that far."
"That's how your stories sound. As though you'd written them without knowing the end" (*S* 204).

In this scene especially, Capote teases the reader with the suspicion that the narrator of *Breakfast at Tiffany's* is himself. There is no doubt about the resemblance, or about the role of this story in Capote's gradual transition from fiction to non-fiction. The rather surprising insertion of Holly's critique on obviously early-Capote writing may be a tribute to the real-life girl who seems to have had more influence on his literary career than all the professional critics put together. For he has followed Holly's advice to the letter. *Breakfast at Tiffany's* itself fills the prescription that he abandon brats and trembling leaves, and *In Cold Blood* has solved the financial problem. Of course, what Capote really found in the Ur-Holly, as in the other women who inspired his heroines, was a new avatar of his constantly unfolding self.

This bizarre literary discussion brings the narrator's friendship with Holly to a temporary close. Spring comes, and one day he sees a man studying Holly's name card and looking up at her window. Later he notices the man following him and whistling Holly's plaintive tune about the *pastures of the sky*. Apparently in his early fifties, he has "a hard, weathered face, gray forlorn eyes" (*S* 205). He joins the narrator at the counter of Hamburg Heaven, explaining, "Son, I need a friend" (*S*

206), and shows him a worn photograph of seven people on the sagging porch of a wooden house—five children and himself with his arm around a plump blond girl. He says the blond girl is "her," and identifies a tow-headed beanpole as "her brother, Fred."

The narrator looks again at "her" and sees the resemblance. "You're Holly's *father*."

The man blinks, frowns. "Her name's not Holly. She was a Lulamae Barnes. Was," he says, "till she married me. I'm her husband" (S 207). He is Doc Golightly, a horse doctor and farmer from Texas, who married Lulamae at the age of fourteen after his first wife's death. She and Fred had appeared one day, having escaped from the "mean, no-count" family that had kept them since their parents died of TB. Doc was kind to his young wife, but after a time she began taking walks. "Every day she'd walk a little further: a mile, and come home. Two miles, and come home. One day she just kept on" (S 209).

When the narrator springs the name "Lulamae" on her, Holly thinks Fred has come and runs down the stairs looking for him. She is disappointed at finding Doc but treats him kindly and, as she admits to the narrator the next day in Joe Bell's bar, lets him take her to bed. Apparently feeling guilty (for the first time in their acquaintance), she explains, "Anyone who ever gave you confidence, you owe them a lot" (S 211). She says they spent the latter part of the night in a bus station, Doc all the while thinking that she was really coming home with him, even though she told him she was not fourteen any more, and that she was not Lulamae. "But the terrible part is (and I realized it while we were standing there) I am" (S 211).

Joe Bell brings them another drink and she says to him, "Never love a wild thing, Mr. Bell . . . the more you do, the stronger they get. Until they're strong enough to run into the woods. Or fly into a tree. Then a taller tree. Then the sky" (S 212). Holly's words, which would be an appropriate text for "A Diamond Guitar," are spoken in a voice slightly blurred with drinking. She offers a toast to the absent Doc: "Good luck: and believe me, dearest Doc—it's better to look at the sky than

116

live there. Such an empty place; so vague. Just a country where the thunder goes and things disappear" (*S* 212).

For various reasons, the narrator doesn't see Holly again for some time. Fired from his job and threatened by the draft, he has his own case of the mean reds. When he sees headlines proclaiming Rusty Trawler's fourth marriage, he assumes that he has married Holly and gets even more depressed. "For I *was* in love with her. Just as I'd once been in love with my mother's elderly colored cook and a postman who let me follow him on his rounds and a whole family named McKendrick" (*S* 213). A while later he buys a paper, finishes the article, and learns that Rusty has married not Holly but Mag Wildwood. Arriving home, he hears a terrible racket in Holly's room but, strangely, no quarreling voices. At his knock the noise stops, but the door remains locked. He is trying to break it down when a frightened José rushes up the stairs accompanied by a doctor and enters the room with his key.

Almost everything in the apartment is broken. Holly is on the bed, staring blindly and "whimpering like an exhausted, fretful child" (*S* 214). The doctor tells her she must sleep, and she says, "He's the only one would ever let me. Let me hug him on cold nights. I saw a place in Mexico. With horses. By the sea" (*S* 214). The doctor gives her an injection and José shows the narrator a telegram from Doc telling Holly that Fred has been killed in action.

Holly does not talk about Fred any more and stops calling her friend by that name. Through the summer she lives in relative isolation. Far from becoming bitter, however, she seems happier than the narrator has ever seen her. She is trying to learn Portuguese and begins most of her sentences with "After we're married—" though José has never mentioned marriage. This is notwithstanding the fact, she informs her friend, that José knows she is six weeks pregnant. She says she is delighted at the fact and even wishes she had been a virgin for José. This leads to a brief survey of her sex life. She denies that she has "warmed the multitudes" that some people suspect; she has, to be precise, had eleven lovers. This is "not counting anything that happened before I was thirteen because, after all, that just *doesn't* count. Eleven. Does that make me a whore?" (S 217). She explains that she doesn't have anything *against* whores. "Except this: Some of them may have an honest tongue but they all have dishonest hearts. I mean, you can't bang the guy and cash his checks and at least not *try* to believe you love him. I never have. . . . I sort of hypnotized myself into thinking their sheer rattiness had a certain allure" (S 218). She concludes that, in fact, Doc and José have been her only "non-rat" romances.

Earlier, in a conversation with Mag Wildwood overheard by the narrator, Holly had said that she liked a man who sees the humor of sex rather than being like "most of them, . . . all pant and puff" (S 195). Insisting she would rather be "natural" than "normal," she emphasized the visual approach and suggested leaving the lights on while making love: "Men are beautiful, a lot of them are, José is, and if you don't even want to look at him, well, I'd say he's getting a pretty cold plate of macaroni" (S 195).

Holly's response to José is not, in fact, very different from the narrator's own appreciation of his handsomeness. What we really come to know of Holly in *Breakfast at Tiffany's* makes the account of her sexual exploits seem as fictional as Tico Feo's admittedly were in "A Diamond Guitar"—a fact of considerable interest in view of the strong similarity between the two characters in other respects. As in Capote's other stories, sexuality is more convincingly negated than affirmed. On the other hand, Holly's efforts to avoid the dishonesty of whores by "making herself love" practically anybody seem never quite successful—even in the case of José, as she goes on to show. Acknowledging that he's not really her idea of "the absolute finito," she lists some of his questionable traits such as worrying about what people think, taking "about fifty baths a day," turning his back to get undressed, making too much noise when he eats, and having "something funny-looking about him when he runs" (S 218).

If, she goes on, she were free to pick anyone in the world, she would more readily select Nehru, Wendell Willkie, or even Garbo. "Why not? A person ought to be able to marry men or

118

women or—listen, if you came to me and said you wanted to hitch up with Man o' War, I'd respect your feeling" (S 218). Holly says she's completely in favor of love, that it "should be allowed." And, she says, she does love José, for he has helped her escape at least to some extent from the mean reds. She has even thrown away her horoscope, having decided the only answer is that good things happen to you only if you're honest.

Not law-type honest—I'd rob a grave, I'd steal two bits off a dead man's eyes if I thought it would contribute to the day's enjoyment—but unto-thyself-type honest. Be anything but a coward, a pretender, an emotional crook, a whore: I'd rather have cancer than a dishonest heart. Which isn't being pious. Just practical. Cancer *may* cool you, but the other's sure to (S 218–219).

Holly's ideal of love is simply not a sexual one, nor is it likely to be satisfied by any real human being she will meet. The ideal relationship she aspires to is approximated by the narrator's own relationship with her: tender but distant, and consisting largely of admiration for her brilliance and strength. That Holly makes honesty to self her guiding principle is not surprising when we remember that on the deepest level she is the Capote-narrator's alter ego, representing for him—as Miss Bobbit did for Billy Bob—the strange, unconventional side of himself. In admiring Holly he is being true to himself, making that act of acceptance that has been the dominant impulse in most of Capote's writing.

The end of summer passes in a blur of pleasantness, for their friendship has reached "that sweet depth where two people communicate more often in silence than in words" (S 219). But as the time for parting draws near, the narrator feels increasingly jealous of José and of Holly's future in general, "infuriatingly left out—a tugboat in drydock while she, glittery voyager of secure destination, steamed down the harbor with whistles whistling and confetti in the air" (S 219). Like Collin at the end of *The Grass Harp*, he feels threatened by the end of one section of his life.

The thirtieth of September, his birthday, is "unlike any other I've lived" (S 219). Holly invites him to go horseback riding in Central Park. Slapping her flat stomach, she says, "Don't think I'm out to lose the heir. But there's a horse, my darling old Mabel Minerva—I can't go without saying goodbye to Mabel Minerva" (S 220). She tells him that she and José will be flying to Brazil in a few days. He follows her down the street in a trance, protesting that she can't just "run off and leave everybody." At the stable she helps hoist him onto an old mare she declares is "safer than a cradle," then mounts her own silvery horse and takes the lead.

The fun lasts only a few minutes, for all at once a gang of Negro boys jump at them from the bushes, throwing rocks, cursing, and whipping the horses. His horse bolts, and Holly chases him through the park and down several blocks of noonday Fifth Avenue traffic before she and a mounted policeman manage to bring him to a stop between them. She puts him into a taxi, expressing serious concern for his welfare. Touched and embarrassed, he mumbles, "honestly. I don't feel anything. Except ashamed. . . . And thank you. For saving my life. You're wonderful. Unique. I love you" (S 222). Holly is a blurred vision: he sees three of her, then four, then faints.

The evening papers are filled with Holly, not as the catcher of a runaway horse but as a "DOPE-SMUGGLING ACTRESS," accused of complicity in Tomato's narcotics racket because of the "innocent" message-bearing which she has, in fact, recently stopped. Under the subheading, "ADMITS OWN DRUG ADDICTION," Holly is quoted as admitting that she has "had a little go at marijuana" and commenting that it is less destructive than brandy, though unfortunately she prefers the latter.

Once again the innocent dreamer becomes a prisoner; as always, she is at odds with a literalistic, moralistic society. One fact not mentioned in the articles is that Holly was arrested in the narrator's bathroom. He was soaking in Epsom salts while she sat on the edge of the tub, "waiting to rub me with Sloan's liniment and tuck me in bed" (S 225). The situation has its similarities to the confrontation between tree-dwellers and town in The Grass Harp. When a burly woman detective barges in and puts her hand on Holly's shoulder, she coolly tells her, "Get them cotton-pickin' hands off of me, you dreary, driveling old bull-dyke," and is slapped so hard "her head twisted on her neck" (S 225).

Holly's wealthy "friends" disappear. The narrator visits her in the hospital and learns that she has "lost the heir" and, in fact, come close to death.

Christ, I nearly cooled. No fooling, the fat woman almost had me. She was yakking up a storm. I guess I couldn't have told you about the fat woman. Since I didn't know about her myself until my brother died. Right away I was wondering where he'd gone, what it meant, Fred's dying; and then I saw her, she was there in the room with me, and she had Fred cradled in her arms, a fat mean red bitch rocking in a rocking chair with Fred on her lap and laughing like a brass band. The mockery of it! But it's all that's ahead for us, my friend: this comedienne waiting to give you the old razz. Now do you see why I went crazy and broke everything? (S 228–229).

The "mean reds," expanding into the "fat mean red bitch," resemble the mad laughing Santa Claus that frightened Sylvia in "Master Misery." Death, which presided over Capote's early stories, is present all through his later ones, though held at bay by friendship and the pursuit of life-sustaining dreams.

Holly is at present facing several preliminary deaths, and her fast-approaching departure will be a sort of death for the narrator. She asks him about José and he hands her a letter in which that individual, frightened by the drug scandal, courteously bows out of her life. She knows in advance what it will say and asks for her purse, explaining, "A girl doesn't read this sort of thing without her lipstick." Finally, "armored" with cosmetics, she scans the letter "while her stony small smile grew smaller and harder" (S 229).

Holly's plan is to use her ticket for Brazil to escape from the country. The narrator tries to dissuade her, arguing that even if she does make it she can never come back. Both of them have visions of "iron rooms, steel corridors of gradually closing doors" (S 231). Finally her departure day arrives, dark with rain. "Sharks might have swum through the air, though it seemed improbable a plane could penetrate it" (S 233). The narrator, eluding police surveillance, cleans out Holly's apartment, and they rendezvous at Joe Bell's bar. Bell has hired a Carey Cadillac to take her to the airport, but gruffly refuses to drink to her "foolishness" and only thrusts some flowers at her before locking himself in the men's room.

Holly shocks the narrator by abandoning her cat in Spanish Harlem. She has never named it, intending to wait until they found a home; now she explains, "Independents, both of us. We never made each other any promises. We never—" (S 236). At a traffic light she jumps out of the car and runs back down the street, looking for the cat. Unable to find him, she finally allows herself to be led back to the car, shuddering. "Jesus God. We did belong to each other. He was mine" (S 236). The narrator promises to find the cat and take care of him, but she whispers, "But what about me? I'm very scared, Buster. Yes, at last. Because it could go on forever. Not knowing what's yours until you've thrown it away. The mean reds, they're nothing. The fat woman, she's nothing. This, though: my mouth's so dry, if my life depended on it I couldn't spit" (S 236).

Holly escapes to Rio and her name gradually disappears from the gossip columns. In the spring a postcard comes: *"Brazil was beastly but Buenos Aires the best. Not Tiffany's, but almost. Am joined at the hip with duhvine $enor. Love? Think so. Anyhow am looking for somewhere to live ($enor has wife, 7 brats) and will let you know address when I know myself. Mille Tendresse"* (S 237). The address never comes, and eventually he moves out of the brownstone because it is "haunted." He wishes he could tell her about the cat. After weeks of searching, he had found him. "Flanked by potted plants and framed by clean lace curtains, he was seated in the window of a warm-looking room: I wondered what his name was, for I was certain he had one now, certain he'd arrived somewhere he belonged. African hut or whatever, I hope Holly has, too" (S 237).

Breakfast at Tiffany's is a showcase for Holly Golightly. O. J. Berman introduced her as a *"real* phony" who honestly "believes all this crap she believes," and the remainder of the story is a gradual exposition of the content of this belief. We learn that her idea of love is a non-sexual focusing of esthetically oriented feeling, just as it was for Randolph, Judge Cool, and Dolly Talbo. Honesty to oneself, or acceptance of one's identity, is as important to her as it came to be for Joel Knox. All her life she has known deprivation and death and fought a desperate battle against fear. It is, finally, the awareness of death that keeps her from feeling at home anywhere and impels her on a constant search for something better. Here at the end of *Breakfast at Tiffany's*—which is, except for the genial "Among the Paths to Eden," Capote's last fictional "word" on life up to the time of *In Cold Blood*—we learn what seems to be Holly's deepest motivating force. Her regret at losing her nameless, battered "slob" of a cat, far from being a sentimental excess on her part (and the narrator's), is an intensely serious expression of a profound fear of relinquishment. Just as the dominant willed movement in Capote's fiction is acceptance—of things, persons, life—so its deepest fear seems to be of the inner principle of rejection that leads one to throw away those few and tenuous possessions life does permit. The fight against death must be carried on even in the innermost recesses of the self.

Holly's values are those of the Capote-narrator: she is a part of himself set free like a broken-stringed kite to wander toward an ambiguous land of dreams and death. Her brief presence is his own breakfast at Tiffany's, his taste of the idyll which always vanishes, leaving pain. Shortly before her departure he achieves a loving acceptance of this fact by an inner movement that parallels that of Collin in the tree house when he felt himself simultaneously receding from Dolly, the Judge, and Verena and embracing them all in a common sympathy. While he and Holly are riding in the park, just before his horse bolts, he feels an unexpected change of mood: "Suddenly, watching the tangled colors of Holly's hair flash in the red-yellow leaf light, I loved her enough to forget myself, my self-pitying despairs, and be content that something she thought happy was going to happen" (S 221). This attitude of blended acceptance and relinquishment sustains him from that time on, through the

123

vaguely sexual but deliberately unheroic climax of the horseback chase and the crisis over Holly's arrest. At the end, like Mr. Belli in "Among the Paths to Eden," he thanks his heroine for the memory and wishes her well.

When *Breakfast at Tiffany's* was published in 1958, Capote was well on his way toward the nonfiction novel. He had gradually shifted himself from the center of his fiction to the edge—from the role of protagonist to that of a highly detached narrator. He had moved from a private dream world to one that was identifiable, topical, even journalistic. He had come increasingly to build his stories around real people he had met, most of them women who resembled the elderly lady who was his first close friend. Outside of the fiction, a long series of developments had been leading him in the same direction. We must now look at these.

Ⅰn *Breakfast at Tiffany's* Capote
has his narrator make this reflection: "The average personality
reshapes frequently, every few years even our bodies undergo a
complete overhaul—desirable or not, it is a natural thing that we
should change" (S 200). Perhaps because he began publishing at
seventeen and his early stories were essentially about childhood,
Truman Capote has always been preoccupied with the necessity
of growth and change. Growing up is the subject of his first
novel, and in 1957 he told an interviewer, "Last summer I read
my novel *Other Voices, Other Rooms* for the first time since it
was published eight years ago, and it was quite as though I were
reading something by a stranger. The truth is, I am a stranger to
that book; the person who wrote it seems to have so little in
common with my present self. Our mentalities, our interior
temperatures are entirely different." [1]

Change, to Capote, is not just something that happens to
you: it is something you do. Near the end of *The Grass Harp*,
Collin reflects, "I've read that past and future are a spiral, one
coil containing the next and predicting its theme. Perhaps this
is so; but my own life has seemed to me more a series of closed
circles, rings that do not evolve with the freedom of a spiral:
for me to get from one to the other has meant a leap, not a
glide" (G 94). Collin eventually makes his leap, northward "to
a city where in my honor pennants flurried" (G 97). His intention is to study law, but we meet him next as the young writer
who narrates *Breakfast at Tiffany's*. Capote's corresponding leap
took him to the *New Yorker* and the literary world he has in-
habited ever since, recently to the accompaniment of flurrying
pennants.

The same element of deliberate design is evident in his account of his stay in Europe during the eight years that followed *Other Voices, Other Rooms:*

For me, Europe was a method of acquiring perspective and an education, a stepping stone toward maturity. But there *is* the law of diminishing returns, and about two years ago it began to set in: Europe had given me an enormous lot, but suddenly I felt as though the process were reversing itself—there seemed to be a taking away. So I came home, feeling quite grown up and able to settle down where I belong—which doesn't mean I've bought a rocking chair and turned to stone.[2]

Of all the calculated leaps Capote has taken in the pursuit of his literary career, by far the most awesome and most amply documented was his swing to the "nonfiction novel." A move carefully planned in both its personal and artistic aspects, it was, like Collin's departure from the South, preceded by a period of faltering: "What weakens me is the lull between, the wait before I know where to jump. After Dolly died I was a long while dangling" (G 94). During the three years that followed the publication of *The Grass Harp* (1951), Capote, apparently not sure where to jump, wrote a play and a musical, both of them unsuccessful, and collaborated on a motion picture. Not the first American novelist to carry on a brief flirtation with the stage, Capote recently gave an interesting explanation of such phenomena:

The real reason serious prose writers become interested in the theater is that it suggests a cameraderie that you don't have in writing a novel, which is necessarily a thing you do alone. They enjoy being taken outside of themselves, the whole thing of going to rehearsals and going out of town. It's not so isolated as when you write a book and then have to wait around for it to be published. It's the only medium in the world where the writer can get an intense, immediate reaction from the audience.[3]

In view of the sustained effort to get "outside of himself" that is evident in Capote's fiction, it is perhaps not very surprising that he should have tried this line of development. At the same time, his dramatic projects seem to have lacked from the beginning the self-determined quality of his other writing. Today he says, probably exaggerating somewhat, that he was "talked into" all of them. The first was a stage version of *The Grass Harp*, presented on Broadway on March 27, 1952, only a year after the publication of the novel. Capote gives the following account of its development:

After *The Grass Harp* was published, I thought it might make a nice opera. Aaron Copland had spoken many times about my doing one with him. I started, but then decided it would be better as a play. . . . I thought Lillian and Dorothy Gish had just the right quality for the two sisters and I did *The Grass Harp* with them in mind. But Bobby Lewis, the director, didn't want them; he was used to a different kind, an Actors' Studio kind of acting. I didn't know anything about the theater, I had never worked in it and I had no confidence in my own judgment. . . .

When we opened out of town I found the whole production heavy-handed. I didn't make any changes, it was the kind of thing you couldn't change around, it was atmospheric writing. Lewis told me it was a well-known fact that playwrights don't know what they've written and that it's for a director to work out, that's what the director was for. The play was a failure on Broadway but then it was put on successfully at Circle-in-the-Square with another director and another cast, and Lillian Gish did get to play it on television. It's still done a lot around the country by college groups.[4]

Though it follows the main lines of the novel with rough faithfulness, the play is only its skeleton and fails to recreate the fragile atmosphere which induced readers to accept the book's bizarre situation and sometimes questionable values. In the novel, it was Collin's all-pervasive love for Dolly, projected through death into a nostalgic past, that created the magic. Deprived of his narrative function, Collin became a problem that Capote tried to solve by conventionalizing him, combining his role with that of Riley Henderson. In the stage version it is Collin who wins Maude Riordan's love and gets shot in the tree house. The last scene, in which Dolly, Verena, and Judge Cool settle their affairs as Collin lies unconscious, could hardly be more different from the elegiac conclusion of the novel.

The Broadway version, which was produced by Arnold Saint-Subber and backed by a Virgil Thompson musical score and scenery and costumes by Cecil Beaton, closed after a month. The following year's off-Broadway production, directed by José Quintero, had an appropriate intimacy but would seem to have been somewhat less successful than Capote suggests. Looking back on the whole episode, Capote recently admitted that he "hadn't enjoyed the experience," but added that it left him with no frustrations, since he had no intention of pursuing the theater as a career.[5]

He did pursue it for a while, however, next by writing—also for Saint-Subber—the musical version of his story "House of Flowers" (1954). He told *Theatre Arts* at the time that he had always wanted to write a musical because, in his view, it was *the* unique form of theater: "A straight play can be done in films, and I suppose it can even be done on television. But a musical needs and uses all of the resources of the theatre—the lights and colors and the sets and the costumes and the living presence of the performers." [6] Capote recently recalled:

I was interested in writing lyrics for the theater. I knew Haiti very well and I liked that kind of West Indian native music. I thought I would do a musical play using a small band of eight and a composer with a knowledge of indigenous music. Saint, on the other hand, was looking for a big-time Broadway composer for a big Broadway musical. Fortunately he came up with Harold Arlen, which turned out to be a very good idea. Harold did a beautiful score. . . .

There was a very distinguished production set-up, Oliver Messel for the sets, Peter Brook to direct—I had wanted him because he'd done 'Ring 'Round the Moon'—and Balanchine for the dances. Pearl Bailey was hired for the part of one madam and the third day of rehearsals she was already acting up, she was being a combination Garbo, Bankhead and Bernhardt rolled into one. I knew she was going to put on her vaudeville act when we opened in Philadelphia. Then Peter Brook left because she couldn't get on with him and Balanchine left and the whole thing was such a shambles, you wouldn't know that a thing could go to pieces in one week.[7]

In the earlier *Theatre Arts* interview, Capote took a larger share of blame for the difficulties. Having written the short story as a preparatory exercise for the play, he next began, he says, writing lyrics and trying to refine the whole work into the desired form. Then Arlen was enlisted to write music and lyrics, and Capote found much of his own work had been in vain. "The musical play is a medium that is full of technical things that I didn't understand and that I still don't understand. I had thought that I was thinking in terms of pacing and variety when I was working alone on the lyrics, but I found that I really didn't know enough about it. When Arlen came in everything had to be changed except for the actual characters and the lyrics for the title song. Even the story had to be changed." [8]

The Capote-Arlen collaboration was apparently a genial, if unusual, one. Capote goes on:

I was living in St. Moritz when Arlen sent me a telegram saying he would do the show. We made a date to begin work in February in New York. But just to let him see what I'd been doing, I started sending him my lyrics right away. After he got them, he sent me some music on phonograph records. I'd listen to the records and write some more lyrics and send them back to him, and he'd mail me more records.

Then I moved to Paris and called him on the phone in Hollywood where he was working on the score of A Star Is Born. He put the phone on top of the piano and played for me what seemed like hours. These calls went back and forth for a month and a half. That's how we wrote the title song. [9]

Peter Brook, meanwhile, was making numerous changes in the script which Capote had worked on for a year in Italy. Capote admitted at the time, "Brook is a very creative force and he's wonderful at cutting. And there was plenty of cutting to be done. I don't usually tend to overwrite, but in this case I had written a full-length play plus a full-length musical. If we'd kept all of my original script, we'd have been in the theatre from eight o'clock until two in the morning." [10] After finishing the musical he summed up the experience this way: "I've always wanted to do it and now I've done it and thank God!" [11]

His 1966 recollection differs considerably in tone: "I kept rewriting the book; I wanted to salvage something because of the big financial investment in the show. I knew that anything artistic had gone down the drain. We'd had a lovely show and then it was wrecked. Lots of 'experts' came down to Philadelphia but all they did was confuse things more. That was when I vowed never again to have anything to do with the theater." [12]

The last statement above is taken from an interview with Irving Drutman that appeared in the *New York Times* in November, 1966. Occasioned by the continuing popularity of *In Cold Blood* and the preparations for the Abe Burrows-Edward Albee musical version of *Breakfast at Tiffany's* (which was soon abandoned), the article—titled "Capote: End of the Affair"— was the public statement of a renouncement of the theater that took place ten years before. For Capote has been as good as his word, never again writing original works or adaptations of his fiction for the stage, though he has continued to be involved in dramatic productions in various marginal ways. He explains:

The basic fact is that as a novelist, short story writer and reporter, I'm on my own and I either get all the praise or all the blame. In the theater, one is a molecule that has to be joined to other molecules to produce a living, breathing thing. I've done it, but I can't really accept it. That's why I'm not partial to the theater. I just don't function well in team sports.[13]

After discussing what Drutman calls his "two shaky excursions into the theatrical rapids," Capote concludes that it is always a mistake for him to try to transpose one of his works into another form. He adds, "Anything I've ever done in films and the theater was commissioned, I was talked into doing it. I've never had an original creative idea that seemed to me a play. I think I'm a good technician, so I could perforce learn to be an adequate playwright, but it's not with me a natural facility." [14]

The tone of mature self-knowledge evident in these assessments is of a piece with the strong, settled quality we have seen increasingly in Capote's fiction. Not at all new, on the other hand, is his sense of the unfittingness of transposing one genre into another. In 1949, the year after he published *Other Voices, Other Rooms*, Capote made a rare appearance as critic to discuss a dance adaptation by Valerie Bettis of William Faulkner's novel *As I Lay Dying*. The brief essay begins:

Art's purpose is the reprocessing of reality, to take our worka-day happenings, take them, translate them, transmit them. When only the original artist is involved, the work must contain at least a certain creative purity since all its accents are his own. That is the only art that matters: the art of the individual; anything else is at best a dubious business. The transposition of one art form into another, for instance, seems to me a corrupt, somewhat vulgar enterprise, even when these arts are related: theatre and film, for example, or the resetting of prose into poetry. Nature being what it is, these experimental inbreedings must logically make for Cretin offspring. Why can't a novel be simply a novel, a poem a poem? [15]

While Capote was doing his own stage adaptations, he often spoke of the difficulty of the task, though the air of disapproval was absent, lulled into silence by whatever combination of motives was operating at the time. That he was temporarily off his own main track he inadvertently revealed in a statement in the 1955 interview: "You write a short story or a novel under a kind of compulsion. You write it even though you yourself can't bear to read it, even if it's the kind of thing that, if you saw it on a publisher's list, you'd say, 'Save me from that!' " [16] He cites *The Grass Harp* as a book he wrote compulsively, even though he hates stories about "old people and children." The *Theatre Arts* interviewer remarks, "When he's writing for the theatre, however, his attitude is entirely different"—and quotes Capote as saying he then wants to write only what he would "long to see." [17]

If Capote made a brief escape from compulsion, he soon submitted to it again, and wisely so. His one remaining extra-curricular project was writing *Beat The Devil* (1954), a United Artists film that starred Humphrey Bogart, Jennifer Jones, and Gina Lollobrigida. The screenplay, a free adaptation of a novel by James Helvick, was jointly written by Capote and John Huston; according to some reports, Capote left before the picture was finished. He has described the experience as "a lark."

At least the one picture I wrote, *Beat The Devil*, was tremendous fun. I worked on it with John Huston while the picture was actually being made on location in Italy. Sometimes scenes that were just about to be shot were written right on the set.

The cast were completely bewildered—sometimes even Huston didn't seem to know what was going on. Naturally the scenes had to be written out of sequence, and there were peculiar moments when I was carrying around in my head the only real outline of the so-called plot. You never saw it? Oh, you should. It's a marvelous joke. Though I'm afraid the producer didn't laugh. The hell with them. Whenever there's a revival I go to see it and have a fine time.[18]

He adds, "Seriously, though, I don't think a writer stands much chance of imposing himself on a film unless he works in the warmest rapport with the director or is himself the director."

His one subsequent piece of movie work, writing the screenplay for *The Innocents* (1961), an adaptation of Henry James's *The Turn of the Screw*, was undoubtedly a labor of respect for an author whom he admires and by whom he has been influenced considerably. Capote stayed clear of the movie version of *Breakfast at Tiffany's* and, in 1966, said he agreed heartily with director Richard Brooks' intention not to confer with him over the filming of *In Cold Blood*. He seems to have given little more than his blessing to the December, 1966, television production of "A Christmas Memory" (which won a George Foster Peabody Award as one of the "very finest TV hours of 1966"), and seems content to play mostly a managerial role in other proposed dramatizations of his work.

The desire for "an intense, immediate reaction from the audience," which Capote said first lured him to the stage, has recently been satisfied by his occasional public readings. Irving Drutman gives an accurate description of Capote's program: "He is a stylish platform entertainer, sometimes performing in sold-out auditoriums seating from 7,000 to 8,000 people, holding his listeners enthralled as he renders, in a winning, childlike treble, the travel piece, 'A Ride through Spain,' a scene from *The Muses Are Heard*, a chapter from *In Cold Blood*, and his nostalgic short story, 'A Christmas Memory.' The program begins at 8:30 in the evening and is in two parts, separated by an intermission."[19] In these readings, Capote makes effective use of his two strongest cards: the fiction itself, and a personal magnetism that almost immediately conquers the preliminary movement of incredulity tinged with aversion which his elfin presence seems to arouse in the average audience. He handles his listeners with consummate skill, often revealing humor in lines where the reader might not—sometimes, I think, should not—see it. A Capote reading is a delight for the audience and apparently for Capote, too. "It is," he says, "just like being in the theatre." [20]

By the time he finished work on "House of Flowers" (1954) Capote was in full flight from Broadway. He says that his serious concern with the nonfiction novel dates from this period.

I'd done the musical "House of Flowers" and was disgusted with the theater; I never had cared much for the theater anyway; and I was furious at having wasted two years on this project which I didn't think was really worth it. To put it mildly. I had been talked into all that and was sick and tired of it. But I'd always written nonfiction and always liked it. Then I suddenly decided that I would do a big one. From that moment on I became very, very interested in the whole idea of doing a nonfiction novel.[21]

Capote had, indeed, always written nonfiction. He was a keeper of journals, and from there it was only a step to the kind of polished vignette found in *Local Color* (1950), a volume he describes as "a small truthful book of travel impressions." [22] It contains pieces on New Orleans, New York, Brooklyn, Hollywood, Europe, Ischia, Tangier, and Spain. His *Selected Writings* (1963), which is equally divided between fiction and nonfiction, includes three sketches from *Local Color*: "New Orleans," "Ischia," and "A Ride through Spain." The first was written in 1943 (the same year as "A Tree of Night," the earliest piece of fiction in the volume), and the last two in 1949, during Capote's European sojourn.

Perhaps the first thing to be observed about these sketches is their stylistic elegance. In his public readings Capote includes "A Ride through Spain," a choreographic rendition of a tragicomic train ride that progressed "so slowly butterflies blew in and out the windows" (S 276); in a soft, precise voice completely at the service of the written word, he projects the carefully sculptured quality of such lines as these:

At each stop cyclones of barefooted women and somewhat naked children ran beside the train sloshing earthen jars of water and furrily squalling Agua! Agua! For two pesetas you could buy a whole basket of dark runny figs, and there were trays of curious white-coated candy doughnuts that looked as though they should be eaten by young girls wearing Communion dresses (S 273).

The earlier "New Orleans" is much more evidently a stylistic exercise. It begins in an atmosphere of hushed, subtropical strangeness: "In the courtyard there was an angel of black stone, and its angel head rose above giant elephant leaves; the stark glass angel eyes, bright as the bleached blue of sailor eyes, stared upward" (S 255). From this quiet beginning the essay moves through a series of contrasting vignettes to a crescendo of blatant sexuality:

And tonight is Saturday. The room floats in cigarette smoke and Saturday-night perfume. All the little greasy wood tables have double rings of chairs, and everyone knows everyone, and for a moment the world is this room, this dark, jazzy, terrible room; our heartbeat is Shotgun's stamping foot, every joyous element of our lives is focused in the shine of his malicious eyes. *I want a big fat mama, yes yes!* He rocks forward on his stool, and, as he lifts his face to look straight at us, a great riding holler goes up in the night: *I want a big fat mama with the meat shakin' on her, yes!* (S 262).

The central fixture in the piece is an elderly lady whom the young narrator visits in her decaying, slum-surrounded mansion. He studies her with an admittedly clinical interest, noting that "she is delightful in her archaic way, amusing, too, though not by intent. . . . Miss Y. speaks in premeditated tones but what she says is haphazard, and her sherry-colored eyes are forever searching the surroundings" (S 257). Except that she is not loved, Miss Y. resembles the heroines of "A Christmas Memory" and *The Grass Harp*.

The transition from journal to sketch is seen most clearly in "Ischia," where it is actually employed as a structural principle. Capote writes: "When one rereads a journal it is usually the less ambitious jottings, the haphazard, accidental notations that, seen again, plow a furrow through your memory. For example: 'Today Gioconda left in the room assorted slips of colored paper. Are they presents? Because I gave her the bottle of cologne? They will make delightful bookmarks.' This reverberates. First, Gioconda. She is a beautiful girl . . ." (S 265). And so on.

"Ischia" recalls the author's stay, with an unnamed companion, on an almost tourist-free Mediterranean island during the months of spring and early summer—a time spent joining in the rhythms of a sleepy village or climbing steep seaside paths "through the grape fields where bees are like a blizzard and lizards burn greenly on the budding leaves" (S 268).

The essay seems designed to typify the quiet periods of creative retirement which in Capote's life have alternated with turbulently social ones. The latter seem to predominate. He told a *Paris Review* interviewer, "I feel slightly as though I've never lived a tranquil moment, unless you count what an occasional Nembutal induces. Though, come to think of it, I spent two years in a very romantic house on top of a mountain in Sicily, and I guess this period could be called tranquil. God knows, it was quiet. That's where I wrote *The Grass Harp*." [23] The period referred to was approximately that of "Ischia," and the place was Taormina, where Capote lived (purely by accident, he says) in a house once occupied by D. H. Lawrence.

In recent years his preferred place of seclusion is his apartment in Verbier, Switzerland, where most of *In Cold Blood* was written. At such times his only companion is Jack Dunphy, a writer and translator who is his closest friend. Capote told *Life:*

Gregariousness is the enemy of art, so when I work I have to forcibly remove myself from other people. I'm like a prizefighter in training: I have to sweep all the elements except work out of my life completely. What I do requires fantastic concentration. I'm so concerned with language and style, right down to the very comma, that any distraction at all is fatal. But you can't be totally alone, or you lose all contact with reality, so even when I'm engrossed and secluded, Jack Dunphy can be there. He's my oldest and best friend, and best critic too. [24]

Truman Capote's professional literary career, inner-directed though it is, was sponsored in its early years by the *New Yorker*, a magazine whose topicality and commercial canniness have played an important part in his swing to nonfiction. It is, Capote says, "the only magazine I know of that encourages the serious practitioners of this art form." [25] When, in 1955, he decided that his first excursion into lengthy reportage should be an account of the Russian tour of an all-Negro production of George Gershwin's *Porgy and Bess*, the *New Yorker* commissioned the project.

The resulting book, *The Muses Are Heard*, is a purportedly objective account of the first part of the tour—from the December 17, 1955, State Department briefing in West Berlin to the December 27 premiere in Leningrad. The touring company was Everyman Opera, Incorporated, and the director was Robert Breen. There were fifty-eight actors in the troupe, and the thirty-six other persons who accompanied them included a psychiatrist and three "journalists," among them Capote.

In keeping with the journalistic nature of *Muses*, the style is relatively functional and unobtrusive, though here and there it slips into the more poetic manner of the earlier fiction and travel sketches. Capote's eye for costume and interior decoration is particularly well suited to his subject. He notes a group of Russian soldiers, "country boys with their heads shaved bald, their drab uniforms sagging in the seat like diapers" (S 372), and in general provides a vivid running commentary on the sartorial clashes that repeatedly occur as this zany group of Americans penetrate into a drab, wintry Russia.

His similes make alien interiors seem familiar. Here, for example, is a Russian restaurant: "The size of a gymnasium, it looked as if it had been done over for a school prom by a decorating committee with Victorian tastes. Plush crimson draperies were looped along the walls. Other-era chandeliers distributed a tropic glare that beat down on a jungle of borscht-stained tablecloths and withering rubber plants" (S 320–21).

There are occasional strong reminders of an earlier Capote, as when a female guide leads the party up a staircase formerly used by ambassadors to the Czar: "In the ectoplasmic wake of those ambassadors our party followed her up marble stairs that curved under a filigree ceiling of green malachite, like a corri-

136

dor under the sea . . ." (S 369). Or this moment during the train ride: "At ten, when I opened my eyes, we were in a wild, crystal world of frozen rivers and snowfields. Here and there, like printing on paper, stretches of fir trees interrupted the whiteness. Flights of crows seemed to skate on a sky hard and shiny as ice" (S 310).

Although Capote narrates the book in the first person, he is obviously aiming at complete objectivity. We can see him skillfully circumventing the need to express his own opinion directly, and though we admire his virtuosity, it is sometimes distracting. Besides presenting an abundance of authentic-sounding dialogue, he several times quotes from the diaries or other written accounts of members of the group.

Since the book is focused on a dramatic performance—one in which the stakes are much higher than usual—the crux of the objectivity problem is Capote's evaluation of the play. Far from evading the issue, he brings it to the fore. Having arrived in his accounts at the moment of the play, he jumps over it in two lines, then sets up the scene in the narrator's memory. Here is the passage:

The curtain, announced for eight, went up at nine-five and came down at eleven-forty. By midnight I was back at the Astoria waiting for a call from Henry Shapiro, the UP correspondent in Moscow who'd said he would telephone me after the premiere to find out "how it went. What really happened." There is no absolute truth in these matters, only opinion, and as I attempted to formulate my own, tried to decide what I was going to tell Shapiro, I stretched on the bed and switched on the light. . . . I seemed still to hear the soft clickety noise of newsreel cameras. And indeed, lying in the dark, it was as though a film were rushing through my head . . . I made a conscious effort to slow the film down, let it start at the beginning (S 390–91).

There follows a long, detailed account of the play and the audience's reception of it—first uncomprehending and silent, somewhat shocked at Breen's erotic touches, then warming to a considerable if not overwhelming enthusiasm. As the show progresses, Capote quotes a whole spectrum of reactions, then formulates his own cautious and tentative verdict: "Though the performance did not sail, perhaps because too much water had already been shipped, at least it floated, wallowed along in a current of less frigid temperature" (S 399). He remembers hearing young Russians humming show tunes outside the theater, and thinks perhaps this lasting effect would justify his calling the performance a success, though not the "bombshell" the Breens had expected.

Finally the phone rings, but at first he doesn't move. Knowing he will be asked to give his verdict on "journalism's unsubtle level," he feels "qualms" (S 400). He prefers, he says, to give a glowing account, and suspects that's what Shapiro wants to hear.

But I let the telephone ring while a plethora of *ifs* plunged around in my head: if the Russians had been able to consult a printed program, if the fanfare and ceremonial aspects had been curtailed, if less had been demanded of the audience, if . . . I quit stalling and picked up the receiver. But the person on the line was Miss Lydia, who said she was sorry, someone had called me from Moscow and been disconnected. I had no more calls that evening (S 400–01).

Capote's method of presenting the big scene frames and highlights it, but is calculated to achieve an even more important end. By focusing in this one section on himself, with the caveat that his reaction can be only a matter of opinion, he maintains in the overall narration the very objectivity he so ostentatiously disclaims for his judgment of the play. But the final effect of all this, especially the strategy of withholding judgment by missing the phone call, is the highly subjective one of damning with faint praise.

One cannot escape the impression that in this instance Capote's elaborate quest for objectivity, for fairness, has turned into a sly rhetorical trick. And the few remaining pages do nothing to dispel this impression. Capote reproduces a cable from the Opera's New York office giving a highly laudatory account of the New York reviews, but also quotes the secretary's remark: "That's not *exactly* how it arrived. The Breens did a little adding and editing. There was one line. '*Times* says scored moderate success.' You can bet Wilva cut that out! Just wants everybody to feel wonderful, and I think that's kind of endearing" (S 403–04).

Capote admits today, agreeing with a number of the reviewers, that *The Muses Are Heard* is a rather "bitchy" piece of writing. (He now describes it as a nonfiction comic short novel.) One might, in fact, rather justly describe *Muses* as Capote's revenge on the theater. His frequent remark that he has never cared much for theater people is borne out by his treatment of director Breen and his wife—though the book is not particularly friendly to the other Americans either.

He treats the Russians both worse and better. Few readers in 1955 were likely to object to his refined ridicule of Miss Lydia, an official interpreter with "straying dishwater hair" and an "embalmed glaze" over her eyes; of the "dragoon of stunted Amazons" who guide the visitors through the Winter Palace; or of Josef ("Call me Joe") Adamov, the on-the-make Radio Moscow representative with his phony New York accent and slightly dusty slang.

On the other hand, some oppressed members of the Russian populace receive deeply sympathetic treatment. In the most striking example, Capote climaxes his account of an evening on the town with this episode: with Orlov, his host, he is sitting in a cafe where one of the entertainers is "a boy who roamed around with a guitar" singing melancholy folk songs. Capote notices that the boy's attention is on him, but doesn't understand why his gaze should be so disturbing until he realizes it reminds him of the "deaf-mute pleadings" in the eyes of a man he saw earlier that evening, beaten and left lying in the snow. Eventually the boy tries to talk to him.

"I . . . you . . . mother . . . man." He knew about ten words of English and he struggled to pronounce them. I asked Orlov to interpret, and as they talked together in Russian it was as though the boy were singing again. While his voice wove some sorrowful prose melody, his fingers tinkered with the strings of the guitar. Tears sprang to his eyes, and he rubbed them away with the flat of his palm, leaving grimy smudges like a child. I asked Orlov what he was saying. "It's not so much interesting. I'm not interested in politics." (S 365)

It seems that the boy, being of English and Polish parentage, is badly treated in Russia and wants Capote to write a letter for him to the British ambassador. Capote, unable to see how he can help him, watches despair "shade the hopeful shine of his wet eyes." At closing time they find him blocking their path to the door. " 'Help,' said the boy, gently catching hold of my sleeve. 'Help,' he said, his eyes full on me, as a waitress, at Orlov's request, pushed him aside to let us by. 'Help, help,' he called after me, a door between us now, and the words a muted sound fading into nothing like the night-falling snow. 'I think he's a crazy person,' said Orlov" (S 366–67).

With this youthful guitarist-prisoner Capote strikes a familiar chord. From Kay of "A Tree of Night" through Tico Feo and Holly Golightly, the guitar is one of the most familiar trademarks of the Capote character. Snow and closing doors also have a way of appearing when Capote writes from the heart. That he did so at times in *The Muses Are Heard* makes it a deeply moving as well as perceptive and timely look behind a then recently erected Iron Curtain. But the price of timeliness—the extent to which the book manifests in Capote that "highly contemporaneous, journalistic mind" that has been attributed to his distant cousin, Edgar Allan Poe—is being paid; it is already becoming dated. Capote's awareness of this liability in the material of *The Muses Are Heard* no doubt strengthened his resolve, when he finally came to the writing of a full-scale nonfiction novel, to pick a subject that would come closer to timelessness.

In *Breakfast at Tiffany's*, published two years after *The Muses Are Heard*, Holly Golightly thinks of her friend, the aspiring young writer, as standing with his nose pressed against a glass, wanting to be "on the inside staring out" (S 194). Truman Capote's career would seem to be everything such a young man could have desired. Certainly Capote began as an outsider in his life and his writing as well. His dispossessed Southern childhood has been amply documented, both in his own fiction and in Harper Lee's *To Kill a Mockingbird*. His subsequent efforts to become an insider are reflected in an almost predictable sequence of literary forms: journalism, fiction becoming more like journalism, then a blend of the two in the nonfiction novel. For journalism is the genre of the insider. *Breakfast at Tiffany's* might have blossomed out of a gossip column, and indications are that Capote's forthcoming novel, *Answered Prayers*, which he told me he planned to finish in 1969, will deal with even more select society. According to the 1966 *Life* article, "It will be based, if indirectly, on Capote's acquaintance with people he knows as Charlie and Oona, Jackie, Babe, Lennie, Bobby and other such noted persons, all of whom can be expected to read it with keen interest." [26] Capote told me that this book, like the preceding ones, will employ a dramatized narrator, but that in this case the narrator will not correspond to himself. The narrator will not, in fact, be a very nice guy. "Maybe this will be my *real* self," he chuckled.[27] Perhaps this novel will be at least a partial fulfillment of the wish expressed by Norman Mailer in this 1959 comment on Capote:

Truman Capote I do not know well, but I like him. He is tart as a grand aunt, but in his way he is a ballsy little guy, and he is the most perfect writer of my generation, he writes the best sentences word for word, rhythm upon rhythm. I would not have changed two words in *Breakfast at Tiffany's* which will become a small classic. Capote has still given no evidence that he is serious about the deep resources of the novel, and his short stories are too often saccharine. At his worst he has less to say than any good writer I know. I would suspect he hesitates between the attractions of Society which enjoys and so repays him for his unique gifts, and the novel he could write of the gossip column's real life, a major work, but it would banish him forever from his favorite world. Since I have nothing to lose, I hope Truman fries a few of the fancier fish.[28]

In 1955 it would have been hard to think of a better way to become an insider than to travel behind the Iron Curtain as a participant in Everyman Opera's well publicized Russian campaign. Interviewing a movie idol is a comparable if more campy undertaking, and the following year Capote did just that. He seems to have come upon the idea in the course of his continuing debate with literary friends about the artistic possibilities of reportage. Contending that an artist can raise any type of journalistic writing to the highest level of literature, he agreed with the New Yorker editors on a Photoplay-type interview of a movie star done in one sitting. Exhibiting his usual flair for combining artistic enterprise with financial acumen and a sense of the colorful gesture, Capote made a bet, exacting the promise of triple payment if he succeeded. "We put some names in a hat and the one I drew out was Marlon. It wasn't quite fair, I suppose, because I already knew him, but once I started, I followed the interview form we had agreed on. It turned out quite successfully. Of course I won the bet." [29]

Like almost all Capote's nonfiction, The Duke in His Domain is partly a travel sketch. The local color in this case is provided by Kyoto, Japan, where Brando was spending part of 1957 on location for the Warner Brothers–William Goetz motion-picture version of James Michener's novel Sayonara. The piece opens with a colorful scene-setting:

Most Japanese girls giggle. The little maid on the fourth floor of the Miyako Hotel, in Kyoto, was no exception. Hilarity, and attempts to suppress it, pinked her cheeks (unlike the Chinese, the Japanese complexion more often than not has considerable color), shook her plump peony-and-pansy-kimonoed figure. There seemed to be no particular reason for this merriment; the Japanese giggle operates without apparent motivation. I'd merely asked to be directed toward a certain room. "You come to see Marron?" (S 405).

Capote told an interviewer, "My work must be held together by a narrative line. Even the Brando piece was narrative." [30] In keeping with the New Yorker agreement, "The Duke in His Domain" is built upon a single interview. Capote achieves depth, however, by filling in the pauses in Brando's monologue with enough background material to yield a reasonably complete account of the actor's life, as well as of the Sayonara project in which he was currently involved. Sometimes this material is simply inserted gratis, amplifying something Brando has said or commenting on an action or an item in his cluttered room. One phase of his past life is presented in the words of "a friend of his, who saw a lot of him in those pre-candy days" (S 428); another in those of "a past tenant on the ducal preserve" (S 439).

The most effective touch in the essay is made possible by the coincidence that Capote had met his subject in 1947, ten years before the time of the interview. By means of a short flashback, he superimposes a younger Brando on the one sitting before him. "Watching him now, with his eyes closed, his unlined face white under an overhead light, I felt as if the moment of my initial encounter with him were being recreated" (S 411). In 1947, Capote recalls, he attended a rehearsal of *A Streetcar Named Desire*, the play that would bring Brando his first general recognition. Its director, Elia Kazan, had some time before declared him to be the best actor in the world. Capote, arriving early and finding only a brawny young man asleep on a table (with the *Basic Writings of Sigmund Freud* open on his chest), took him for a stagehand. Looking more closely, he found the face to be strangely unsuited to the body.

For this face was so very untough, superimposing, as it did, an almost angelic refinement and gentleness upon hard-jawed good looks: taut skin, a broad, high forehead, wide-apart eyes, an aquiline nose, full lips with a relaxed, sensual expression. Not the least suggestion of Williams' unpoetic Kowalski. It was therefore rather an experience to observe, later that afternoon, with what chameleon ease Brando acquired the character's cruel and gaudy colors, how superbly, like a guileful salamander, he slithered into the part, how his own persona evaporated—just as, in this Kyoto hotel room ten years afterward, my 1947 memory of Brando receded, disappeared into his 1957 self (S 412).

The obvious theme is Capote's familiar one of change. He reflects that the Brando now before him "was, of course, a different person—bound to be." He is balding, physically heavier, richer, and far more famous.

Those were some of the alterations a decade had made. There were others. His eyes had changed. Although their *caffe-espresso* color was the same, the shyness, any traces of real vulnerability that they had formerly held, had left them; now he looked at people with assurance, and with what can only be called a pitying expression, as though he dwelt in spheres of enlightenment where they, to his regret, did not (S 412).

Capote paints his portrait of Brando with detachment, but also with fundamental sympathy—sympathy of a kind he does not bestow on the only other person who appears on the scene, Brando's friend and literary assistant, whom Capote calls "Murray." "A subdued-looking youngish man," Murray tries to arrange a session for later in the evening to discuss the actor's current writing project (a film script entitled A *Burst of Vermilion*). "Tell ya, Mar, s'pose I go over this down in my room, and maybe we'll get together again—say, around ten-thirty?" (S 407). Then he departs, almost tripping on the train of the maid's kimono. Periodically he interrupts the conversation with phone calls until Brando gently dismisses him for the night. Capote treats him less gently, and more like the Americans in *The Muses Are Heard*.

James Dean, the young actor whose spectacular career had ended the previous year in an automobile crash, is discussed at some length, having apparently pursued Brando for a time. Capote refers to him as "The All-American 'mixed-up kid,' the symbol of misunderstood hot-rodding youth with a switch-blade approach to life's little problems" (S 431). Brando he seems both to respect as an artist and to feel a certain kinship with as a person. There is something of the wistful outsider in Brando even after he has become a self-styled duke in his domain, and one suspects that Capote may feel a bit this way himself. The essay closes on a scene that fixes its delicate balance of admiration and unPhotoplayish irony. Capote's last sight of Brando is not at the hotel but on an immense theater sign he passes on his way home through an early morning street: sixty feet tall, rivaling in size the greatest of the Buddhas. "Rather Buddha-like, too, was his pose, for he was depicted in a squatting position, a serene smile on a face that glistened in the rain and the light of a street lamp. A deity, yes; but, more than that, really, just a young man sitting on a pile of candy" (S 444).

The year (1958), following the publication of "The Duke in His Domain," saw the appearance of *Breakfast at Tiffany's*, which opens with "a brownstone in the East Seventies where, during the early years of the war, I had my first New York apartment" (S 162). Around the time he was writing these lines Capote was moving into a large, yellow brick house at Number 70 Willow Street in Brooklyn Heights. His move had prompt journalistic results in the form of an essay published in *Holiday* in 1959: "A House on the Heights." The title is appropriate in suggesting a sense of arrival at some sort of eminence, for if the young writer in *Breakfast at Tiffany's* was standing on the outside looking in at Manhattan's expensive glitter, he now seems to consider his position much more central.

Often a week passes without my "going to town," or "crossing the bridge," as neighbors call a trip to Manhattan. Mystified friends, suspecting provincial stagnation, inquire: "But what do you *do* over there?" Let me tell you, life can be pretty exciting around here. Remember Colonel Rudolph Abel, the Russian secret agent, the biggest spy ever caught in America, head of the whole damned apparatus? Know where they nabbed him? Right here! smack on Fulton Street! Trapped him in a building between David Semple's fine-foods store and Frank Gambuzza's television repair shop (S 450).

The democratic chumminess of this passage is only half the picture, socially speaking, for another charm Brooklyn Heights had for Capote in the mid-fifties was its postwar resumption of the aura of an earlier period when "brigades of the gifted— artists, writers," had made it their home. First there were Hart Crane and Thomas Wolfe, then, in the early forties, all together in a house on Middagh Street, W. H. Auden, Richard Wright, Carson McCullers, Paul and Jane Bowles, Benjamin Britten, and stage designer Oliver Smith—along with "an authoress of murder entertainments—Miss Gypsy Rose Lee, and a Chimpanzee accompanied by Trainer" (S 447-448).

After admitting that he may be taking "too Valentine a view" of his new home (he has been called "the last of the old-fashioned Valentine makers"), Capote sets out to depict the

Heights as a timeless oasis amid the tawdriness of greater Brooklyn—a place of gardens, clear seaside air, playing children. The house itself, bought shortly before by an unnamed friend, won him at first sight. (The friend was probably Oliver Smith, who later, in this same house, gave painting lessons to Jackie Kennedy.) Capote, who usually gets what he wants, plied his friend with his own martinis and showed him the wisdom of sharing the house.

He writes lovingly of the twenty-eight rooms, each with a fireplace; the hardwood floors and thick walls; the staircase "floating upward in white, swan-simple curves to a skylight of sunny amber-gold glass" (S 449). The back part of the house is like a projection of Capote's imagination:

French doors led to a spacious rear porch reminiscent of Louisiana. A porch canopied, completely submerged as though under a lake of leaves, by an ancient but admirably vigorous vine weighty with grapelike bunches of wisteria. Beyond, a garden: a tulip tree, a blossoming pear, a perched black-and-red bird bending a feathery branch of forsythia (S 449).

The essay is not primarily about the house, however; it is about Capote's Brooklyn Heights friends—the non-literary ones —a colorful multitude from wealthy aristocrats to dock workers. Capote is, if not the duke of his domain, at least its ranking gadabout, gaining entree, one way or another, to every kind of dwelling. There is, for example, the store owned by Mr. George Knapp, "known to his friends as Father," and his wife Florence. Father Knapp's occupations, both dear to Capote's heart, are those of world traveler and collector of odds and ends.

Cards arrive: he is in Seville, now Copenhagen, now Milan, next week Manchester, everywhere and all the while on a gaudy spending spree. Buying: blue crockery from a Danish castle. Pink apothecary jars from an old London pharmacy. English brass, Barcelona lamps, Battersea boxes, French paperweights, Italian witch balls, Greek icons, Venetian blackamoors, Spanish saints, Korean cabinets; and junk, glorious junk, a jumble of ragged dolls, broken buttons, a stuffed kangaroo . . . (S 450-451).

When a *Paris Review* interviewer sought out Capote in 1958, she found him in the big yellow house, which she notes he had "recently restored with the taste and elegance that is generally characteristic of his undertakings." [31] Also characteristically, he was "head and shoulders inside a newly arrived crate containing a wooden lion"—an item quite possibly from Father Knapp's collection.

The personage who dominates the essay is not Father Knapp but Mrs. Cornelius Oosthuizen, "a tall intimidating replica of frail unforbidding Miss Marianne Moore (who, it may be re- called, is a Brooklyn lady too)" (*S* 452). Capote gained admit- tance to her mansion by delivering a pound of dog meat that had been sent to him by mistake. The old lady is devoted to animals, and shows Capote a graveyard containing several generations of them.

Look below, there in the garden. Under the heaven tree. Those markings: graves are what you see, some as old as my childhood. The seashells are goldfish. The yellow coral, canaries. That white stone is a rabbit; that cross of pebbles: my favorite, the first Mary—angel girl, went bathing in the river and caught a fatal chill. I used to tease Cornelius, Mr. Oosthuizen, told him, ha-ha, told him I planned to put him there with the rest of my darlings. Ha-ha, he wasn't amused, not at all (*S* 454).

Mrs. Oosthuizen, who has several counterparts in Capote's writing, is associated in this essay with some familiar images. The garden with its heaven tree recalls "The Headless Hawk"; that story's strange heroine, as well as her cousin Holly Go- lightly, comes to mind when Mrs. Oosthuizen's cats are de- scribed as "scarred battlers with leprous fur and punch-drunk eyes," and when, on the next page, we read of the St. George alley: "a shadowy shelter for vagrants . . . wino derelicts wan- dered over the bridge from Chinatown and the Bowery . . . orphaned, gone-wild creatures: cats, as many as minnows in a stream . . ." (*S* 454–455).

Capote concludes the essay with three Brooklyn Heights episodes recalled by jottings in the "hieroglyphic shambles I call my journal" (S 455). "Took T&G to G&T" reminds him of a favorite restaurant, Gage & Tollner, a devotedly maintained relic of 1874.

Another notation, "At last a face in the ghost hotel!" jolts the reader back to *Other Voices, Other Rooms*. The ghost hotel is a seemingly haunted riverfront building, the romantic destination of many of Capote's walks. He had almost come to believe it deserted when one day he saw a man appear briefly at one of its windows.

The phrase "Thunder on Cobra Street" eludes him for a while, but then he remembers the experience behind it and turns it into the essay's exciting climax. The street referred to is one that runs steeply down to the dockyards—"not a true part of the Heights neighborhood" but lying "like a serpent at the gates, on the outmost periphery" (S 459). It is ruled by a gang of juvenile delinquents called "Cobras," and Capote (who habitually casts himself in disarmingly non-heroic roles) admits that he visits it rarely and with a thumping heart. On one such occasion the sky was threatening rain as he walked along among rope-skipping children and lounging elders. The expensive camera he was carrying attracted the attention of the group of "dull-faced" Cobras; without looking he felt that they had "uncoiled" and were sliding toward him, whistling, then calling, "Hey huh, Whitey, lemmeseeduhcamra" (S 460). As the street grew silent, he was uncertain what to do.

The ending combines the exhilarating flight from young Central Park hoodlums in *Breakfast at Tiffany's* and the final, deluged scene of "The Headless Hawk":

Thunder salvaged the moment. Thunder that rolled, crashed down the street like a truck out of control. We all looked up, a sky ripe for storm stared back. I shouted, "Rain! Rain!" and ran. Ran for the Heights, that safe citadel, that bourgeois bastion. Tore along the Esplanade—where the nice young mothers were racing their carriages against the coming disaster. Caught my breath under the thrashing leaves of troubled elms, rushed on: saw the flower-wagon man struggling with his thunder-frightened horse. Saw, twenty yards ahead, then ten, five, then none, the yellow house on Willow Street. Home and happy to be (S 460).

Brooklyn Heights was "home" until 1965, when Capote moved back across the bridge and took up lodgings in the new United Nations Plaza co-op apartments, where one of his neighbors was Robert F. Kennedy. He reportedly still maintains a brownstone in Brooklyn Heights, as well as the apartment in Switzerland and two beach houses on Long Island. The latter three are hideaways for work, but the New York home fulfills an equally important need of Capote-the-erstwhile-outsider: to be at the center of things, where the action is: "When I'm flying my flag in town," Capote says, "there's nobody in the world more sociable than I am." [32]

Friendship is probably as important to him as his writing, and certainly quite inseparable from it. It is, as mentioned before, the real theme of "A House on the Heights." It was "a friend" who brought him to the yellow house; Capote is, implicitly, among the friends who call Mr. George Knapp "Father"; even Mrs. Cornelius Oosthuizen has "condescended to distinguish" him with her "acquaintance." There are the two mysterious friends T&G whom he took to G&T; and the possession of "waterfront friends" enables him to lunch on ships of various nations and share coffee on tugboats. In Capote's fiction, too, friendship is a recurrent motif, and "friends" describes the relationship between the Capote-narrator and his various heroines.

Capote's conversation is liberally sprinkled with references to his friends. Hardly a name is mentioned—particularly a well-known one—without the reply, "He (or she) is a friend of mine." Ten months after the publication of In Cold Blood, Capote gave this aspect of his life an expression unlikely to be surpassed. Deciding that he "just wanted to give a party for my real friends," [33] he staged a spectacular Black and White Masked Ball at New York's Plaza Hotel. According to writer Leo Lehrman (a friend), Capote was planning as early as 1945 to give such a party someday—"if I ever have a lot of money." [34] In Cold Blood brought in the money, and on November 28, 1966, he produced what Life magazine alternately described as "the party of the decade . . . the party of the century, or . . . the biggest and most glorious bash ever." [35]

A black and white decor, suggested by Cecil Beaton's setting from the Ascot scene of "My Fair Lady," was maintained throughout—from the prescribed masks, some of which were said to have cost over $600, to the two orchestras (Peter Duchin and the all-Negro Soul Brothers). Capote proved himself a super-insider by writing his own international social register to people this affair; the number was originally set at 400, then extended to 500 because of complaints from the uninvited— "People are practically committing *suicide*." [36]

Despite the host's claim that it was to be a "no-publicity" affair, the guest list inevitably appeared in the *New York Times*, and the ball was reported nationally for several days by all the news media. Among those invited, most of whom accepted, were Governor Rockefeller, Mayor Lindsay, several Kennedys (Rose, Jackie, Robert, Ted), Ambassador and Mrs. Llewellyn Thompson, the Walter Lippmanns, the Henry Fords, Lynda Bird Johnson, Mrs. W. Averell Harriman, Baron and Baroness de Rothschild, the Henry Fondas, the Joseph Alsops, Gloria Vanderbilt, the John Steinbecks, the William Buckleys, Greta Garbo, Frank and Mia Sinatra, Sammy Davis, Jr., Tallulah Bankhead, James Baldwin, The Marquis and Marchioness of Dufferin and Ava, Kay Graham (to whom the party was dedicated, in return for a similar favor), Gloria Guinness, Lee Radziwill, Count and Countess Rudolfo Crespi, Arthur Schlesinger, Jr., McGeorge Bundy, Lauren Bacall, Jerome Robbins, Edward Albee, Marianne Moore, Norman Mailer, Nicholas Katzenbach, John Sherman Cooper, Jacob Javits, Alice Roosevelt Longworth, George Plimpton, Roddy McDowall, Margaret Truman Daniel, the Maharajah and Maharani of Jaipur, the William S. Paleys, Peter Lawford, Adolph Green, Mrs. William Rhinelander Stewart, Cleveland Amory, Janet Flanner, Andy Warhol, Douglas Fairbanks, Princess Luciana Pignatelli, Richard Avedon, the Sargent Shrivers, Edmund Wilson, the Lionel Trillings, and several residents of Kansas whom Capote met while working on *In Cold Blood*. Contemplating the brilliant and varied gathering, Capote remarked, "I really don't think anyone else could have done it—could have brought all these people together—because nobody else *knows* them all." [37]

Many people were annoyed by Capote's party, finding it

ostentatious, extravagant, artificial. Max Lerner saw it as an illustration of historian Daniel Boorstin's dictum that the events of our time turn out, all too frequently, to be pseudo-events.[38] Cleveland Amory, author of *Who Killed Society?* called it "almost a joke."[39] To some extent it was all these things, and probably intended so by Capote. For him and a lot of others it was also apparently great fun.

Virtuosity, as Shana Alexander has remarked,[40] is one of Capote's main characteristics; and if he seems to collect people the way he collects *virtu*, he does so with a high degree of the requisite skills. Capote may be snippy, prissy, caustic, and numerous other things, but he is also a charming person who is genuinely interested in other people and has inspired strong affection in a remarkable number of them. In "The Duke in His Domain," a former friend of Marlon Brando says something about the actor which seems to me to fit Capote himself:

He makes you feel you're the only person in the room. In the world. Makes you feel that you're under his protection and that your troubles and moods concern him deeply. You have to believe it; more than anyone I've known, he radiates *sincerity*. Afterward, you may ask yourself, 'Is it an act?' If so, what's the point? What have you got to give him? Nothing except—and this *is* the point—affection. Affection that lends him authority over you. I sometimes think Marlon is like an orphan who later on in life tries to compensate by becoming the kindly head of a huge orphanage. But even outside this institution he wants everybody to love him (S 440).

Capote adds the footnote that "within the clique over which Brando presides he is esteemed as an intellectual father, as well as an emotional big brother. The person who probably knows him best, the comedian Wally Cox, declares him to be a 'creative philosopher, a very deep thinker,' and adds, 'He's a real liberating force for his friends'" (S 440).

Time magazine, reporting the Black and White Ball, concedes, "Capote's friends are nothing if not loyal—in fact, some of them feel he has changed their lives forever by opening new vistas."[41] Mrs. William Paley says, "He's opened up avenues for me—he made me read Proust, the whole thing." Jackie Kennedy calls him a "loyal friend." Bennett Cerf, Capote's publisher at Random House, declares, "I do things for Truman that I wouldn't do for any other writer. I love him—my wife and I *both* love Truman. Always have. Boys, men who like men's men, girls, women, heterosexuals, homosexuals, hermaphrodites—he endears himself to all of them." [42]

One of the most striking things about Truman Capote is what Barbara Long has described as "the singular integration of his literary and life styles." [43] Paralleling his sustained effort to bring his art closer to real life is an equally strong tendency to make his life artistic. He says of his new apartment, "You have to envisage it all at once. It's like writing a book. In an apartment, an atmosphere is important, and I've worked very hard on this one." [44]

Showing an interviewer around his Bridgehampton house, he said, "Rooms are terribly important to me. They're extensions of myself. And rooms and the things in them are extensions of my art. Do you see how all of this is an extension of me? All of this is part of the perfection I achieve in my writing." [45]

The pattern extends to people as well:

I move in all worlds. I'm not snobbish, but I like people who are accomplished, people who are terribly brilliant or terribly amusing or terribly beautiful. I do *not* have an addiction to rich people. I have a lot of rich friends because they have great taste. One of the first things that interests me in anybody is the spectrum of their tastes. I call it the pursuit of excellence. An artist can't be a snob—they cancel each other out. But still, you wouldn't want to eat just a *rather* good oyster.[46]

"The pursuit of excellence" has involved a pursuit of publicity—a subject on which Capote is often less than candid. Bennet Cerf calls him "an absolute genius at promoting himself," [47] and others have echoed the tribute, sometimes in less affectionate tones. Quizzed by *Newsweek* about his busy promotion of *In Cold Blood*, he chortled, "A boy has to hustle his book." [48] The most obvious motive behind this is money, a subject on which Capote has always been much more frank.

He represents, in fact, the ultimate combination of artistic integrity and open avowal of the profit motive.[49] *Breakfast at Tiffany's* contains what seems in retrospect to be an official statement of Truman Capote's fiscal policy. Holly Golightly advises the narrator, "You'd better make money. You have an expensive imagination" (S 204), and Capote has taken her advice. He is, he says, "physically incapable" of writing anything for which he is not certain of being well paid. He will explain at considerable length that two million dollars is not an excessive reimbursement for *In Cold Blood*, since a lot of talent and six years of hard work went into it. An even more recent example of his financial *sang froid* is recorded in *Time*, August 5, 1966: "Serious writers aren't supposed to make money, but I say the hell with that. My next book will be called A *Christmas Memory*. It's 45 pages long, and it's going to cost $5 and be worth every cent. How do you like that for openers?" In Capote's opinion, talent and hard work deserve to be rewarded; at the same time, he believes that money should be earned. "I have a peculiar attitude toward money. I don't think it's right for me to put $500 on a ball at Monte Carlo, and win money for doing it. Nor do I think it's right that I should lose my money." [50]

The goal that young Collin had in mind as he started northward at the end of *The Grass Harp* is the goal that Truman Capote has achieved—success in the American style: fame and fortune. Not only has he matched the Horatio Alger success story; he has gone it one better: "Businessmen may have a kind of genius, but their work never lasts. A book can be burned, but it always survives somehow. It's the only real source of power. . . . The only *real* achievement is artistic or intellectual." [51] Success is finally this, power, and Capote is acutely aware of it. An element of deliberate self-aggrandizement runs through every phase of his career, even his friendships. (In *The Grass Harp*, Dolly left Collin with the advice to love, because "that is owning.") Caught in a particularly expansive mood by an *Esquire* interviewer, Capote talked to her about *her* writing career, revealing much about the way he has created his own.

Nobody ever helped me. I did it all myself. . . . One-third of success is talent, talent that is self-discipline and concentration;

153

the rest is using it. Then you reach a point when you don't need anything from the others. You have complete power over your life. You're at one with yourself and the world. . . .

But it's so important to *build* a career. Don't waste anything. Plan. Be seen in the right publications. *Mademoiselle, Vogue.* . . . After a few years you can demand more money from magazines than they ever thought they had. . . .

Never get an agent. I know more about getting money than anyone in the business. I know more about publishing than most people who make their living at it. I know how to build a book, to promote it. I've never written a sentence for free, and I never intend to. *Life* wanted to quote a thousand words for their picture spread of my book. I suppose they thought they were doing me a big favor by publicizing the book, but I made them pay for those words. After all, those were *my* words. That's what it's all about, isn't it? I write the words, people want to read them; somebody's got to pay for them.[52]

So inseparable is the habit of exaggeration from Capote's grandiose vision and very considerable achievement that seasoned Capote-watchers are accustomed to a certain credibility gap. But, like it or not—and many, for various reasons, don't—his peculiar combination of ambition, talent, and eccentricity abounds in front-page appeal and earning power. "People never understand this. They see only the paradox. Here is this hard-working writer: here is this man who is such a materialist. But can't you see? The materialism in my life is just another extension of my art?"[53]

O n November 16, 1959, one year after the publication of *Breakfast at Tiffany's* and only months after "A House on the Heights" appeared in *Holiday*, Truman Capote picked up a copy of the *New York Times* and noticed on an inside page a short article that began: "Holcomb, Kan. Nov. 15 (UPI) A wealthy wheat farmer, his wife and their two young children were found shot to death today in their home. They had been killed by shotgun blasts at close range after being bound and gagged. . . ." Three days later, Capote was in Kansas attending the funeral of the murder victims and embarking on the most spectacular undertaking of his career. Artistically, he had set the stage carefully:

The decision was based on a theory I've harbored since I first began to write professionally, which is well over 20 years ago. It seemed to me that journalism, reportage, could be forced to yield a serious new art form: the "nonfiction novel," as I thought of it. Several admirable reporters—Rebecca West for one, and Joseph Mitchell and Lillian Ross—have shown the possibilities of narrative reportage; and Miss Ross, in her brilliant "Picture," achieved at least a nonfiction novella. Still, on the whole, journalism is the most underestimated, the least explored of literary mediums. . . .

Not that I'd never written nonfiction before—I kept journals, and had published a small truthful book of travel impressions: "Local Color." But I had never attempted an ambitious piece of reportage until 1956, when I wrote "The Muses Are Heard". . . . It was published in the New Yorker, the only magazine I know of that encourages the serious practitioners of this art form. Later, I contributed a few other reportorial finger-exercises to the same magazine. Finally, I felt equipped and ready to undertake a full-scale narrative—in other words, a "nonfiction novel." [1]

But the decision to write a major nonfiction novel was not a purely artistic one; it was an attempt at a profound personal change—an especially long "leap" from one circle of life to another. For Capote has also said:

If you've been training yourself since you were—let me see . . . I began to write so-called seriously certainly by the time I was fifteen, and I'd already been writing four years. . . . I saw everything in literary or writing terms. I was a highly trained and accomplished writer by the time I was eighteen. All I had to do then was something to myself. As far as technical ability, I could write as well when I was eighteen as I can today. I mean technically. But I had to do something to myself.[2]

Capote felt that he was not the only writer needing a change: "It seems to me that most contemporary novelists, especially the Americans and the French, are too subjective, mesmerized by private demons; they're enraptured by their navels, and confined by a view that ends with their own toes. If I were naming names, I'd name myself among others. At any rate, I did at one time feel an artistic need to escape my self-created world. I wanted to exchange it, creatively speaking, for the everyday objective world we all inhabit."[3]

Capote is not alone in lamenting the self-absorption of the modern writer. Many observers, like him, tend to blame the writer for this state of affairs; others blame the world. Jonathan Baumbach, one of the most capable surveyors of the current literary scene, titles his study of several contemporary American novelists (not including Capote) *The Landscape of Nightmare*, and introduces it in this slightly hysterical way:

To live in this world, to live consciously in this world in which madness daily passes for sanity is a kind of madness in itself. Yet where else can we go? We are born into this nightmare and we do our best (with a sense of initiative, duty, and honor—with no sense at all) to make the worst of it. And for all our massive efforts at self-extinction we continue to survive—a cosmic joke. Our novelists, unlike our journalists who (practical people) believe in the world they see, have tried to make sense—to make art—out of what it's like to live in this nightmare.[4]

In Baumbach's opinion, the novelist who, next to Faulkner, has recently succeeded best in making artistic sense out of this world is Saul Bellow; to judge from the beginning of his chapter on Bellow, Truman Capote typifies for him a class of writers who have failed:

Saul Bellow is a rarity among American novelists. He is not a child prodigy. I say *is* not because most of our "marvelous boys" have, in the face of time, stalwartly refused to age, have instead become elder statesmen–child prodigies, senile innocents, imaginary boys in real bull rings. Bellow was twenty-nine when his first novel, *Dangling Men* (1944), was published. At twenty-nine so many of our talented writers had already indicated that their most significant work was behind them that they had neither other voices nor other rooms, only new dust jackets for the nostalgic recreations of their earlier works. What is so remarkable about Bellow's career is that, while continuing to grow as a writer, he has risked transaction, each time out, with a different uncharted territory of the novel.[5]

In view of his scorn for journalists, it is doubtful whether Baumbach would accept *In Cold Blood* as an entry in the race— though at first glance it seems to fill his prescription almost too neatly. Bellow himself has recently asked the novelist to come out of his isolation. Upon receiving the 1964 National Book Award for *Herzog*, he issued this challenge to his fellow writers:

The fact that there are so many weak, poor, and boring stories and novels written and published in America has been ascribed by our rebels to the horrible squareness of our institutions, the idiocy of power, the debasement of sexual instincts, and the failure of writers to be alienated enough.

The poems and novels of these same rebellious spirits, and their theoretical statements, are grimy and gritty and very boring too, besides being nonsensical, and it is evident now that polymorphous sexuality and vehement declarations of alienation are not going to produce great works of art either.

There is nothing left for us novelists to do but think. For unless we think, unless we make a clearer estimate of our condition, we will continue to write kid stuff, to fail in our function, we will lack serious interests and become truly irrelevant. . . .

We live in a technological age which seems insurmountably

hostile to the artist. He must fight for his life, for his freedom, along with everyone else—for justice and equality, threatened by mechanization and bureaucracy.

This is not to advise the novelist to rush immediately into the political sphere. But in the first stage he must begin to exert his intelligence, long unused. If he is to reject politics, he must understand what he is rejecting. He must begin to think, and to think not merely of his own narrower interests and needs.[6]

Bellow's complaint is much like Capote's—even, it seems, to the extent of having the early Capote in mind as one of the prime offenders. Their proposed solutions, however, are characteristically different. Capote's orientation has never been toward the speculative or the political. If his problem was immersion in a too-narrow personal world, his attempt at broadening was to be made also on the personal level. He recently concluded a list of the qualifications of the nonfiction novelist with the observation that "above all, the reporter must be able to empathize with personalities outside his usual imaginative range, mentalities unlike his own, kinds of people he would never have written about had he not been forced to by encountering them inside the journalistic situation. This last is what first attracted me to the notion of narrative reportage." [7]

A large cast of characters was one criterion Capote kept firmly in mind during his two-year search for a subject for his nonfiction novel. Another was timelessness. "The difficulty," he says, "was to choose a promising subject. If you intend to spend three or four or five years with a book, as I planned to do, then you want to be reasonably certain that the material will not soon 'date.' The content of much journalism so swiftly does, which is another of the medium's deterrents. A number of ideas occurred, but one after the other, and for one reason or another, each was eventually discarded, often after I'd done considerable preliminary work." [8]

The subject of crime was not at all essential to the original concept, as he told a *Life* interviewer.

I don't think that crime is all that interesting a subject. What could be more cut and dried, really, than two ex-convicts who set out to rob a family and end up killing them? The important thing is the depth you can plunge to and the height you can reach. The art form I've invented allows for great flexibility that way. I could have written about all sorts of other things—some I even started to do. There are two that I won't talk about, because I may still do them some day, but one I will mention—though I may finish that too. That one was a nonfiction novel about a New York cleaning woman, one who did several people's apartments without ever having met the people—she got the job through some employment agency and they gave her the keys and all. I actually found such a woman, a very nice one, and I'd make her rounds with her to talk to her and even help her clean. I was going to follow her around some time, to find out what she thought about her various employers judging by what she saw of how they lived, and then finally interview *them*—to contrast her view of their lives with theirs. It could have worked out quite effectively, I think.

My theory, you see, is that you can take *any* subject and make it into a nonfiction novel.[9]

In practice, Capote is considerably more selective than this would suggest. A good deal of light is thrown on his requirements and techniques by a statement he made in 1966:

The other day someone suggested that the break-up of a marriage would be an interesting topic for a nonfiction novel. I disagreed. First of all, you'd have to find two people who would be willing—who'd sign a release. Second, their respective views on the subject-matter would be incoherent. And third, any couple who'd subject themselves to the scrutiny demanded would quite likely be a pair of kooks. But it's amazing how many events *would* work with the theory of the nonfiction novel in mind—the Watts riots, for example. They would provide a subject that satisfied the first essential of the nonfiction novel—that there is a timeless quality about the cause and events. . . . The requisite would also be that you would have had to live through the riots, at least part of them, as a witness, so that a depth of perception could be acquired.[10]

Just why the brief article about the Clutter murder attracted Capote will always remain something of a mystery, though not as deep as one might at first suppose. Understandably, his own explanation of it varies slightly from time to time. In 1966 he told me:

At the time I decided to do *In Cold Blood* I had been thinking for a long time, looking for a huge canvas. Then, I was reading the *New York Times*, and just for no reason, at that very same moment, because it never had crossed my mind, I thought, maybe that's it . . . take a crime of a certain kind, and really go into it with Dostoievskian thoroughness. That would be a good framework to make my big experiment with. And while I'm sitting there, my mind is idly looking at this item. I said, Why not this crime? There wasn't anything about it that appealed to me especially other than the thought coming at the same time. And the idea.[11]

George Plimpton records Capote's recollection of the episode this way: "The story was brief, just several paragraphs stating the facts. . . . There was nothing really exceptional about it; one reads items concerning multiple murders many times in the course of a year." Asked why, then, he picked this particular subject, Capote said:

I didn't. Not immediately. But after reading the story it suddenly struck me that a crime, the study of one such, might provide the broad scope I needed to write the kind of book I wanted to write. Moreover, the human heart being what it is, murder was a theme not likely to darken and yellow with time.
    I thought about it all that November day, and part of the next; and then I said to myself: Well, why not this crime? . . . Of course it was a rather frightening thought!—to arrive alone in a small, strange town, a town in the grip of an unsolved mass murder. Still, the circumstances of the place being altogether unfamiliar, geographically and atmospherically, made it that much more tempting. Everything would seem freshly minted—the people, their accents and attitudes, the landscape, its contours, the weather. All this, it seemed to me, could only sharpen my eye and quicken my ear.[12]

Judging from these two accounts, it would seem that in the choice of the Clutter murder as his subject Capote's prime considerations were timelessness, unfamiliarity of setting, and a large cast of characters. Even in 1962, when he had been working on the book for two years, he told *Newsweek*, "My book is not a crime story. It's the story of a town." [13]

A somewhat different impression is given by his remarks to *Saturday Review* interviewer Haskel Frankel in 1966: Capote said that after two years of searching for a subject it "suddenly occurred" to him that a crime might serve his purpose best.

Once I had decided on the possibility of a crime—and I am not interested in crime per se; I hate violence—I would half-consciously, when looking through the papers, always notice any item that had a reference to a crime. Well, one day in November 1959 I was thumbing through the *New York Times* and I saw this little headline, just a few paragraphs about this case. It was sort of as though one had been sitting for a long time watching for a certain kind of bird—if you were a bird-watcher—to come into view, and there it was. Almost instantaneously I thought, well, this is maybe exactly what I want to do, because I don't know anything about that part of the world. I've never been to Kansas, much less western Kansas. It all seems fresh to me. I'll go without any prejudices. And so I went.[14]

It is a rare person, at least among contemporary Americans, who is immune to the fascination of violence, and the book Capote finally wrote suggests that his interest in it goes somewhat deeper than he suggests here. That he enjoys true accounts of a kind not necessarily excluding violence is evident in a casual remark he made in *The Muses Are Heard*. In his Russian hotel room he found a pile of anti-Communist pamphlets, "most of which purported to be the case histories of individuals, primarily Germans, who had gone behind the iron curtain, either voluntarily or as the result of force, and had not been heard from again. It was absorbing, as only case histories can be, and I would have read through the lot uninterruptedly if the telephone hadn't rung" (*S* 295).

He gave a fuller account of his reading habits in the *Paris Review* interview, which took place about two years after he wrote *The Muses Are Heard* and two years before he read about the Clutter murders. Asked if he read a great deal, he replied, "Too much," confessing in particular a "passion for newspapers." Then he added, "I enjoy thrillers and would like someday to write one. Though I prefer first-rate fiction, for the last few years my reading seems to have been concentrated on letters and journals and biographies." [15] This reading diet is about what one would expect of an emerging nonfiction novelist. Today Capote seems not to relate his desire to write a thriller to *In Cold Blood*; still, the connection is there.

After reading the newspaper account of the Kansas murders, Capote hesitated for a day and a half before deciding it was what he wanted. Aside from doubts about the suitability of the subject and some apprehension about difficulties he might encounter on the scene, there was little to hold him back. He had kept himself "footloose." He is not averse to living in motels and has a taste for spur-of-the-moment departures. "Sometimes I just get in the car and drive. Recently I felt like taking a little ride, so I packed a bag, and found myself in Chicago. I don't know anyone there. I lived in a very nice hotel, read a few books, went to museums, and drove back a week later. I like to do that sometimes." [16]

When he decided to write the book he arranged with the *New Yorker* to back the project in return for first-publication rights, as they had done with *The Muses Are Heard*. The amount settled on was reportedly $70,000. Among the book's acknowledgments Capote includes the *New Yorker*'s William Shawn, "who encouraged me to undertake this project and whose judgment stood me in good stead from first to last." Deciding that his friend Harper Lee could be of help and might enjoy the experience, he phoned her in Monroeville, Alabama, and invited her along as "assistant researchist."

"When he first called me," she told *Newsweek*, "he said it would be a tremendously involved job and would take two people. The crime intrigued Truman, and I'm intrigued with crime, and boy, I wanted to go. It was deep calling to deep." [17] Capote's version is that "she had been thinking about doing a nonfiction book, and wanted to learn my techniques of reportage, so she asked to come along." [18]

Capote and Miss Lee went by train to St. Louis, then to Manhattan, Kansas, where they rented a car to drive the 400 miles to

Garden City. "It was twilight when we arrived. I remember the car-radio was playing, and we heard: 'Police authorities, continuing their investigation of the tragic Clutter slayings, have requested that anyone with pertinent information please contact the Sheriff's Office. . . .' If I had realized then what the future held, I never would have stopped in Garden City. I would have driven straight on. Like a bat out of hell." [19]

As he had hoped, Capote found Kansas "as strange to me as if I'd gone to Peking." [20] The opening page of *In Cold Blood* gives the reader what must have been his own first impression of it. "The land is flat, and the views are awesomely extensive; horses, herds of cattle, a white cluster of grain elevators rising as gracefully as Greek temples are visible long before a traveler reaches them" (C 3).[21] Capote describes Holcomb, the scene of the murders, at length—noting its precise geographical location, socioeconomic structure, and physical appearance. It is "an aimless congregation of buildings" (C 3) lining the Santa Fe Railroad tracks, surrounded by prairies and wheat fields. Though its citizens are mostly prosperous farm ranchers, the few public buildings are run-down.

Down by the depot, the postmistress, a gaunt woman who wears a rawhide jacket and denims and cowboy boots, presides over a falling-apart post office. The depot itself, with its peeling sulphur-colored paint, is equally melancholy; The Chief, the El Capitan go by every day, but these celebrated expresses never pause there. No passenger trains do—only an occasional freight. Up on the highway, there are two filling stations, one of which doubles as a meagerly supplied grocery store, while the other does extra duty as a cafe—Hartman's Cafe, where Mrs. Hartman, the proprietress, dispenses sandwiches, coffee, soft drinks, and 3.2 beer (C 4).

Holcomb is a suburb of Garden City, a town of eleven thousand, and it was there that Capote set up his headquarters. Capote says that anyone who has crossed America by car or train has probably passed through Garden City, "but it is reasonable to assume that few travelers remember the event" (C 33). Yet he concludes that the town is "probably remembered with nostalgia by those who have left it" and provides, for those who have remained, "a sense of roots and contentment" (C 33–34).

If Kansas was strange to Capote, Capote was just as strange to Kansas. He had, appropriately, brought along his passport for identification, and had also provided himself with several letters of introduction from Dr. James McCain, president of Kansas State University at Manhattan. Jane Howard reports that in November, 1959, only two people in Garden City, high school English teachers, had read any of Capote's books.[22] Harper Lee recalls, "It looked as if the case would never be solved. Everyone was looking at his neighbors, wondering if they could be murderers—the killings seemed so motiveless. You'd see porch lights on all night. We were given the cold shoulder. Those people had never seen anyone like Truman—he was like someone coming off the moon." [23] A Holcomb resident's recollection is typical: "We did feel pretty put off by Truman at first, with that funny little voice of his and the way he dressed and all, but after we'd talked to him only for an hour, we just got so we thoroughly enjoyed him." [24] Rudy Valenzuela, a Garden City photographer who worked with Capote, recalls, "I first thought, 'Here's a little fellow who's going to get trampled by the newsmen.' But as you got to know him you became intrigued with this soft-shoe super-intelligence that sort of sneaks up on you. Now everyone here has a great admiration and respect for the little guy—even those who wouldn't swing in the same tree." [25] Postmistress Myrtle Clare, who was one of his favorites, recalls admiringly, "He was just as quick as any man afoot. Just like a flash of lightning, he was here, there, everywhere." [26]

Among the friendships Capote eventually established in Kansas, probably the closest was that with Alvin Dewey, the detective in charge of the case, and his wife Marie. Mrs. Dewey says, "Oh, I just feel so sorry for anybody who doesn't know Truman. Do you know he calls up long distance every couple of days? You know he once called us up all the way from *Switzerland* just to say he missed us?" [27] When it is suggested that he was cynically using them and others for his book, she retorts, "He's far above that. He's something more than any of us. He was always aboveboard." [28] She adds that Capote "had to go on his own" in Kansas—that "maybe it was one of the first times that being Truman Capote didn't get him things handed on a silver platter. But when we went to New York after his book was done, we found that Truman was no different there than he was here. All those famous people we met there—Jackie Kennedy, Barbara Paley, Bennett Cerf, Arlene Francis—they love Truman just as we did in Garden City. He enriched our lives." [29] A skeptical *Time* magazine concedes, "A diminutive, eccentric and lisping presence on Midwest territory, whose citizens at first scarcely knew what to make of him, Capote commanded the attention and ultimately the respect of everyone he approached, including the killers." [30]

This double-take pattern seems to be universal when people meet Capote—whether individuals, families, or huge lecture audiences. The *Paris Review* interviewer who visited him in 1958 in his ornate Brooklyn home noted that "at first glance" he seemed all quaintness and innocence. "He is small and blond, with a forelock that persists in falling down into his eyes, and his smile is sudden and sunny. His approach to anyone new is one of open curiosity and friendliness. He might be taken in by anything and, in fact, seems only too ready to be. There is something about him, though, that makes you feel that for all his willingness it would be hard to pull any wool over his eyes and maybe it is better not to try." [31] A Kansas man puts it, "That little Truman, he's got plenty on the ball all right, even if he never did finish high school. That little rascal's as smart as a whip." [32]

Some Kansans were offended by Capote's investigations, others by the book that followed, but an editorial by Stuart Awbrey, editor of *The Hutchinson News,* probably gives an accurate view of the prevailing attitude—at least among those who knew Capote personally. "We came to know the author, a man of grace and intellect. Foreign to our ways and our land, sophisticate by reputation . . . the alien immersed himself in his Finney County surroundings where his rare intuition took over to provide an understanding the natives themselves often lack." [33]

One of Capote's wisest moves was taking Harper Lee with

him to help break the ice. "She is a gifted woman," he says, "courageous, and with a warmth that instantly kindles most people, however suspicious or sour." [34] He sums up her contribution: "She kept me company when I was based out there. I suppose she was with me about two months altogether. She went on a number of interviews; she typed her own notes, and I had these and could refer to them. She was extremely helpful in the beginning, when we weren't making much headway with the townspeople, by making friends with the wives of the people I wanted to meet. She became friendly with all the churchgoers." [35] In addition to her first stay in Garden City, Miss Lee later stopped for a week on her way to California. Some observers have wondered why Capote did not acknowledge her work more, but he answers that she "simply did not help me that much. She's the first to admit it." [36] And he did dedicate the book to her: the dedication reads: "For Jack Dunphy and Harper Lee with my love and gratitude." (If Miss Lee was thinking of writing a nonfiction novel herself, she has changed her mind; she informed me in a letter written December 11, 1966, that such a project was definitely not among her plans.)

It took about a month for Holcomb and Garden City to accept Truman Capote. He reflects:

I think they finally just realized that we were there to stay— they'd have to make the best of it. Under the circumstances, they were suspicious. . . . But then after it all quieted down—after Perry and Dick were arrested—that was when we did most of the original interviews. Some of them went on for three years— though not on the same subject, of course. I suppose if I used just 20 per cent of all the material I put together over those years of interviewing, I'd still have a book two thousand pages long! [37]

"Capote probably listens as attentively and compassionately as anyone alive," *Life* Magazine's Jane Howard has written. "Tell him something one month, something seemingly trivial and monumentally forgettable, and the next month you hear him weave it, verbatim, into another unrelated conversation.

'I'm not interested in my own idiosyncrasies, whatever they may be,' Capote says. 'What interests me—what I dwell on and dream of—are not the little nuances of my own life but the lives of people around me.' " [38] By the time Capote went to Kansas to begin the interviews for *In Cold Blood*, he had turned his natural gift into a precision instrument.

Long before I started *In Cold Blood*, I taught myself to be my own tape recorder. It wasn't as hard as it might sound. What I'd do was have a friend talk or read for a set length of time, tape what he was saying, and meanwhile listen to him as intently as I could. Then I'd go write down what he had said as I remembered it, and later compare what I had with the tape. I got better and better at it, and I started doing finger exercises that led up to this book, like my interview with Marlon Brando and the long piece I did on a *Porgy and Bess* company's tour of Russia. Finally, when I got to be about 97% accurate, I felt ready to take on this book. [39]

Capote feels that his refusal to take notes or use a tape recorder contributed to the accuracy of *In Cold Blood*, since these aids tend to intimidate people and make them say "what they think you *expect* them to say."

But I'm terribly, terribly clever about that. When somebody is telling me something a little bit wobbly, his eyes shift from right to left, and I ask him to go over that part another time. There were lots of people that I interviewed repeatedly, until I was absolutely sure I had it right—especially in the case of conversations the Clutters had had. Nobody who knew them, and nobody else for that matter, has accused me of misquoting. I'm certain that I have it all perfectly. [40]

His practice in Kansas was to record the interview material within three hours, then file and cross-index it. "Funny enough, I seldom had to look at my notes after that: I had it all in my head." [41] Since most of the interviewees were busy ranchers or teachers, he explains, "Usually I'd go out to someone's farm about four in the afternoon and have a long interview, then go back to the motel, write up my notes, go to sleep, and next morning type them up. It was very cold, and most interviews were after dark, and a lot of them were conducted in the living room with the TV going full blast. I don't think I've been in a house in Kansas where the TV wasn't going perpetually." [42]

The mother of Susan Kidwell, Nancy Clutter's best friend, recalls, "Truman handled Susan with great care. He'd ask her the same question over and over, and never took any notes. When she got tired, he'd immediately cut it off. Sometimes he'd come to the apartment just to ask one question." [43]

A fact that must be kept in mind when reviewing the early months of Capote's investigations is that neither he nor anyone else knew how things would turn out. He was at first, as he said, writing the story of a town, and for all he knew, the rampant suspicion that the killer was a local person might have proved true, and In Cold Blood a very different sort of book. It might, in fact, quite possibly never have been written. It was a long time before Capote reached the firm resolve to finish it, and there are indications that in the early stages he kept at least a part of himself aloof from the case. Alvin Dewey remembers, "At first he said he came out to write a story and it made no difference to him whether the crime was solved or not. But later he would say to me, 'Do you know this or that?' and I'd be amazed at the things he was digging up." [44] Considerably more cold-blooded is the attitude attributed to Capote by Kenneth Tynan, who tells of a New York dinner party he attended in 1960 at which "Capote regaled [us] with a dazzling account of the crime and his friendship with the criminals. I said they seemed obviously insane and he agreed they were 'nuts.' And what would happen to them? 'They'll swing, I guess,' he said." [45]

This kind of personal detachment is absent from Capote's later statements about his work on the book. One of his avowed reasons for undertaking the task was that it would require him to empathize with numerous people outside his usual imaginative range, and while this involvement would naturally have been a slowly developing thing, there seems to have been no doubt in Capote's mind or those of the other principals that it was eventually achieved. To Capote, it was essential to the writing of the nonfiction novel that the reporter not simply observe from the outside but relive the experience with the participants in order to acquire the necessary depth of perception. "The book wasn't something reconstructed from some great distance. . . . I lived the whole thing. The whole investigation of the case, the capture of the boys, the trial, all of the years on Death Row. All I really had to reconstruct, in an historical way, was the last days of the Clutter family's lives. It's not so awfully difficult to do— I was there three days after the murder, and I could talk to everybody who had seen the family." [46]

Capote's involvement in the case, no matter how deep, always coexisted with artistic detachment. The climax of his emotional implication, his presence at the hanging of the killers, was preceded by two days of vomiting and followed by convulsive weeping—"And yet, for the entire three days I was throwing up and crying and carrying on, in another part of my mind I was sitting and quite coolly writing the story." [47] Any kind of artistic writing requires some such discontinuity between experience and expression, and Capote has always laid heavy stress on the fact. In the 1958 *Paris Review* interview, when reference was made to the "unusual detachment" of *The Muses Are Heard*, Capote stated that he did not consider the style of that book markedly different from the style of his fiction.

Perhaps the content, the fact that it is about real events, makes it seem so. After all, *Muses* is straight reporting, and in reporting one is occupied with literalness and surfaces, with implication without comment—one can't achieve immediate depths the way one may in fiction. However, one of the reasons I've wanted to do reportage was to prove that I could apply my style to the realities of journalism. But I believe my fictional method is equally detached—emotionality makes me lose writing control: I have to exhaust the emotion before I feel clinical enough to analyze and project it, and as far as I'm concerned that's one of the laws of achieving true technique. If my fiction seems more personal it is because it depends on the artist's most personal and revealing area: his imagination.[48]

Another remark Capote made on the same occasion seems to suggest a difference between *In Cold Blood* and his earlier journalistic efforts: "The *Porgy and Bess* articles are not relevant to this issue. That was reporting, and 'emotions' were not much involved—at least not the difficult and personal territories of feeling that I mean." [49]

The Clutter case was to demand a kind of reporting that *would* penetrate deeply into these difficult and personal territories of feeling. Still, the writing would have to be done coldly. Capote seems satisfied that it was. Asked by George Plimpton whether his emotional involvement was a problem, he replied, "Yes, it was a problem. Nevertheless, I felt in control throughout. However, I had great difficulty writing the last six or seven pages. This even took a physical form: hand paralysis. I finally used a typewriter—very awkward as I always write in longhand." [50]

Herbert and Bonnie, Nancy and Kenyon Clutter were murdered in their isolated farm home during the night of Saturday, November 14, 1959. Two older daughters, one married and one soon to be, were living elsewhere at the time. The victims' bodies were discovered shortly after nine o'clock on Sunday morning by Susan Kidwell, Nancy's best friend, and Nancy Ewalt, another friend of Nancy's who usually accompanied the Clutter family to Methodist services in Garden City. By that time the two vagabond ex-convicts who had committed the murders were hundreds of miles away in eastern Kansas, on the first leg of a six-week journey that would take them to Acapulco and Miami.

The first person suspected by Garden City authorities was Bobby Rupp, Nancy's high school sweetheart, who watched television with the Clutters on Saturday night and left at eleven, according to the last entry in Nancy's diary. He was soon cleared of suspicion, as was Alfred Stoecklein, the Clutters' resident hired man and the only other likely suspect for many weeks.

As the days passed, Holcomb and Garden City settled into a gradually deepening mood of fear and suspicion. "In a way, that's the worst part of the crime," one woman reflected. "What a terrible thing when neighbors can't look at each other without kind of wondering" (C 70). Hardware stores sold out of locks and bolts, and in many homes lights were kept burning all night. A school teacher analyzed the situation: "Feeling wouldn't run half so high if this had happened to anyone *except* the Clutters.

Anyone *less* admired. Prosperous. Secure. But that family represented everything people hereabouts really value and respect, and that such a thing could happen to them—well, it's like being told there is no God. It makes life pointless. I don't think people are so much frightened as they are deeply depressed" (C 88).

By the time Truman Capote and Harper Lee reached Garden City, three days after the crime, the Finney County sheriff had turned the case over to Alvin Dewey, Garden City representative of the Kansas Bureau of Investigation. Dewey, with his fellow agents, was settling down to a painstaking and dedicated investigation. Capote quotes him as calling it "a personal proposition": he and his wife were, the detective said, "real fond of Herb and Bonnie," and "saw them every Sunday at church, visited a lot back and forth. But even if I hadn't known the family, and liked them so well, I wouldn't feel any different. Because I've seen some bad things, I sure as hell have. But nothing so vicious as this. However long it takes, it may be the rest of my life, I'm going to know what happened in that house: the why and the who" (C 80).

By the time the criminals were caught, Dewey had grown accustomed to receiving crank calls, confessions from drunks, and abuse from frightened people; he had lost twenty pounds, was smoking sixty cigarettes a day, and had developed an obsession with the case that worried his wife and friends. Not long afterward he suffered a heart attack.

Perry Smith and Dick Hickock spent Sunday afternoon in Olathe, near Kansas City—Perry in a hotel and Dick with his family, who thought he had been visiting his sister in Ft. Scott and noticed nothing unusual about him except his sleepiness. Five days later they cashed almost two hundred dollars' worth of bad checks in Kansas City and set out in a stolen car for Mexico. After a week in Mexico City they moved on to Acapulco; then, almost out of money, they returned to Mexico City and took a bus to Barstow, California. They hitchhiked across Nevada and Wyoming into Nebraska, where their plans to rob and kill a businessman who had picked them up were frustrated by his stopping for another hitchhiker. In Idaho they stole another car and against Perry's wishes drove to Kansas City, the only place Dick felt confident he could freely distribute bad checks.

Kansas City was more dangerous than they thought, for several days earlier an informer named Floyd Wells had given their names to the authorities. Eleven years before, Wells had worked for Mr. Clutter for a year; later, in June, 1959, in the Kansas State Penitentiary on a robbery charge, he had met Dick. During the month they celled together, Wells told Dick about Mr. Clutter, passing on his own impression of the rancher's wealth and his erroneous belief that there was a wall safe in Mr. Clutter's study. Dick in turn mentioned his friend Perry and outlined in considerable detail his plan to rob the Clutter house, killing everyone in it.

Narrowly eluding the K.B.I. agents who were closing in on them in Kansas City, Perry and Dick drove to Miami Beach, where they spent the week of Christmas. Then, again low on money, they headed west with no particular plans. In Texas they picked up two hitchhikers, a sickly old man and his grandson, a pleasant, talkative twelve-year-old. Dick insisted on dropping the pair at evening, and they drove on, having settled on Las Vegas as their destination. It was there, on Wednesday, December 30, that they were arrested.

They were kept in the Las Vegas City Jail for a week and were separately interrogated there on Jananuary 2 by Dewey and three other K.B.I. agents. In an effort to surprise them into confessions, they were first led to believe they were wanted only for parole violation, then suddenly confronted with the murder charge. Neither confessed during the first questioning, but later the same day Dick declared that Perry had killed all four of the Clutters. On January 6 the detectives drove Smith and Hickock to Garden City in separate cars, and on the way Perry was goaded into a lengthy confession that differed from Dick's only in his claim that the latter had killed the two women.

Late that evening the convoy arrived at the Finney County Court House, where Capote, standing in the crowd of newsmen and local citizens, had his first view of the accused killers.

Although none of the journalists anticipated violence, several had predicted shouted abuse. But when the crowd caught sight of the murderers, with their escort of blue-coated highway patrolmen, it fell silent, as though amazed to find them humanly shaped. The handcuffed men, whitefaced and blinking blindly, glistened in the glare of flashbulbs and floodlights. The cameramen, pursuing the prisoners and the police into the courthouse and up three flights of stairs, photographed the door of the county jail slamming shut. (*C* 248).

The most crucial and difficult part of Capote's work began the following day. Already on terms of mutual trust with the police, he secured permission to interview the prisoners if they would consent to talk to him. A photographer presented his request, but the men refused. Deciding that fifteen minutes with each of them "would be time enough to make my pitch," he sent another message offering them fifty dollars each if they would see him for that amount of time. (Capote oiled the wheels in a similar manner with many of his other interviewees, paying them moderate sums in exchange for legal releases permitting him to make use of their names and statements in the book and movie that would probably be made from it.)[51]

This time he succeeded in convincing both men that they might as well talk to him, and from then on he had their cooperation. "I had a very easygoing rapport with Dick right from the start," he told *Life* magazine, "but Perry was more difficult. He'd let me interview him a lot, but he was very surly. Sometimes he'd look at me as if he'd like to kill me. But finally one day, a couple of months after we'd met, he suddenly said, 'Maybe it's true, maybe you really *are* interested in me as a person—maybe you don't just want to write a book to exploit me.' From then on he was cooperative. They were both very honest with me and I was with them, too." [52]

Capote has also given a fuller account:

I saw Perry first, but . . . he couldn't have been less communicative. It was always easier with Dick. He was like someone you meet on a train, immensely garrulous, who starts up a conversation and is only too obliged to tell you *everything*. Perry became easier after the third or fourth month, but it wasn't until the last five years of his life that he was totally and absolutely honest with me, and came to trust me. I came to have great rapport with him right up through his last day. For the first year and a half, though, he would come just so close, and then no closer. He'd retreat into the forest and leave me standing outside. I'd hear him laugh in the dark. Then gradually he would come back.[53]

An important later step in Capote's research was his retracing of the long path the two men followed during the six weeks after the murders—a feat made possible by Dick's almost photographic recall of the details of the trip.

Dick had an absolutely fantastic memory—one of the greatest memories I have ever come across. The reason I know it's great is that I lived the entire trip the boys went on from the time of the murders up to the moment of their arrest in Las Vegas—thousands of miles, what the boys called 'the long ride'. . . . Dick could give me the names and addresses of any hotel or place along the route where they'd spent maybe just half a night. He told me when I got to Miami to take a taxi to such-and-such a place and get out on the boardwalk and it would be southwest of there, number 232, and opposite I'd find two umbrellas in the sand which advertised 'Tan with Coppertone.' That was how exact he was.[54]

In March, 1960, Hickock and Smith were convicted and sentenced to hang, and in April they were transferred to the Kansas State Penitentiary for Men at Lansing, 400 miles from Garden City. With difficulty, Capote secured permission to continue his interviews with them. These eventually numbered over two hundred. In addition, he began writing to each of them twice a week and supplying them with books and magazines. Perry developed an interest in several of Capote's favorite authors, especially Thoreau. The prisoners were permitted to write twice a week and faithfully did so.

This intimate relationship with the condemned men continued and intensified during a five-year period in which a series of appeals led to three postponements of the execution date (October 25, 1962; August 8, 1963; February 18, 1965). Finally,

Capote was present, at the request of the prisoners themselves, at their execution on April 14, 1965. "It wasn't a question of my *liking* Dick and Perry," he explains; "that's like saying 'Do you like yourself?' What mattered was that I knew them, as well as I know myself." [55]

The process of coming to know these two men so well was undoubtedly the most difficult part of a project that Capote has called the most painful of his entire life. It was, in fact, almost too painful. "After I had worked on it for three years, I almost abandoned it. I'd become so emotionally involved that it was really a question of personal survival, and I'm not kidding. I just couldn't bear the morbidity all the time. There's just so much you can give to art. Nevertheless I didn't abandon it." [56] Yet he adds, "If I had known what that book was going to cost in every conceivable way, emotionally, I never would have started it, and I really mean that." [57]

The hardest part of all came at the end, when the decision had long been made and the writing was almost finished. "Going back to Kansas to watch the execution was undoubtedly the most intense emotional experience in my life. . . . I spent the whole two days before the execution in my motel room throwing up. Telegrams kept arriving from the prison, saying 'Where are you?' and I couldn't leave the room. But somehow when the time came I got myself together and went there, and spoke to them." [58]

I certainly didn't want to go, and the state of Kansas had even tried to prevent me, but of course if Dick and Perry wanted me, it was legal, and I had to be there. I first saw them in what is called the holding room, where they were served their last meal—which needless to say they didn't eat. Then they were strapped into these leather harnesses. After that I had to hold up their cigarettes for them to smoke. They were trembling violently, not from fear but from being terribly nervous.

Perry talked about Thoreau and asked me did I believe this and did I believe that. He told me to be sure I got his personal possessions, which he had willed to me, and at the end he handed me a 100-page farewell letter. Dick kept talking, right up to the end, about his mother—he felt very sad about her—and some old girl friends. Up to the end he kept making jokes: that was his defense. They were both an unbelievable color from spending all those years in cells. They had an extraordinary phosphorescence, so that they were practically glowing in the dark.[59]

After Dick had been hanged, Perry asked permission to speak once more to Capote. "He kissed me and told me '—*adios, amigo!*' and then he was hanged. I cried for two and a half days afterward." [60] "I couldn't stop. It was convulsive, like hiccups. Finally, they had to call a doctor to the prison to give me something, and get me on a plane home. And I flew all the way back to New York holding a pillow over my face because, you know, the tears just kept coming." [61]

Capote paid for the modest headstones that mark the graves of Perry and Dick in a private cemetery near the prison. The four-hundred-mile distance between their graves and those of the Clutters in Garden City is symbolic of the situation he was placed in by the project as a whole. "It was such a schizophrenic experience jumping from the Garden City people one day to the criminals the next. It was in many ways the hardest thing I've done in all my life." [62] The comment on Capote's experience by one New York friend is certainly accurate: "Truman dwelled so deeply on the lives of those people, good guys and bad guys both, that he and it are hooked on each other for life." [63]

In material terms, the result of Capote's years of hard work and emotional stress was six thousand pages of notes and an accumulation of boxed and filed documents bulky enough to fill a small room to the ceiling. Here were the facts of the case, recorded about as fully and accurately as is humanly possible. What Capote did with these facts he has described in the following way: "I've often thought of the book as being like something reduced to a seed. Instead of presenting the reader with a full plant, with all the foliage, a seed is planted in the soil of his mind." [64] The name Capote has given to his new genre— the "nonfiction novel"—is a contradiction in terms, suggesting that he might be viewed less as a gardener-in-reverse than as a magician who has just pulled a rabbit out of a hat.

The analogy is apt in several ways, and consistent with much of Capote's career. Barbara Long predicted that his big year would be different from those of other writers.

The years of the others—Mailer, Baldwin, Bellow, *et al.*—centered around the books themselves and the visions of life promulgated by the authors, and not how the books had come to be written or the mechanics by which they had become Big Book of the Year. And the public had not been interested in what kind of car Mailer might drive, which salad dressing Baldwin preferred, how Bellow's living quarters were furnished. No, the Year of Capote would celebrate the singular integration of his literary and life styles. His book would be discussed, but less as a literary landmark than as a triumphant coup by Capote.[65]

In Cold Blood might be called a remarkably successful attempt at an impossible job. Capote has professed surprise that no one else has done quite the same thing, but it is really not surprising at all. Critics have, for the most part, tended to classify *In Cold Blood* as simply an extreme form of a familiar class of writing, the documentary novel. (The definite sound of this term is rather illusory, since the documentary novel is a particularly ill-defined subtype of a large class, the novel—itself never strong on definition.) It is interesting to note, however, that Capote does not classify his book this way, but tends always to speak of it as something unique. This sometimes involves him in apparent contradictions, as when, at different points in the same interview, he makes the following statements:

Several admirable reporters—Rebecca West for one, and Joseph Mitchell and Lillian Ross—have shown the possibilities of narrative reportage; and Miss Ross, in her brilliant 'Picture,' achieved at least a nonfiction novella. . . .
The nonfiction novel should not be confused with the documentary novel—a popular and interesting but impure genre, which allows all the latitude of the fiction writer, but usually contains neither the persuasiveness of fact nor the poetic altitude fiction is capable of reaching. The author lets his imagination run riot over the facts! If I sound querulous or arrogant about this, it's not only that I have to protect my child, but

that I truly don't believe anything like it exists in the history of journalism.[66]

If the documentary novelist is doomed to wander between the fixed poles of journalistic factuality and imaginative power, Capote has tried to force the poles together. He has done this, he feels, by living his way so deeply into the real-life events that his eventual incorporation of them in a novel would have as much "poetic altitude" as any of his more purely imaginative works.

It is a fascinating ideal: to reach a point at which the inner reality coincides with the outer and the free use of the artist's shaping power results not in distortion but in heightened fidelity. In its pursuit, Capote made demands on himself of a kind seldom made by novelists, who are usually content to use the material picked up in the course of a life that wanders as it will. He literally placed his life at the service of his art, making himself, as he remarked to me, "merely the instrument" to observe the Clutter murder case and "to transfer this life into art." [67] Where the average documentary novelist would keep his research distinct from his deepest personal life, Capote transplanted his deepest personal life to Kansas, knowing—as In Cold Blood was finally to prove—that the real meanings of the book would be framed at that deep level. Of all the deliberate "leaps" he has made in his art-centered life, this was surely the most daring. Few writers are "foot-loose" enough for this kind of journey.

Capote's aim eluded his grasp, as it would have eluded anyone's. The book he finally wrote, failing to attain that charmed circle in which fact and fiction would blend, falls back into a category which may as well be labeled "documentary novel"— though it must be added that In Cold Blood is certainly one of the finest specimens of that "impure genre" and quite possibly the best piece of artistic journalism ever written.

There is a sense, however, in which Capote's achievement is not so important as his aim. Neither his literary career nor In Cold Blood itself can be adequately understood without some

178

knowledge of what he hoped to achieve in the nonfiction novel. Capote himself seems, with the supreme self-confidence that artists must breathe like air, to feel that he *has* achieved it. His extravagant claims for the book are more than mere expressions of his natural flamboyance and high-pressure salesmanship. Confidence in his technical ability is not a new thing with Capote; what is new is his assurance that he has done an immense piece of social groundwork successfully, not only on the level of accurate reporting but on the deeper level of personal understanding. Stated simply, it is the conviction that his talent for writing and his talent for friendship have been fully and triumphantly integrated.

The foundation of *In Cold Blood* was to be "immaculate" factuality. Asked if such details as Dick's swerving the car to hit a dog were his own invention, Capote replied, "No. There was a dog, and it was precisely as described. One doesn't spend almost six years on a book, the point of which is factual accuracy, and then give way to minor distortions." [68] Capote's emphasis on this kind of accuracy, as evidence of the ironclad truthfulness of the book as a whole, places him in an awkward position. To begin with, his diligent critics and disgruntled subjects have inevitably turned up small errors in *In Cold Blood*. For example, it has been asserted by those concerned that he exaggerated Bobby Rupp's basketball prowess and gave an inaccurate account of the sale of Nancy's horse Babe.

More important, the thoughtful reader rightly considers complete factual accuracy in a book of this sort a patent impossibility. Awareness of the author's necessary role of selection and arrangement should be enough to reduce the question to minor importance, given Capote's excellent record for accuracy. But even to know how accurate he is, the reader is dependent on extra-textual evidence—must constantly be aware of the diligent researcher hovering in the wings. Capote's recognition of the reader's need to know whether Dick really swerved to hit that dog is surely one of the main reasons for the numerous interviews he has granted in connection with the publication of *In Cold Blood.*

Accuracy on the factual level is meant to undergird Capote's really important concern: objectivity with regard to the internal action. The main business of any novel, fiction or nonfiction, is with moral action—or at least with the question of whether moral action is possible. The moral action in *In Cold Blood* is the murder of four people and the execution of two, and our chief interest is in the motivation of the actors and the significance of what happens to the sufferers. It takes more than research to ascertain "facts" of this kind, and yet this was Capote's main job. Though his statements about the book would seem to place him as staunchly "against interpretation" as Susan Sontag herself, he, too, had to interpret. The observer of any facet of life is necessarily an interpreter, and the artist is one preeminently. Neither the undisputed factuality of the book nor the author's claims for it should be allowed to obscure the fact that what *In Cold Blood* presents is Truman Capote's view of the facts. Here, just as in *The Grass Harp* or *Breakfast at Tiffany's,* he had to decide what the book was to say, then direct every smallest part of it toward that end.

Capote has acknowledged this, as when he said to me, "One has a great bundle of material, then you choose and select to make the impression you want." Asked what principle he followed in the selection, he replied unhesitatingly, "What is relevant. I always know the end first of all; I usually write the end first of all—what the end is in theory, at least—and build along toward it." [69] His account of the construction of *In Cold Blood* is in keeping with this. "I worked for a year on the notes before I ever wrote one line. And when I wrote the first word, I had done the entire book in outline, down to the finest detail. Except for the last part, the final dispensation of the case—that was an evolving matter." [70]

Asked by George Plimpton how he managed, while keeping himself "out of it," to present his point of view about why Perry Smith committed the murders, he answered:

Of course, it's by the selection of what you choose to tell. I

believe Perry did what he did for the reasons he himself states—
that his life was a constant accumulation of disillusionments and
reverses and he suddenly found himself (in the Clutter house
that night) in a psychological cul-de-sac. The Clutters were such
a perfect set of symbols for every frustration in his life. As Perry
himself said, 'I didn't have anything against them, and they
never did anything wrong to me—the way other people have all
my life. Maybe they're just the ones who had to pay for it.' Now
in that particular section where Perry talks about the reason for
the murders, I could have included other views. But Perry's happens to be the one I believe is the right one, and it's the one that
Dr. Satten at the Menninger Clinic arrived at quite independently, never having done any interviews with Perry.

I could have added a lot of other opinions. But that would
have confused the issue, and indeed the book. I had to make up
my mind, and move towards that one view, always. You can say
that the reportage is incomplete. But then it has to be. It's a
question of selection, you wouldn't get anywhere if it wasn't for
that. . . . I make my own comment by what I choose to tell and
how I choose to tell it. It is true that an author is more in control of fictional characters because he can do anything he wants
with them as long as they stay credible. But in the nonfiction
novel one can also manipulate: if I put something in which I
don't agree about I can always set it in a context of qualification
without having to step into the story myself to set the reader
straight.[71]

The seeming contradiction between such admissions as these
and Capote's claims to objectivity can be resolved only by reference to his conviction that, through painstaking investigation
and deep personal sympathy with those involved, he reached a
correct judgment about the Clutter case. For the book to be a
complete success on Capote's terms, the reader would have to
share this conviction. A partial help toward this end might be
a second volume, to accompany each copy of In Cold Blood,
describing the entire process of writing the book; better still
would be a meeting with the author himself, yet even this, however persuasive, would not be quite enough. At best we are back
with Capote the magician, bowing at the completion of a stun-
ning but never quite believable trick. The analogy is not perfect,
for Capote is in dead earnest and asks to be taken so.

As a novelist, he has no other choice. Unlike the illusionist, whose effect derives from the audience's intense awareness of deception, the novelist asks for—indeed compels—that willing suspension of disbelief of which Coleridge spoke. Henry James stated the principle: "Really, universally, relations stop nowhere, and the exquisite problem of the artist is eternally but to draw, by a geometry of his own, the circle within which they shall happily appear to do so." [72] Having once made his judgment about the Clutter case, Capote had to try, with every technical means available to him within the book itself, to "create total credibility," as he says—to give the impression that he was representing not one man's view but the facts. To do this with any degree of success requires of the novelist an act of complete faith in his own mind and its creations; yet in the case of the nonfiction novelist this inevitably suggests culpable deception. The author's defense against this charge can only be to give, outside the work itself, all the evidence he can of his integrity. Lacking the hypothetical second volume, Capote has nevertheless attempted to present such evidence in a number of published interviews, and seems to have succeeded to the satisfaction of all but a few critics. Still, no matter how admirable his personal credentials are, artistically they are finally beside the point.

Within the book itself, granted Capote's fundamental control, he has succeeded in giving a strong impression of objectivity. The very subject he chose made possible an effective show of impartiality through sympathetic portrayal of both victims and killers. Capote says he answered Perry's questions about his motive for writing the book by telling him that "it didn't have anything to do with changing the reader's opinion about anything, nor did I have any moral reasons worthy of calling them such—it was just that I had a strictly aesthetic theory about creating a book which could result in a work of art." [73]

In terms of narrative technique, Capote kept himself out of the book, having learned the advisability of this from his work on *The Muses Are Heard*. "My feeling is that for the nonfiction-novel form to be entirely successful, the author should not appear in the work. Ideally. Once the narrator does appear, he has to appear throughout, all the way down the line, and the I-I-I intrudes when it really shouldn't. I think the single most difficult thing in my book, technically, was to write it without ever appearing myself, and yet, at the same time, create total credibility." [74]

It is understandable that Capote had difficulties, for he had placed himself in the position of having to stay out of the book and in it—or at least behind it—at the same time. This is because, with regard to credibility, fiction and nonfiction work in almost directly opposite ways: the journalist must always be an eyewitness or have access to eyewitness accounts.

For example, an early scene in *In Cold Blood* begins as follows:

"Good grief, Kenyon! I hear you."
As usual, the devil was in Kenyon. His shouts kept coming up the stairs: "Nancy! Telephone!"
Barefoot, pajama-clad, Nancy scampered down the stairs. There were two telephones in the house—one in the room her father used as an office, another in the kitchen. She picked up the kitchen extension: "Hello? Oh, yes, good morning, Mrs. Katz" (C 17).

One might wonder at first how Capote reconstructed this dialogue, since the only persons present were dead before he reached Kansas. But someone else could have heard the words: Mrs. Katz—and with her, Capote did talk. We breathe a sigh of relief and admiration: the invisible reporter is on the job.

In the conventional novel, on the other hand, the reader "believes" whatever is told him unless it is patently unbelievable (improbable). It is precisely when an eyewitness narrator is introduced that the question of limited credibility arises. Dramatized narrators have their uses, of course, and Capote's fiction shows a steadily increasing employment of them. But for works of large scope—and a new largeness of scope was his first aim in the nonfiction novel—what is needed is the illusion of omniscience, best conveyed by impersonal narration.

James Joyce said that the author should "refine himself out of existence." That Capote considered this good advice for the nonfiction novelist is made clear by the remark quoted above, and also by one made to me during a discussion of *In Cold Blood:* "My narrator is always an observer. He's better the less he participates in the action. He is the omniscient eye. I always try to make him the object sitting there vibrating—seeing, observing." With regard to the Clutter case, he saw himself as "merely the instrument to transfer this life into art." [75]

The few shadowy appearances Capote does make in *In Cold Blood* serve as reminders both of his authoritative presence and of his remarkable overall success in keeping himself authorially "out of" the book. They occur when he is quoting statements made to him and not ascribable to any other source. Larry Hendricks' long account of the finding of the bodies is told, for example, to "an acquaintance," and on one or two other occasions Capote appears as "a friend" or "a journalist." One section near the end of the book consists mostly of a long statement made by Dick Hickock to Capote, describing the execution of Lowell Lee Andrews and commenting on Perry Smith. It begins, " 'That was a cold night,' Hickock said, talking to a journalist with whom he corresponded and who was periodically allowed to visit him" (C 331), and later includes the following: " 'But honest to God, I've done my damnedest to get along with Perry. Only he's so critical. Two-faced. So jealous of every little thing. Every letter I get, every visit. Nobody ever comes to see him except you,' he said, nodding at the journalist, who was equally well acquainted with Smith as he was with Hickock" (C 335).

Capote considers these intrusions unfortunate but unavoidable, and the reader finds them only slightly disturbing. Ironically, their purpose is not to introduce Capote's opinions but rather to tie in statements made by others.

The limitations I have ascribed to *In Cold Blood* are inherent in the very concept of a nonfiction novel. Viewed as fictional art, any such work would be found lacking in that self-containedness which the artifact should possess; viewed as reportage, it would always seem to present spurious claims to truth. These flaws are pervasive, setting up disturbing vibrations all through the book. On the other hand, the ores refined in the heat of Capote's intention did turn, if not into pure gold, at least into a very high grade alloy. *In Cold Blood* is a remarkable blend of compassion and craftsmanship, of life and art, possessing large measures of the factual persuasiveness and poetic altitude its author sought. It is also, as I hope to show, the product of an amazing collaboration between design and chance and, for Capote, between the new and the old.

· IX. *IN COLD BLOOD* ·

The form Truman Capote gave his nonfiction novel was well chosen from both the journalistic and the artistic points of view. *In Cold Blood* is written in small sections, eighty-five in number, varying in length from ten lines to twenty-five pages, with most between three and ten pages. Journalistically this gives, more effectively than a smoothly flowing account could do, the impression of a great multiplicity of events skillfully encompassed. The abrupt scene-shifting often has the effect of an up-to-the-minute news bulletin. Capote says he wrote the small parts separately—enough to fill a 700-page book had he so desired—and put them "in a box" like pieces for a mosaic. Each, he told me, is "a very defined small story of its kind." [1]

Some are especially satisfactory as distinct compositions, and Capote has chosen several for reading on his *In Cold Blood* recording and in public appearances.

Among these is the episode when Perry and Dick pick up two hitchhikers on a Texas highway. It begins, "Perry noticed them first—hitchhikers, a boy and an old man, both carrying homemade knapsacks, and despite the blowy weather, a gritty and bitter Texas wind, wearing only overalls and a thin denim shirt" (C 207). Dick finally agrees to pick them up, and as they ride, the boy explains his technique for spotting empty soft drink bottles beside the road. They begin an amiable competition, and by nightfall the car is loaded: "The trunk was filled, the back seemed a glittering dump heap; unnoticed, unmentioned by even his grandson, the ailing old man was all but hidden under the shifting, dangerously chiming cargo" (C 210). They have supper at a restaurant and then, because Dick refuses to carry the pair farther, the pleasant episode comes to an end. After shaking hands with Dick and Perry and wishing them a Happy New Year, the boy is left standing beside the highway as he "waved them away into the dark" (C 211). Within a few hours they are arrested in Las Vegas.

Capote sometimes speaks of the artistic quality of *In Cold Blood*, as of his earlier work, in terms of poetic power or ability to exert an emotional effect on the reader without the latter's being aware of the process. As an example of this he cites the short section, near the middle of the book, in which Alvin Dewey wanders alone through the deserted Clutter house.

Inside, the house was warm, for the heat had not been turned off, and the shiny-floored rooms, smelling of a lemon-scented polish, seemed only temporarily untenanted; it was as though today were Sunday and the family might at any moment return from church. . . . In the parlor, a sheet of music, "Comin' Thro' the Rye," stood open on the piano rack. In the hall, a sweat-stained gray Stetson hat—Herb's—hung on a hat peg. Upstairs in Kenyon's room, on a shelf above his head, the lenses of the dead boy's spectacles gleamed with reflected light. (C 152).

The atmosphere of intense nostalgia, of silent, haunted rooms, is one Capote handles well. He makes the scene vivid with sensory images—the warmth, the scented polish—and precise, intimate details recalling the departed tenants.

As Dewey pauses at an upstairs window, he notices, out in a wheat field, a scarecrow on which an old dress of Bonnie's flutters in the wind. It reminds him of a dream his wife described to him a few mornings before. In it she was in her kitchen preparing supper when Bonnie Clutter walked through the door. Invited to taste the shrimp gumbo boiling on the stove, she had refused to move, only shaking her head, wringing her hands, and repeating, "To be murdered. To be murdered. No. No. There's nothing worse. Northing worse than that. Nothing" (C 154). Bonnie's empty dress flapping in the winter field climaxes the motif of absence, and the dream contains the book's most powerful expression of the pathos of the Clutters' victimization.

From the chill despair of this scene, Capote shifts abruptly to Perry and Dick, striding down a highway "deep in the Mojave Desert" and chanting, "Mine eyes have seen the glory of the coming of the Lord . . ." (C 155). Aside from simple chronology, this kind of cinematic contrast is the leading structural technique employed by Capote through most of *In Cold Blood*. He has denied consciously using film techniques in this book, yet he also said, not long before starting it, "I think most of the younger writers have learned and borrowed from the visual, structural side of movie technique. I have." [2] Movie critic Dwight Macdonald has called attention, somewhat overemphatically, to cinematic traces in *In Cold Blood*: "the Griffith crosscutting in the first chapter between the Clutter family and the steadily approaching death car, the 'establishing' long shots of the Kansas milieu, the psychological close-ups of the killers, the death-row prison background, with the other condemned killers playing bit grotesques counterpointed against the decent, normal home life of the chief detective and his wife." [3]

The most obvious advantage of the vignette structure, cinematic or not, is the way it enables Capote to reinforce the contrast between victims and killers by repeated jolts from one group to the other, especially in the section preceding the murders. Minutes before Perry and Dick reach the Clutter house, they are shown at a gas station where Perry has been nursing his grotesquely injured legs in the men's room. "Perry gripped the edge of the washbasin and hauled himself to a standing position. His legs trembled; the pain in his knees made him perspire. He wiped his face with a paper towel. He unlocked the door and said, 'O.K. Let's go.' " Then "Nancy's bedroom was the smallest, most personal room in the house—girlish, and as frothy as a ballerina's tutu. Walls, ceiling, and everything else except a bureau and a writing desk, were pink or blue or white" (C 55–56). This juxtaposition vividly anticipates the rapidly approaching moment (not to be described in detail until much later in the book) when these men will enter Nancy's bedroom with intentions of rape and murder.

In Cold Blood is divided into four equal sections entitled

"The Last to See Them Alive," "Persons Unknown," "Answer," and "The Corner." These headings, like the title of the book itself, have the journalistic flavor and are, indeed, taken from the verbal matrix of the case rather than from Capote's imagination. All, however, are rich with a multiple suggestiveness that is the result of his artistry. As Capote told Perry Smith, though without explaining fully, the book's title has a "double meaning," referring both to the murders and the executions, with the ironic emphasis falling heavily on the latter. Capote has always enjoyed disturbing the complacent. Here he shows us that the familiar phrase "in cold blood," if it means anything, doesn't mean quite what we thought it did.

"The Last to See Them Alive" provokes a similar double take. It refers at first glance to the various acquaintances who saw the Clutters on their last day, but its final reference is to the killers, whose eyes Capote has reproduced at the front of the book. Mrs. Dewey, when her husband showed her their photographs, felt "transfixed by Hickock's eyes." She was "reminded of a childhood incident—of a bobcat she'd once seen caught in a trap, and of how, though she'd wanted to release it, the cat's eyes, radiant with pain and hatred, had drained her of her pity and filled her with terror." " 'Think of those eyes,' she said. 'Coming toward you' " (C 164–165).

Part One covers the day of the murder, recounting the activities of each of the four Clutters and tracing the gradual approach of the killers as they drive across Kansas toward Holcomb. Since the book's point of view is the "public" or journalistic one rather than that of the killers, no account of the murder is given here. Bobby Rupp's departure from the house shortly before midnight is followed by the discovery of the bodies on the following morning. One of the many strokes of good luck that Capote brilliantly capitalized on was the fact that among the first arrivals was the Holcomb citizen probably best qualified to describe the experience: the high school English teacher and aspiring writer, Larry Hendricks. Capote reproduces his long account, describes the first wave of panic as the news spreads, and concludes Part One with Perry and Dick four hundred miles away, sleeping.

Part Two, "Persons Unknown," introduces detective Alvin Dewey and covers the first month of investigations, meanwhile following Hickock and Smith as they pass hot checks in Kansas City, take a grotesquely idyllic vacation in Mexico City and Acapulco, and return as far as the Mojave Desert. To Holcomb they are the "persons unknown," but the reader is coming to know them well through Capote's slowly accumulating history of their lives. At bottom they will, of course, remain unknown.

This part of the book, unlike the other three, contains no very dramatic events. On the Kansas scene, its purpose is to convey a sense of the passing of time and to dramatize the fear and suspicion that fill the Holcomb area, where the concept of "persons unknown" expands ominously to include next-door neighbors. Underlying the immediate fear is a deeper emptiness. The experience struck one Holcomb woman as "like being told there is no God. It makes life seem pointless. I don't think people are so much frightened as they are deeply depressed" (C 88). These feelings are, finally, brought to poignant life at the end of the section in Mrs. Dewey's bleak dream of Bonnie Clutter.

Capote titled Part Three simply "Answer," refusing to bestow on the accusation of Smith and Hickock that definitive rightness it would seem to possess. The section begins with the introduction of Floyd Wells, the informer, and his statement to authorities implicating Dick and Perry. Detectives travel to question members of the suspects' families and follow up other leads, but narrowly miss their quarry in Kansas City as the latter head for Miami Beach.

Christmas comes, unseasonably mild and brilliant, and Capote uses Bobby Rupp's memories to provide a vivid reminiscence of the Clutters. Uneasy at home, Bobby goes out for a jog across the wheat fields. Without intending to, he approaches a familiar spot. "The cider-tart odor of spoiling apples. Apple trees and pear trees, peach and cherry: Mr. Clutter's orchard, the treasured assembly of fruit trees he had planted" (C 206). Looking at the house, Bobby notices that "the first threads of decay's cobweb were being spun. A gravel rake lay rusting in the driveway; the lawn was parched and shabby. That fateful Sunday, when the sheriff summoned ambulances to remove the murdered family, the ambulances had driven across the grass straight to the front door, and the tire tracks were still visible" (C 206). Again the details, especially the last, give the impression of absence.

The arrest in Las Vegas soon follows, first revealed to the reader through Mrs. Dewey's long recollection of the arrival of the news and the mixed reaction of her husband. The event itself is anticlimactic.

Neither Perry nor Dick was aware of the police vehicle trailing them as they pulled away from the post office, and with Dick driving and Perry directing, they traveled five blocks north, turned left, then right, drove a quarter mile more, and stopped in front of a dying palm tree and a weather-wrecked sign from which all calligraphy had faded except the word "OOM."
"This it?" Dick asked.
Perry, as the patrol car drew alongside, nodded (C 215).

The prisoners are questioned separately in the Las Vegas jail. Dick finally confesses to the crime but insists that it was Perry who actually committed all four of the murders. Perry's own confession, the dramatic high point of the book, comes as a result of prodding by Dewey during the drive to Garden City. Capote heightens the effect of immediacy by narrating the confession scene in the present tense.

According to Perry's painstaking recital, he himself had at first wanted to give up the Clutter project, but Dick, angry at the thought of so much wasted effort, persuaded him to go ahead. When Mr. Clutter insisted that he did not have a safe, Perry believed him and again wanted to leave. "But Dick was too ashamed to face it. He said he wouldn't believe it till we searched the whole house. He said the thing to do was tie them all up, then take our time looking around. You couldn't argue with him, he was so excited. The glory of having everybody at his mercy, that's what excited him" (C 239). Perry still wanted to leave. "And yet—How can I explain this? It was like I wasn't part of it. More as though I was reading a story. And I had to know what was going to happen. The end. So I went back upstairs" (C 240).

Perry's careful recital of their methodical handling of the Clutters reveals in his own behavior a surprising strain of gentleness—laying the bound Mr. Clutter on an empty mattress box, providing a pillow for Kenyon's head, talking gently to Nancy about dancing and horses. When Dick told him that he intended to rape the girl, Perry, disgusted, warned that Dick would have to kill him first. After tying and gagging the family, they stopped for another discussion. Perry, fed up with Dick's bragging, asked for the knife and said, "All right Dick. Here goes"—intending, by his account, only to call Dick's bluff. Kneeling painfully down beside Mr. Clutter, he felt shame and disgust, and remembered that *"they'd* told me never to come back to Kansas" (Italics Capote's).

But I didn't realize what I'd done till I heard the sound. Like somebody drowning. Screaming under water. I handed the knife to Dick. I said, 'Finish him. You'll feel better.' Dick tried—or pretended to. But the man had the strength of ten men—he was half out of his ropes, his hands were free. Dick panicked. Dick wanted to get the hell out of there. But I wouldn't let him go. The man would have died anyway, I know that, but I couldn't leave him like he was. I told Dick to hold the flashlight, focus it. Then I aimed the gun. The room just exploded. Went blue. Just blazed up. Jesus, I'll never understand why they didn't hear the noise twenty miles around" (C 244).

Capote writes, "Dewey's ears ring with it . . ." and summarizes the continuing account the detective hears:

Kenyon's head in a circle of light, the murmur of muffled pleadings, then Hickock again scrambling after a used cartridge; Nancy's room, Nancy listening to boots on hardwood stairs, the creak of the steps as they climb toward her, Nancy's eyes, Nancy watching the flashlight's shine seek the target ("She said, 'Oh, no! Oh, please. No! No! No! No! Don't! Oh, please don't! Please!' I gave the gun to Dick. I told him I'd done all I could do. He took aim, and she turned her face to the wall"); the dark hall, the assassins hastening toward the final door. Perhaps, having heard all she had, Bonnie welcomed their swift approach (C 244–245).

The entire confession scene has been narrated from Dewey's point of view, and Capote now comments, "Sorrow and profound fatigue are at the heart of Dewey's silence" (C 246). The detective has, for the most part, attained his goal of learning what happened in the Clutter house that night—yet the confessions have failed to satisfy his "sense of meaningful design." He sees the crime as "a psychological accident, virtually an impersonal act; the victims might as well have been killed by lightning" (C 246). The only difference is that they suffered prolonged terror, and this Dewey cannot forget, though he can look at Perry without anger and even with some sympathy for his life of loneliness and futility. "Dewey's sympathy, however, was not deep enough to accommodate either forgiveness or mercy. He hoped to see Perry and his partner hanged—hanged back to back" (C 246).

By this point in the book, the reader has come very close to accepting Dewey, at least in his more contemplative, less professional moments, as a spokesman for the author. Capote does not, as with so many others, set the detective's speculations about the deeper meanings of the events in a "context of qualification." The inconclusiveness of "Answer" is here evident in Dewey's inability to shape the how's and why's of the case into a meaningful design. When, at the end of the book, Capote brings matters at least somewhat closer to a final resolution, it will again be in the mind of Dewey.

Part Three, meanwhile, ends with a short section describing the arrival of the prisoners in Garden City. Capote once commented to me that he often thinks of his writing in musical terms; for example, he is fond of "glissando endings" that avoid the climactic organ note.[4] He cited the end of In Cold Blood as an example, but the end of Part Three would serve as well. The passage begins with one of his more gratuitous, though strictly factual, touches—a description of two Garden City tomcats "who are always together" and whose daily ceremony is to scavenge the grilles of parked cars in search of "slaughtered birds" picked up on the highway. Their unvarying daily itinerary takes them to Courthouse Square, "another of their hunting grounds—a highly promising one on the afternoon of Wednesday, January 6, for the area swarmed with Finney County vehicles that had brought to town part of the crowd populating the square" (C 246).

Capote's familiar affection for stray cats (*Breakfast at Tiffany's*, "A House on the Heights")—his habit of identifying them with wild, wandering souls like Holly Golightly—is evident here, though muted, in the resemblance between these "thin, dirty strays with strange and clever habits" and Perry and Dick. Later, Perry watches the cats from his cell window and finds the experience painful: "Because most of my life I've done what they're doing. The equivalent" (C 264).

The crowd in the square awaiting the delayed arrival of Dewey and his colleagues with their prisoners "might have been expecting a parade, or attending a political rally" (C 247). By six o'clock, however, fewer than three hundred persons remain, for with this day's sunset the Indian Summer has come to an end. When the prisoners finally arrive the crowd falls silent, "as though amazed to find them humanly shaped. The handcuffed men, whitefaced and blinking blindly, glistened in the glare of flashbulbs and floodlights" (C 248). Afterward, no one lingers. "Warm rooms and warm suppers beckoned them, and as they hurried away, leaving the cold square to the two gray cats, the miraculous autumn departed too; the year's first snow began to fall" (C 248).

Part Four is entitled "The Corner," after the prisoners' name for the execution chamber at the Kansas State Penitentiary. With the departure of the mild autumn weather that furnished the backdrop for all the principal events up to this point, the drama, in a sense, ends as well. All that remains is for the legal process to grind its slow way along, pushing Perry and Dick ever deeper into a corner and finally to their deaths. Until the trial, the prisoners are kept in the Finney County jail, from which both make abortive plans to escape. Judge Roland Tate, acting within the letter of Kansas law, refuses to permit them to be sent to the state hospital for extensive psychiatric tests, ordering instead an examination by three local physicians, who, after "an hour or so of conversational prying" (C 268), decide that neither man suffers from mental disorder.

The week-long trial itself is accurately presented by Capote as not very exciting, the outcome almost a foregone conclusion. The state-appointed defense attorneys had secured the volunteer services of Dr. W. Mitchell Jones, a highly qualified criminal psychologist from the state hospital, who interviewed both prisoners on the day before the trial and asked them to write short autobiographical accounts. They occupy themselves with this task during the first day in court, and Capote reproduces the accounts at length, concluding one section with Dick's closing words: "My lawyer said I should be truthful with you as you can help me. And I need help, as you know" (C 279).

Dr. Jones appears as a witness for the defense but is restricted by the M'Naghten Rule to simply stating his opinion as to whether the accused "knew right from wrong" at the time of the commission of the crime. In Dick's case he answers yes, but in Perry's he says he is uncertain.

In each case Capote gives the remainder of the statement Dr. Jones would have made "had he been permitted' to do so. Concerning Dick, the psychiatrist concludes that, while mentally alert and in contact with reality, "he shows fairly typical characteristics of what would psychiatrically be called a severe character disorder. It is important that steps be taken to rule out the possibility of organic brain damage, since, if present, it might have substantially influenced his behavior during the past several years and at the time of the crime" (C 295).

The doctor's indecision in Perry's case results from his opinion that Perry "shows definite signs of severe mental illness. His childhood, related to me and verified by portions of the prison records, was marked by brutality and lack of concern on the part of both parents. He seems to have grown up without direction, without love, and without ever having absorbed any fixed sense of moral values" (C 296–297). Dr. Jones finds two traits of Perry's especially pathological: a " 'paranoid' orientation toward the world" and "an ever-present, poorly controlled rage," usually in the past directed at authority figures. He also detects an element of confusion in Perry's thinking, and "a 'magical' quality, a disregard of reality." He concludes, pending further examination, that Perry should be classified as "paranoid schizophrenic" (C 298).

This diagnosis of Perry Smith is not surprising to one who knows the history of his life, and Capote has seen to it that the reader knows it well, devoting considerably more space to him than to anyone else in the book. Perry was one of four children born to Tex John Smith and his wife Flo, itinerant rodeo performers, who, when Perry was five, were forced by illness to settle near Reno, Nevada. A year later they separated, and the children went with their mother to San Francisco. After a period of gradual deterioration, she died, and Perry was sent to a Catholic orphanage and later to a Salvation Army shelter. His father, who called himself the Lone Wolf, had begun a life of wandering around the western states and Alaska. For a while Perry lived with his father in Reno, finishing the third grade—as far as his education was ever to go. Then for six years they lived in a trailer, never staying long in one place.

Perry inherited his father's restlessness and also his dreams of finding gold. During later years he carried with him "all his worldly belongings: one cardboard suitcase, a guitar, and two big boxes of books and maps and songs, poems and old letters, weighing a quarter of a ton" (C 14). He was "an incessant conceiver of voyages," and the trip he and Dick took to Mexico after the murders was largely the result of the fantasies he had absorbed from men's magazines about buried and sunken treasure, "flights of parrots" over tropical beaches, and a life of perfect ease and freedom. By that time he had already done a lot of traveling, having served in the Merchant Marine and later the Army during the Korean conflict.

Periodically he went searching for his father, and after his discharge from the Army he spent some time with him in Alaska. This reunion was delayed by a serious motorcycle accident that placed him in the hospital for six months and on crutches for another six. At the time of the Clutter murders, Capote notes, "his chunky, dwarfish legs, broken in five places and pitifully scarred, still pained him so severely that he had become an aspirin addict" (C 31).

He finally reached his father in Alaska, but the visit came to a violent end. When Perry's father snatched one of their last biscuits out of his hand, berating him for his greediness, the younger man lost control: "My hands got hold of his throat. My hands—but I couldn't control them. They wanted to choke him to death" (C 136). His father broke loose, ran for his gun; and announced to his son, "Look at me, Perry. I'm the last thing living you're ever gonna see" (C 136). Then, realizing the gun was unloaded, he sat down and cried. Perry took a long walk and returned to find himself locked out and all his possessions lying in the snow. He left, taking only his guitar.

Not long afterward, in 1955, Perry was arrested for burglary. (It was not the first time: his first arrest was at the age of eight, and he had spent a considerable part of his youth behind bars.) It was while in the Kansas State Penitentiary for larceny, jailbreak, and car theft that Perry met Dick Hickock.

The rest of the Smith family had, for the most part, done badly, too. When the thought occurred to Perry, as it occasionally did, that there was "something wrong" with him, he was inclined to blame it on his origins, recalling that his mother had died of alcoholism, one sister had jumped from a hotel window, a brother had "one day driven his wife to suicide and killed himself the next" (C 111). Among the numerous sections of *In Cold Blood* devoted to Perry is one of twenty-five pages, the longest in the book. In it, Capote has quoted in full two documents from Perry's treasured box: a long biographical sketch of him written by his father for the Kansas Parole Board, and an exhortatory letter from his sister Barbara, the one member of the family who had led a reasonably normal life. A measure of love is apparent in both, but it was hardly reciprocated by Perry. Once, angry and drunk, he told his sister, "Oh, the man I could have been! But that bastard never gave me a chance. . . . *You* went to school. You and Jimmy and Fern. Every damn one of you got an education. Everybody but me. And I hate you, all of you—Dad and everybody" (C 185). Later he told Dick that his only regret about that night in the Clutter house was that his sister hadn't been there.

There was another document in Perry's box, appended to

Barbara's letter and entitled "Impressions I Garnered From the Letter." It was written by Willie-Jay, an effeminate older man, chaplain's assistant in the penitentiary, who had taken a sentimentally apostolic interest in the young prisoner with intellectual and artistic yearnings. Perry felt that Willie-Jay saw him as he saw himself—"exceptional," "rare," "artistic"—and was the only person in the world who really "gave a damn" about him. But Willie-Jay had, in a sense, let him down. Just before accepting Dick's 1959 invitation to collaborate on a "really big score," Perry had gone to visit his prison mentor only to learn that he had been released and had left town five hours before. The news left Perry "dizzy with anger and disappointment" (C 45).

When Perry decided to rendezvous with Dick Hickock, it was not with a sense of joining a "friend" such as Willie-Jay had been, or a few other men at various times in his life. The relationship was less a deep personal harmony than a strong but uneasy attraction of opposites. Capote remarks that the two "had little in common, but they did not realize it, for they shared a number of surface traits. Both, for example, were fastidious, very attentive to hygiene and the condition of their fingernails" (C 30). Both, too, had been injured in highway accidents. Though Dick's injury was less serious than Perry's, it had the effect of making his face seem "composed of mismatching parts. It was as though his head had been halved like an apple, then put together a fraction off center" (C 31).

In spite of their similarities, Perry saw in Dick primarily someone intriguingly unlike himself. In Capote's version of Perry's thoughts: "When you got right down to it, Dick's literalness, his pragmatic approach to every subject, was the primary reason Perry had been attracted to him, for it made Dick seem, compared to himself, so authentically tough, invulnerable, 'totally masculine'" (C 16). Dick was aggressively heterosexual and successful with women; Perry, on the other hand, considered sex "filthy." A fastidious disgust with people who "can't control themselves sexually" lay behind his firm opposition to Dick's plan to rape Nancy Clutter. Several times, in fact, he prevented Dick from seducing young girls.

While both men were above average in intelligence, it was

Dick who was the organizer. Dick planned the robbery of the Clutter house and the disposal of the witnesses; he was willing—at least in words—to kill a dozen people if necessary and "blast hair all over them walls" (C 22). Shrewdly, he had decided that Perry was "that rarity, 'a natural killer'—absolutely sane, but conscienceless, and capable of dealing, with or without motive, the coldest-blooded deathblows" (C 55). The events in the Clutter house destroyed most of Perry's admiration for Dick and gave the latter a frightening new insight into his companion. From that time on, their relations were severely strained, each thinking several times of killing or abandoning the other. The trial and imprisonment did not bring them significantly closer, though some of their liking for each other endured. Separated from Dick, Perry felt "all by myself. Like somebody covered with sores. Somebody only a big nut would have anything to do with " (C 260).

After recording Dr. Jones's diagnosis of Perry Smith, Capote goes even more thoroughly into the subject of Perry's psychological condition, pointing out that Dr. Joseph Satten of the Menninger Clinic, "a widely respected veteran in the field of forensic psychiatry," consulted with Dr. Jones and endorsed his conclusions. Dr. Satten considered the crime "essentially the act of Perry Smith, who, he feels, represents a type of murderer described by him in an article: 'Murder Without Apparent Motive—A Study in Personality Disorganization'" (C 298), which appeared in The American Journal of Psychiatry for July, 1960. The study, based on four cases, deals with "murderers who seem rational, coherent, and controlled, and yet whose homicidal acts have a bizarre, apparently senseless quality," and theorizes that "those individuals are predisposed to severe lapses in ego-control which makes possible the open expression of primitive violence, born out of previous, and now unconscious, traumatic experiences" (C 299).

Capote notes that according to the article, the murderers themselves "were puzzled as to why they killed their victims, who were relatively unknown to them, and in each instance the murderer appears to have lapsed into a dreamlike dissociative trance from which he awakened to 'suddenly discover' himself assaulting the victim" (C 299). He quotes at length from the article, which attributes to the individuals studied such characteristics as feelings of inferiority and severe sexual inhibition together with, in some cases, overt homosexuality. Dr. Satten writes, "The murderous potential can become activated, especially if some disequilibrium is already present, when the victim-to-be is unconsciously perceived as a key figure in some past traumatic configuration. The behavior, or even the mere presence, of this figure adds a stress to the unstable balance of forces that results in a sudden extreme discharge of violence, similar to the explosion that takes place when a percussion cap ignites a charge of dynamite" (C 301).

Capote points out that Dr. Satten believes it was only the murder of Mr. Clutter that "mattered psychologically" to Perry, the others following necessarily as a result of the first; when Perry attacked Mr. Clutter he was

under a mental eclipse, deep inside a schizophrenic darkness, for it was not entirely a flesh-and-blood man he "suddenly discovered" himself destroying, but "a key figure in some past traumatic configuration": his father? the orphanage nuns who had derided and beaten him? the hated Army sergeant? the parole officer who had ordered him to "stay out of Kansas"? One of them, or all of them.

In his confession, Smith said, "I didn't want to harm the man. I thought he was a very nice gentleman. Soft-spoken. I thought so right up to the moment I cut his throat" (C 302).

Capote concludes, with a veiled allusion to himself, "So it would appear that by independent paths, both the professional and the amateur analyst reached conclusions not dissimilar" (C 302).

The foregoing passage presents the deepest, most authoritative look that was taken into the motivations of Perry Smith. By placing it where he does, Capote emphasizes the court's refusal to look as deeply as possible as the trial moved inexorably to its conclusion. In several other ways as well he manages to imply strongly that the trial of Smith and Hickock was not all that it should have been. He describes the concluding statement of one of the two defense attorneys as "a mild, churchly sermon," then quotes briefly from the other, a discourse on the barbarity and ineffectuality of capital punishment, observing that during it "not everyone was attentive; one juror, as though poisoned by the numerous spring-fever yawns weighting the air, sat with drugged eyes and jaws so utterly ajar bees could have buzzed in and out" (C 303).

The prosecution, on the other hand, "woke them up." Logan Green vividly recreates the murder scene, with Nancy's last cries for mercy and Bonnie's listening as her family dies and the killers approach. Nearing his climax, Capote observes, Green "gingerly touched a boil on the back of his neck, a mature inflammation that seemed, like its angry wearer, about to burst" (C 305). Green concludes by reminding the jury that "some of our enormous crimes only happen because once upon a time a pack of chicken-hearted jurors refused to do their duty" (C 305). As he sits down, a colleague says, "That was masterly, sir."

Capote notes that some listeners were "less enthusiastic," and records a conversation between two newsmen, one of whom considers the trial unfair and alludes to Perry Smith's "rotten life" as an extenuating factor. The other reporter answers, "Many a man can match sob stories with that little bastard. Me included. Maybe I drink too much, but I sure as hell never killed four people in cold blood." The first man replies, "Yeah, and how about hanging the bastard? That's pretty goddam cold-blooded too" (C 306). Capote's reporting of this brief exchange shows unmistakably where his feelings lie. As usual he allows both sides to speak, but here—as in the book's title—there is no question as to which side has the last word.

Judge Tate announces the death sentences, telling the jurors they have performed "a courageous service." Leaving the courtroom, Perry says to Dick, "No chicken-hearted jurors, they!" and they laugh loudly. Back in his cell, as the jailor's wife later recalls, Perry weeps like a child and holds her hand, saying, "I'm embraced by shame" (C 308).

Once the prisoners have been transferred to the state penitentiary, Capote compresses the passing five years into about thirty pages. He gives brief case histories of three other inmates of death row. He summarizes the continued attempts of Smith's and Hickock's federally appointed lawyers to reverse the decision of what they consider a "nightmarishly unfair trial," then mentions that a last clemency appeal was denied by Governor William Avery—"a rich farmer sensitive to public opinion"—and concludes: "And so it happened that in the daylight hours of that Wednesday morning, Alvin Dewey, breakfasting in the coffee shop of a Topeka hotel, read, on the first page of the *Kansas City Star*, a headline he had long awaited: DIE ON ROPE FOR BLOODY CRIME" (C 337).

Having thus returned Alvin Dewey to the center of the stage, Capote employs his point of view throughout the next section, the last of the book. It begins, "Dewey had watched them die," and first gives his impressions of the bleak execution chamber, the "self-consciously casual" and often insensitive remarks of the witnesses. The sound of rain on the roof, "not unlike the rat-a-tat-tat of parade drums," coincides with Hickock's arrival. He enters "handcuffed and wearing an ugly harness of leather straps" (C 338). As the long order of execution is read to him, Dick's eyes, "enfeebled by half a decade of cell shadows," search the little audience for members of the Clutter family. On learning that none are present, he is disappointed, "as though he thought the protocol surrounding this ritual of vengeance was not being properly observed" (C 338). Asked if he wants to make a last statement, Dick says that he has "no hard feelings" and shakes hands cordially with Dewey and with the three other K.B.I. agents who did most to capture him. He hangs for twenty minutes, then "a hearse, its blazing headlights beaded with rain, drove into the warehouse, and the body, placed on a litter and shrouded under a blanket, was carried to the hearse and out into the night" (C 339). One of the agents remarks, "I never would have believed he had the guts. To take it like he did. I had him tagged a coward" (C 339).

Perry enters, at first "jaunty and mischievous," then grave. Capote notes his "sensitive eyes" and manacled hands, the fingers inky and stained with color, for he has recently done many self-portraits and paintings of other prisoners' children. He begins his last remarks with some force.

"I think," he said, "it's a helluva thing to take a life in this manner. I don't believe in capital punishment, morally or legally. Maybe I had something to contribute, something—" His assurance faltered; shyness blurred his voice, lowered it to a just audible level. "It would be meaningless to apologize for what I did. Even inappropriate. But I do. I apologize" (C 340).

Dewey shuts his eyes, then hears "the thud-snap that announces a rope-broken neck." Hickock's execution had not disturbed him, but Perry, "though he was the true murderer, aroused another response, for Perry possessed a quality, the aura of an exiled animal, a creature walking wounded, that the detective could not disregard" (C 341). He remembers his first meeting with Perry in Las Vegas—"the dwarfish boy-man seated in the metal chair, his small booted feet not quite brushing the floor. And when Dewey now opened his eyes, that is what he saw: the same childish feet, tilted, dangling" (C 341).

This is, literally the book's last word about Dick Hickock and Perry Smith, and it is typical of the way they are presented throughout. Though portrayed at some length and even permitted to speak on occasion, Dick emerges as an unsympathetic character—shrewd, mean, able to take care of himself. It is Perry who haunts the memory, overshadowing not only Dick but everyone else.

Capote agrees heartily with Rebecca West's observation, made in her essay on *In Cold Blood*, that it is "not so easy to write about the dynamically good as about the dynamically bad." [5] Though one may agree that, as she goes on to say, "Mr. Capote represents the victims of the murder as brilliant, powerful, and important in their goodness," the fact remains that there is little complexity—hence, comparatively little interest—in their portrayal. The same may be said of Dick, whom we tend to dismiss much as Dewey does. Although the Clutters are admirable in many ways, and Nancy in particular has a powerful charm, the dominant thing about them in the book is their violent and pathetic fate. The action which brings this about—the central action in the book—is performed by Perry Smith. But our feeling for Perry does not, as in the case of Raskolnikov or even of Clyde Griffiths, derive principally from his commission of a gravely immoral act—from his "dynamic badness"—but rather from his amoral, pathetic blending of violence and aspiration. In addition to being a murderer by "psychological accident," Perry is a childlike dreamer, a romantic wanderer.

Perry's physical appearance is that of a grotesque child. Seated, he reveals "the shoulders, the arms, the thick, crouching torso of a weight lifter," but standing ("no taller than a twelve-year-old child"), he suggests "a retired jockey, overblown and muscle-bound" (C 15). Perry spends a lot of time in front of mirrors, for he is "enthralled" by his own face. "It was a changeling's face, and mirror-guided experiments had taught him how to ring the changes, how to look now ominous, now impish, now soulful; a tilt of the head, a twist of the lips, and the corrupt gypsy became the gentle romantic" (C 15). From his Cherokee mother he inherited "dark, moist eyes" and plentiful black hair. The father's Irish strain is less evident, but an "uppity Irish egotism takes control when he sings."

Perry has a repertoire of two hundred hymns and ballads, some composed by himself, and one of his dreams is to be a Las Vegas nightclub singer. He has chosen a stage name: "Perry O'Parsons, the One-Man Symphony." Even in a literal sense, he lives in dreams. One in particular has recurred all during his life. In it he sees himself in an African jungle, moving toward a solitary tree that exudes a sickening odor.

Only, it's beautiful to look at—it has blue leaves and diamonds hanging everywhere. Diamonds like oranges. That's why I'm there—to pick myself a bushel of diamonds. But I know the minute I try to, the minute I reach up, a snake is gonna fall on me. . . . But I figure, Well, I'll take my chances. . . . So I go to pick one, I have the diamond in my hand, I'm pulling at it, when the snake lands on top of me. We wrestle around, but he's a slippery sonofabitch and I can't get a hold, he's crushing me, you can hear my legs cracking. Now comes the part it makes me sweat even to think about. See, he starts to swallow me. Feet first. Like going down in quicksand (C 92).

At this point there always comes glorious relief in the form of a giant yellow bird, a "sort of parrot, which first appeared in his dreams when he was seven years old"—a bird " 'taller than Jesus, yellow like a sunflower,' a warrior-angel who blinded the nuns with its beak, fed upon their eyes, slaughtered them as they 'pleaded for mercy,' then gently lifted him, winged him away to 'paradise' " (C 93). Over the years, the nuns were replaced by other authority figures, but always there was the same final ascent, sometimes taking the form simply of "a sense of power, of unassailable superiority" (C 93).

This dream of Perry's is associated in his mind with suicide, a way out chosen by Fern and Jimmy, and one which has increasingly seemed to Perry "not just an alternative but the specific death awaiting him" (C 202). After his arrest this preoccupation grows. In the Garden City jail he dreams that he has cut his wrists and ankles and is lifted by the great yellow bird above an angry, powerless sheriff. The closest Perry actually comes to suicide is a fourteen-week hunger strike during his first summer in the penitentiary. He is kept alive by intravenous feeding, and when a postcard from his father revives some of his feeling for life, he decides, "Anybody wanted my life wasn't going to get any more help from me. They'd have to fight for it" (C 320). In prison he often dreams of voices crying, "Where is Jesus? Where?" and on one occasion wakes up shouting, "The bird is Jesus! The bird is Jesus!" (C 319).

Perry's aspiration to artistic success takes several forms. He says of himself, "I had this great natural musical ability. . . . I liked to read, too. Improve my vocabulary. Make up songs. And I could draw. But I never got any encouragement" (C 133). Capote describes a portrait of Jesus he did in prison as "in no way technically naive" (C 42). During his talks with Capote, when the latter insisted that his only intention in writing In Cold Blood was to create a work of art, Perry would remark, "What an irony, what an irony." Capote explains, "I'd ask what he meant, and he'd tell me that all he ever wanted to do in his life was to produce a work of art. . . . 'And now, what has happened? An incredible situation where I kill four people, and you're going to produce a work of art.' " [6]

As imprisonment forces upon Perry the realization that neither his dreams of "diving deep in fire-blue seas toward sunken treasure" nor those of artistic success will ever come true, "Perry O'Parsons" begins to appear in a new dream. He is performing in a Las Vegas nightclub, and ends his act by tap-dancing up a flight of gold-painted steps to take a bow. But there is no applause from the large audience, mostly male and mostly Negro.

Staring at them, the perspiring entertainer at last understood their silence, for suddenly he knew that these were phantoms, the ghosts of the legally annihilated, the hanged, the gassed, the electrocuted—and in the same instant he realized that he was there to join them, that the gold-painted steps had led to a scaffold, that the platform on which he stood was opening beneath him. His top hat tumbled; urinating, defecating, Perry O'Parsons entered eternity (C 319).

There is much in the life and character of Perry Smith to arouse sympathy, and Capote has skilfully emphasized it. Perry asks, "Why did I do it?" with an air of sincere questioning, and even when he admits to a visitor his lack of remorse about the murders, his words have a disarming frankness.

Am I sorry? If that's what you mean—I'm not. I don't feel anything about it. I wish I did. . . . The good people of Kansas want to murder me—and some hangman will be glad to get the work. It's easy to kill—a lot easier than passing a bad check. Just remember: I only knew the Clutters maybe an hour. If I'd known them, I guess I'd feel different. I don't think I could live with myself. But the way it was, it was like picking off targets in a shooting gallery (C 290–291).

When Alvin Dewey presents his testimony in court, making public for the first time the events detailed in Perry's confession, Capote handles the scene so as to contrast Perry with Dick and consequently place him in the best light possible. Among the facts revealed are that Perry prevented Dick from raping Nancy Clutter and that he has made a change in his confession admitting that he, not Dick, killed Nancy and Mrs. Clutter. As

Dewey explains, "He told me that Hickock . . . didn't want to die with his mother thinking he had killed any members of the Clutter family. And he said the Hickocks were good people. So why not have it that way" (C 286). Capote notes, "Hearing this, Mrs. Hickock wept" (C 286).

He also records her later remark to a woman reporter: "I can't make any excuses for what he did, his part in it. I'm not forgetting that family; I pray for them every night. But I pray for Dick, too. And this boy Perry. It was wrong of me to hate him; I've got nothing but pity for him now. And you know—I believe Mrs. Clutter would feel pity, too" (C 288).

This is not the only time Capote permits us to view Perry through the eyes of motherly women. Earlier, when Perry and Dick were first placed in the Garden City jail, he employed another feminine observer, Josephine ("Josie") Meier, the wife of the undersheriff. He describes her as "a direct and practical woman who nevertheless seems illuminated by a mystical serenity" (C 251), thus qualifying her as an observer worthy of respect. Mrs. Meier and her husband occupied an apartment adjacent to the jail, and her kitchen was joined directly to the cell in which Perry was placed. Before he was there a full day, she had reached the conclusion that "he wasn't the worst young man I ever saw" (C 253). Capote concludes his account of the trial with another short section devoted to Mrs. Meier, and again the focus is on Perry. "I never had much truck with Dick," she says. "But Perry and I got to know each other real well. . . . He hated the whole world. But the morning the men came to take him to the penitentiary, he thanked me and gave me a picture of himself. A little Kodak made when he was sixteen years old. He said it was how he wanted me to remember him, like the boy in the picture" (C 308).

Perry's aloneness—"the solitary, comfortless course" of his life—is one of Capote's persistent themes. When the killers flee from Kansas, Dick leaves behind several "whom he claimed to love: three sons, a mother, a father, a brother." Perry, however, leaves "nothing behind, and no one who might deeply wonder into what thin air he'd spiraled" (C 106). One of the entries in his private diary reads, "My acquaintances are many, my friends are few; those who really know me fewer still" (C 146)). During one of Capote's prison visits, Dick tells him that he is the only real visitor Perry ever has, and mentions that Perry's father was invited to visit him in prison but never showed up. "Sometimes you got to feel sorry for Perry. He must be one of the most alone people there ever was. But. Aw, the hell with him. It's mostly every bit his own fault" (C 335). At his death, Perry willed all his belongings to Truman Capote. Dewey, watching Perry's childish, dangling feet, sees him as Capote has presented him: "an exiled animal, a creature walking wounded."

Witnessing the execution does not bring Dewey the "sense of climax, release, of a design justly completed" that he had expected. Rather, "he discovered himself recalling an incident of almost a year ago, a casual encounter in Valley View Cemetery, which, in retrospect, had somehow for him more or less ended the Clutter case" (C 341).

Capote uses this recollected scene to conclude *In Cold Blood*. He describes the cemetery, situated on high ground above the town, as "a dark island lapped by the undulating surf of surrounding wheat fields" (C 341). On a May afternoon, at a time "when the fields blaze with the green-gold fire of half-grown wheat," Dewey had spent several hours weeding his father's grave. He was four years older now than he had been at the time of the murders; he had bought a new house in town, and his sons were almost grown. Strolling along the paths, he noticed recent graves, among them that of Judge Tate, who had died of pneumonia several months before. "Deaths, births, marriages —why, just the other day he'd heard that Nancy Clutter's boy friend, young Bobby Rupp, had gone and got married." Approaching the Clutter monument, he found another visitor already standing there near "the wheat field's bright edge"—"a willowy girl with white-gloved hands, a smooth cap of dark-honey hair, and long, elegant legs." It was Susan Kidwell, whom he had last seen as a child at the time of the trial. They chatted, and Dewey learned that she was home on vacation from the University of Kansas. Glancing across the prairie, Susan said, "I love it. I'm really happy. . . . Nancy and I planned to go to college together. We were going to be roommates. I think about it sometimes. Suddenly, when I'm very happy, I think of all the plans we made." Dewey watched Susan "as she disappeared down the path, a pretty girl in a hurry, her smooth hair swinging, shining—just such a young woman as Nancy might have been. Then, starting home, he walked toward the trees, and under them, leaving behind him the big sky, the whisper of wind voices in the wind-bent wheat" (C 343).

Years before, just after Smith and Hickock confessed, Dewey had felt that their revelations still "failed to satisfy his sense of meaningful design" (C 245). He thought of the crime as a "psychological accident, virtually an impersonal act"; the victims might as well have been struck by lightning—except for the single fact that they had suffered prolonged terror. At that time, as later at the execution, he had looked on Perry Smith with "a measure of sympathy," though not with forgiveness or mercy.

Even after the hangings, his uneasiness continues. To Dewey's mind, particularly since he is a lawman theoretically in favor of capital punishment, there is no easy escape from the dilemma. If the Clutters were victims of a brutal accident, the same was true of their victimizer, Perry Smith. From his childhood to his execution at the hands of a righteous state, he had suffered.

In this final section of the book, the thought of Perry merges with that of Nancy—her absence made vivid by Susan's presence—and the sad undertones that their fate obtrudes on the world of births and marriages gives *In Cold Blood* its poignant impact and such "resolution" as it achieves. Sadness at the way things vanish and innocence suffers in this world, repeatedly associated with images of the wheat fields, has been growing all through the book. It has, in fact, been growing for much longer than that in the writings of Truman Capote.

From the time Capote began his fictional "growing up" through the use of a dramatized narrator, a nostalgic mood has colored that narrator's memory of the heroine after she dies, like Buddy's friend—or Miss Bobbit or Dolly—or vanishes, like

Holly Golightly. Its purest embodiment is "A Christmas Memory," and it is probably for the story's emotional tone as well as its "trueness" that Capote likes it so well.

But the fictional passage most similar to Dewey's final scene in the cemetery is the one that concludes *The Grass Harp*. The field of grass near cemetery hill, which autumn winds fill with "sighing human music, a harp of voices," frames that story much as autumn Kansas wheat fields frame Capote's account of the Clutter tragedy. Dolly tells Collin, "Do you hear? that is the grass harp, always telling a story—it knows the stories of all the people on the hill, of all the people who ever lived, and when we are dead it will tell ours, too" (G 9). At the end of the story, after Dolly has died and Verena has become a pathetic wanderer, Collin and the Judge take a last walk down the River Woods road to the "summer-burned, September-burnished field. A waterfall of color flowed across the dry and strumming leaves; and I wanted then for the Judge to hear what Dolly had told me: that it was a grass harp, gathering, telling, a harp of voices remembering a story. We listened" (G 97).

Asked about the similarity of this passage to the closing lines of *In Cold Blood*, Capote admitted that he "lifted" it almost word-for-word.[7] The choice could hardly have been a casual one. Dolly Talbo and Perry Smith were both victims, both dreamers. Even the practical Nancy Clutter is, by Susan's reference to the plans they had shared for college, cast as a dreamer of unfulfilled dreams. And Nancy Clutter and Perry Smith are far from being the only sufferers in *In Cold Blood*. With the exception of Alvin Dewey, who comes increasingly to serve as the book's center of consciousness, all of the major characters are—like almost all of Capote's fictional characters—victims. This is the single fact about the Clutters that would have been clear to Capote from the moment he noticed the article in his New York newspaper, and one could safely assume that the killer or killers, if found, had been victimized, too.

Capote's decision to write the book was not, of course, made once and for all at the moment he learned of the Clutter murders. He says that he researched for eight months before really committing himself to the task. "And then something in the whole material appealed to something that has always been inside me anyway, waiting there. It was Perry that made me decide to do it really. Something about Perry turned the whole thing, because Perry was a character that was also in my imagination." [8] It is in the portrayal of Perry Smith that Capote's achievement comes closest to his ideal for the nonfiction novel: a perfect identification of the inner vision with the outer reality. "Dick," he says, "is a person I never could have dreamed up or written. Got to know him fairly well. Small-time chizzler. I understand him perfectly. Much too banal for my taste. But I think I brought him off pretty well." Perry, on the other hand, "could absolutely step right out of one of my stories." [9]

Capote succeeded best with Perry, not only because the latter resembled his fictional characters, but because in his similarity to these childlike dreamer-victims he resembled the author's imaginative projection of himself. Capote obviously thought of Perry as similar to himself even in physical appearance. In the book he makes much of Perry's small stature and speaks of his "changeling's face." Of himself he has said, "I'm about as tall as a shotgun and just as noisy. I think I have rather heated eyes. I have a very sassy voice. I like my nose but you can't see it because I wear these thick glasses. If you looked at my face from both sides you'd see they were completely different. It's sort of a changeling face." [10]

Capote does not stop at the superficial parallels between Perry's life and his own. When Perry, resentful of his questioning, challenged him to tell about his *own* sex life, Capote did. "I told him honestly in great detail all about myself—some of my own problems were very close to his. He could see I was very sincere." [11] Harper Lee has said authoritatively, "Perry was a killer, but there was something touching about him. I think every time Truman looked at Perry he saw his own childhood." [12]

That Capote should find such a "congenial" character in the Clutter case might be explained in two ways: either he distorted Perry in the book, or he was remarkably lucky. George Plimpton, in his interview with Capote, asked this very relevant question: "Is it one of the artistic limitations of the nonfiction novel that the writer is placed at the whim of chance? Suppose, in the case of "In Cold Blood," clemency had been granted? Or the two boys had been less interesting? Wouldn't the artistry of the book have suffered? Isn't luck involved?" [13]

Capote's reply seems to minimize the role of luck. Admitting that he "never knew until the events were well along whether a book was going to be possible," he went on to say that if the principals had been "uninteresting or completely uncooperative" he could have "stopped and looked elsewhere, perhaps not very far." He might, he said, have written a nonfiction novel about any of the other prisoners in the Kansas penitentiary's death row. As an answer to Plimpton's question, Capote's observation that he wrote the book because of Perry Smith would have been more to the point.

The evidence suggests, in fact, that chance plays an immensely important role in the writing of the nonfiction novel—another reason, no doubt, why the field is so thinly populated. Although Capote had tried other subjects, nothing had worked until the Clutter case, and even that choice depended finally on the presence of Perry. Moreover, without the help of Dick's photographic memory, Capote would have been hard put to reproduce in detail the career of the killers between the murder and the arrest. I would even suggest, without in the least intending to imply that Capote personally desired or neglected opportunities to avert the execution, that the book might very likely not have been completed without that particular conclusion. The extreme difficulty experienced in the writing of the last few pages may well reflect a profound conflict between human anguish and artistic necessity.

Understandably, readers have been reluctant to trust to Capote's luck, suspecting that in writing the book he must have changed Perry to fit his own conception. The most extensive criticism so far aimed at the factuality of In Cold Blood, particularly in its portrayal of Perry, is that of Phillip K. Tompkins in the June 1966 Esquire. Tompkins feels that Capote remained too closely bound to the structural requirements of the novel to achieve an accurate presentation of the facts of the case, and charges that, with an artistry that several times led to distortion of fact, he has created "a multitude of short, internal dramas with effective final curtains. He has achieved a theatrical climax in his confession scene. He has created a heroic, poetic villain—a villain capable of evoking considerable sympathy (as Hollywood was quick to realize)." [14] Observing correctly that "it is Perry Smith—not the victims, the investigators, the lawyers, not even the pair of killers—who dominates this book," [15] Tompkins concentrates on Capote's portrayal of Perry.

From his own study of documents relating to the Clutter case, he concludes that Perry Smith was a man accustomed to violence, "an obscene, semiliterate and cold-blooded killer," and that Capote, unable to understand this side of a man who in other respects was strikingly similar to himself, transformed him into "an outcast and accursed poet" who could kill only under the influence of what Capote has termed a "mental eclipse" or "brain explosion."

Tompkins faults Capote on a number of details. Using what appears to be reliable evidence, he shows that Capote altered details of Perry's long confession in a manner that heightened the dramatic effectiveness of the scene. He adduces the somewhat less convincing testimony of Mr. and Mrs. Wendle Meier that Mrs. Meier never said she had seen worse men than Perry; that she saw little of Perry and never heard him cry; that he never held her hand or said "I'm embraced by shame"; and, finally, that they never told Capote any of these things. Tompkins says that Capote did not hear Perry's last words, and quotes accounts by newsmen who did hear them to show that Perry never apologized for his crime. He says Capote is inaccurate in suggesting that Perry killed all four of the Clutters, since two of the men best acquainted with the case, attorney Duane West and Alvin Dewey, still believe that Dick killed the two women.

Tompkins devotes most attention, however, to the murder scene. Against Capote's account he sets the official court record of Dewey's testimony—which, he says, agrees in essentials with that of another detective and with the official transcript of the confession Perry made but later refused to sign:

. . . So they debated who was going to do what and who was going to start it, and finally Smith said, 'Well,' he says, 'I'll do it' . . . and he said he put this knife in his hand with the blade up along his arm so that Mr. Clutter couldn't see it and he . . .

told him that he was going to tighten the cords on his hand, and he said he made a pretense to do that and then he cut Mr. Clutter's throat. Smith said that after doing that he got up and Hickock said to him, 'Give me the knife,' and he said about that time they heard a gurgling sound coming from Mr. Clutter and Smith said that Hickock . . . plunged this knife into Mr. Clutter's throat, either once or twice. . . . He said that after Hickock stepped away from Mr. Clutter that Mr. Clutter jerked one arm loose, his left arm, I believe, and he put it to his throat to try to stop the bleeding, and . . . Smith said that he could see that Mr. Clutter was suffering and told Hickock that that was a hell of a way to leave a guy, because he felt he was going to die anyway, so Smith said he said to Hickock, 'Shall I shoot him?' and Hickock said, 'Yes, go ahead,' so Smith said that he shot Mr. Clutter in the head while Hickock held the flashlight. . . .[16]

Tompkins concludes from this that, aside from numerous small discrepancies, Dewey's account differs crucially from Capote's in showing Smith as committing the murder "with *full consciousness and intent* (italics Tompkins').[17] He also makes the following points:

Should we believe he suffered a "brain explosion" when he poised the rock to open the head of the Omaha salesman? And again when he wished out loud that he could have killed his sister along with the Clutters? And when he planned with Hickock two other murders which Capote told the *Times* he chose to omit from the book? Capote appears to have fallen into the trap of believing that operational definition of insanity one frequently hears: "Anyone who can kill *has* to be insane." [18]

Tompkins does not accuse Capote of deliberate misrepresentation. While allowing for the possibility that Perry lied or erred in his recollections, he inclines to the view that Capote himself unconsciously reshaped certain details through an overwhelming need to create a work of fictional art. And he concludes that Capote has indeed "told exceedingly well a tale of high terror in his own way"—a tale that will be valued as a work of art after his excessive claims to accuracy have been forgotten.

Tompkins' revelations, while rather disturbing to our faith in the overall accuracy of *In Cold Blood*, should not be too surprising. It was only to be expected that Capote would be inaccurate in some details and would select and arrange the evidence to suit his aim. (In fairness to Capote it should be remembered that, if he has suppressed some evidence, he has also included much of that which Tompkins used against him.) Capote has admitted that he designed the book to fit his interpretation. His fundamental claim is that he is accurate on the deepest level—that he has presented the real Perry Smith. He told me: "All I can do is show you his letters. You read the letters of Perry Smith and you know darn well that my portrait of him is absolutely accurate, and it's not a sentimental distortion on my part, of identifying with him. I *did* identify with him to a great degree. Never did deny it. It's also quite true that my portrait of him is absolutely one hundred per cent the way he was." [19]

It is this sense of identification with Perry that seems to give Capote his strongest assurance of accuracy. He also told me: "Perry almost never used to have to finish a sentence with me, because I always knew exactly what he was talking about. He'd start to tell me something about his life and I'd be miles ahead of him." [20]

It should not require Tompkins' help to teach the reader a degree of skepticism toward this kind of assurance. Certainly Capote must have changed Perry at least slightly in the book. Probably he also, as some have suggested, changed Perry himself during their long friendship, making him a bit more of a "Capote hero" even before putting him into the book. On the other hand, if he has failed to give us the "real" Perry Smith, so have Tompkins and the law courts, with their facile classification of him as an "obscene, semiliterate and cold-blooded killer." Tompkins, though convincing on some points, is no more satisfying—in fact far less so—than Capote. (A similar though less severe oversimplification is evident in Capote's own handling of Dick, whom he is inclined to classify as a "small-time chizzler.")

Capote's deep sympathy for Perry makes *In Cold Blood* a powerful work of art and a probing and admirable attempt to understand a human being. If it is less than completely successful, so are all such efforts.

· X. THE CAPOTE PARADOX ·

1. Close-up

There is a passage at the end of Henry James's story "The Middle Years" that impressed Truman Capote so deeply that he had Randolph quote part of it in *Other Voices, Other Rooms*. Having approached the hour of his death, the novelist Dencombe finally accepts the fact that the brilliant "later period" he has hoped for will not be permitted him, and that he must be content with the "little spell" he has been allowed to cast: "A second chance—*that's* the delusion. There never was to be but one. We work in the dark—we do what we can—we give what we have. Our doubt is our passion, and our passion is our task. The rest is the madness of art."

While Randolph speaks the words in a mood of resignation, Capote has taken them as a challenge. Unwilling to identify himself with Randolph, a wounded artist washed up in one of the backwaters of life, he has tried "in the madness of art" to give himself a second chance. He told *Newsweek*: "The thing about American writers is that they burn themselves out by remaining whatever they start out as. They don't have a second chance. But I gave myself a second chance. But it was terribly hard." [1]

Capote describes himself as a very slow-developing writer, pointing out that in his fiction he was always stuck about ten years back in terms of the emotional experience he could encompass artistically. (A glance at the stories bears this out remarkably well.) His stated purpose in attempting a nonfiction novel was to achieve an artistic and personal liberation—to escape from his private imaginative world into the larger world of reality. He believes that in writing *In Cold Blood* he achieved that purpose. Today he speaks of having come over the hump, of being able now to apply his artistic intelligence to a wide range of contemporary experience.[2]

The reader who picks up Capote's factual account of a Kansas murder case hardly expects it to have much in common with his fictional accounts of haunted Southern childhoods. Capote himself has recently been talking so much about the new that one might suppose he, too, felt the old had been pretty thoroughly left behind. He now seems, for example, to consider his artistry predominantly objective, rather than subjective as before. When I asked him whether there wasn't something superficial in his approach to the nonfiction novel he made this careful reply:

I found that as soon as I began to do reportage . . . I could write about all kinds of people that I never would have been stimulated to write about inside of an imaginative situation. When they were presented to me inside of a situation that I had to encompass journalistically, it was necessary for me to encompass *them,* and broadened my whole horizon of the kind of person I can handle or am interested in. . . . I would never have written about most of these people, and yet in the end I became completely and totally involved with them, creatively and personally, and could not have been more interested. This is not superficiality. There is something superficial about the setup, setting oneself up to do that, as though it doesn't come from some deep inner thing. But that's not what artistic understanding is. It just depends on your degree of sensitivity and sensibility and intelligence—is limited only by them. The more sensitive and intelligent you are, the wider and wider possible range of people you can encompass.[3]

Although the emphasis here, as elsewhere, is on change, it will be noted that Capote never claims to have made a complete break with his artistic past. He will, in fact, when questioned on the point, quite emphatically say the opposite. "Who wants a complete break with anything? I don't want a complete break. . . . It all goes together. It's all one piece. . . . It's quite simple to see parallels in the things; I chose what was naturally attractive to me." [4]

That there should be a continuity in his work is, of course, inevitable; yet Capote's complacent recognition of the fact comes as something of a surprise. One would expect him to be disappointed at the realization that *In Cold Blood*, his "second chance," proved feasible and successful only by coming to resemble his earlier work. But he is not. He seems, in fact, to be completely satisfied with it.

His satisfaction becomes understandable only when one is in a position to see, as we are now, how remarkably the book fulfills the design of Capote's literary career so far. When one realizes how many lines in this design were pointing toward just such a book—especially toward his ideal concept of it— it becomes less surprising that Capote should have undertaken so unusual a project and that he should claim for it an *absoluteness* of success that goes somewhat beyond the limits of possibility.

While Capote can take well-deserved pride in *In Cold Blood* as a genuine enlargement of his artistic scope, his deepest satisfaction probably derives from its being something even more important to him: a vindication of his imagination. In its portrayal of Perry Smith and in its pervasive theme of victimization, the book is a factual echo of Capote's earliest fiction.

That fiction began, as we have seen, with a series of "dark" stories in each of which the rather unattractive protagonist was trapped in a cage of childhood fears. Near the end of the dark period, in "Master Misery," there appeared a new tendency to see the protagonist (though doomed, like the others) as a somewhat admirable *dreamer*, together with a concomitant scorn for conventional society. Preference for the unconventional may be seen as a new development of a motif present earlier in the stories: the protagonist's own tendency to escape involvement with troublesome characters by dismissing them as "crazy." Another innovation in "Master Misery" is that the ever-present bogeyman becomes slightly ambivalent, a not-completely-threatening father.

Perry Smith closely resembles the protagonists of these early stories, as do the other characters of *In Cold Blood* insofar as they are sufferers and dreamers. Perry's most important deviation from the pattern is the "brain explosion" in which he lashes out at the father figure—an act which serves only to confirm his subjection. If Perry remains a trapped child, however, he can hardly be blamed for it: like Sylvia in "Master Misery," he has been robbed of his dreams. Capote is in these early stories, too, of course, though only a part of him. "They're not about me," he has said. "They're very objective portraits of various states of mind—not necessarily my state of mind at all." [5] But he adds, "Yes, those early works were written at a great sort of pressure. Why do you think they're so riddled with anxiety, so neurotic? . . . You must remember how young I was when I wrote those stories." [6] As Harper Lee suggests, when Capote looked at Perry Smith he saw his own dream-trapped childhood.

He had come a long way from that childhood. By a literary process both instinctive and highly deliberate, he had from the beginning been making his escape from its private world. Not content with skillful patternings of fear and constriction such as "Miriam," he had searched for the proper forms to embody a maturing consciousness and sensibility—and in his first novel he began to find them: if the material of *In Cold Blood* is to some extent a return to Capote's childhood and a real-life confirmation of his earliest imaginative creations, its technique, its artistic and ideological presuppositions—even the very fact of its being written—are the almost predictable consequences of directions that Capote began to take in this second phase of his career.

Other Voices, Other Rooms, which Capote describes as "very important to me . . . in my development as a writer," [7] dramatizes the liberation of the Capote protagonist through confrontation of the father after removal from the protective care of the mother. (Capote writes of Perry Smith that he several times "set out to find his lost father, for he had lost his

mother as well" [C 131]. Perry, of course, failed in his search.)
The mysterious figure that looms over Joel is still the ambivalent father-bogeyman or protector-destroyer, but now with the
two sides more equally balanced. The boy's maturation consists
in a gradual emergence from dependence on the one, combined with dependence on the mother figure, and fear of the
other.

This maturation pattern is uneasily balanced against the
fact that the central figure in Joel's experience ceases to be
the threatening and protecting parent only to become Randolph, a social outcast and spiritual cipher, yet on one symbolic
level both father and mother to the boy. The novel's implication that both material and moral decay is negated by love
and by acceptance of one's proper place, while partially undercut by opposite currents in the book itself, remains its dominant
theme and principal weakness. A closely related problem is an
inadequately defined narrative point of view—an unreliability
of the narrator not adequately compensated for by firm handling of other elements—which finally obscures the book's
meaning.

What are we to think of Randolph? He is portrayed as
radically defective, yet often seems to speak with authority. I
asked Capote about Randolph and received the following
reply: "I think he's a cripple who has some very sensitive insights because of his isolation and crippledness. . . . Yes, I
believe a lot of the things that he says, but I don't think that
Randolph is a whole person, or even sane." [8] In the novel,
Joel's sweeping final acceptance passes over such distinctions
in a disturbing way.

But whatever may be said of Joel's acquiescence in the life
of Skully's Landing, it must be recognized as the first appearance of a tendency that will characterize Capote's work up to
and including *In Cold Blood*: acceptance of the unconventional, of the misfit in others and in oneself. I asked Capote if
this weren't the dominant thing about the novel and he replied, "That's the point of it, isn't it? It's one of the points.
That a rather eccentric, sensitive boy has to make some acceptance in his life one way or the other, about himself sexually,

physically, morally." [9] One who has made the choice that Joel makes would never again be inclined to dismiss another human being as "crazy"—or as an "obscene, semiliterate and cold-blooded killer."

The tendency toward acceptance that first appears in *Other Voices, Other Rooms* is part of a broad movement in the author's work that expresses itself in several other recurrent motifs and has, at least implicitly, a rather coherent philosophical foundation. The kind of love Joel is initiated into finds its perfect object in Randolph, a completely dependent, completely receptive individual in whom sexual distinctions are virtually nonexistent. The desire to obliterate such distinctions, along with all the other classifications that society imposes on persons, is apparent in all of Capote's work. Closely related to it is a movement away from morality in the narrow sense toward a more spiritual standard. His heroines—Miriam, Sylvia, Idabel, Miss Bobbit, Dolly Talbo—are always shocking people, and they are always right; their way proves always to be the most practical or at least the most pleasant. When "morality" and convention enter the stories, they enter to be refuted by someone with a vision that transcends them.

There is, indeed, a strain of American transcendentalism in Capote, which reminds us that his "student" Perry Smith developed, in his last days, a strong admiration for Thoreau. Behind transcendentalism is Platonism, which Frank Baldanza has seen as a common heritage of Capote and some of his fellow Southern writers, particularly Carson McCullers. They are, he suggests, "natural" Platonists temperamentally inclined to interpret reality in the Platonic manner, and probably influenced as well by direct or indirect contact with the philosopher's writings. Baldanza describes their works as "parables on the nature of love" and adds, "They share with Plato's *Symposium* and *Phaedrus* in particular that curious tone of purely and absolutely spiritual love which grows out of a diffused and circumambient atmosphere of sexuality that never clearly manifests itself." [10]

Randolph and Judge Cool, Capote's two principal lecturers on the nature of love, certainly reflect the Platonic side of the Western mentality; and Dolly Talbo and his other heroines seem to be both highly committed seekers for and actual representatives of the transcendent realm. The maturing of Joel Knox, which we have seen to be the turning point in Capote's fiction, assumes broad relevance when viewed—as Baldanza views it—as a recapitulation of the "passage from the Heraclitan flux of constant change to the Platonic absolute of love, . . . a momentous achievement of Greek intellectual history." [11]

The spiritual liberation that took place in Capote's work at the time of *Other Voices, Other Rooms* was bound up with another movement that was to reach its ultimate development in *In Cold Blood:* a turning outward to the world of social experience. There are hints of a real world in the neighborhood of Skully's Landing, and the later stories contain more and more realistic treatments of more and more recognizable settings. In style, the stories gradually become less poetic. Their tone becomes less subjective, their atmosphere less thickly crowded with a dreamlike profusion of symbols. Most important, there is a new protagonist at the center of the stories, and this person is usually a woman. Capote had always tended to use feminine protagonists, but in the early work gender did not matter especially, since all the main characters were mirror-images of a single isolated consciousness. The attitude taken toward this captive protagonist ranged from pity to a scorn that was really self-hatred.

Slowly, however, a polarity began to reveal itself. Implicit criticism began to be directed mostly at male characters (Vincent, Walter), and women became the objects of compassion and eventually even of admiration (D.J., Sylvia). Immediately after *Other Voices, Other Rooms*, this heroine achieved a major breakthrough to freedom. Still a sufferer at the hands of life, she was now predominantly a dreamer—an unconventional childlike wanderer whose integrity in the search for an ideal happiness gave her strength to resist the encroachments of society.

While this heroine had obviously been evolving in Capote's imagination, and in fact is, from beginning to end, a projection of himself, a crucial difference from this time on is that her portrayal begins to be based on real girls and women whom Capote has known. Thus the new heroine illustrates most clearly how

Capote's liberation is related to a shift—at least partial—from inner to outer experience. *Other Voices, Other Rooms* is the first of his works that has the flavor of factual autobiography, though he describes it as a Gothic dream. While maintaining that the book is not literally true, he says that it is "made of all sorts of things from my childhood." [12] Specifically, it deals with one of his first friendships, that with Harper Lee, and some of the experiences they shared.

In her much more literal way, Miss Lee treated some of the same experiences in *To Kill a Mockingbird*. Capote says that the first part of her book is quite literally true. And, he says, "In my original version of *Other Voices, Other Rooms* I had that same man living in the house that used to leave the things in the trees; and then I took that out. He was a real man, and he lived just down the road from us; we used to go and get those things out of the trees; everything she wrote about it is absolutely true. But you see, I take the same thing and I transfer it into some Gothic thing, a dream, done in an entirely different way." [13]

In Capote's book Harper Lee was transmuted into Idabel Thompkins, whom Joel learns to accept as she is, to pity, and to love. His learning to accept and love his father and Randolph seems much more created and symbolic, and relates most directly to his acceptance of himself. Yet even this seems intimately bound to, or conditioned by, Capote's new extroversion.

From the time of *Other Voices, Other Rooms*, most of Capote's stories are based on his "Platonic" relationships with real women. "I like women. I enjoy their minds," he has said. Age makes no difference, but always his women are to some extent victims and dreamers, and often they share Miss Bobbit's tough unconventionality. "Children on Their Birthdays," published in the same year as the novel, makes use of the young Capote's infatuation for a real girl who he claims was named June Bug Johnson. "A Christmas Memory," his favorite story, can be taken as the archetype of the relationship. It records his friendship with the elderly cousin who cared for him between the ages of four and ten, and who obviously had a profound formative influence on his imagination. Even in *In Cold Blood* Capote tends to favor the use of women observers.

When I mentioned this similarity, he remarked, "Naturally, I was drawn to them for that reason. It's quite simple to see parallels in the things; I chose what was naturally attractive to me. The postmistress and her mother were two fantastic cases anyway—I couldn't let them go by." [14] I asked him if these various friendships weren't similar to that with the elderly cousin, and he answered:

Yes, and almost all the girls I've known. I've told you "Children on Their Birthdays" was a real little girl; then I had that relationship with Harper Lee. She was a tough little kid that I was stomping on and training and raising up to be something. And then I met the girl who is Holly Golightly, who lived in the building with me. My relationship with them has always been like that. And in this new novel of mine it's the same thing, only on a much bigger scale, to put it mildly. [15]

In the stories, Capote usually describes the relationship as one of being "friends," and his usual definition of a friend is "one to whom you can tell everything." In *In Cold Blood* he says of Nancy and Susan, "Thus, the girls were no longer always together, and Nancy deeply felt the daytime absence of her friend, the one person with whom she need be neither brave nor reticent" (C 21). The tendency in a love relationship of this kind is toward the breaking down of the distinction between self and other—the Platonic identification of the friend as the missing half of the self. Hence, as we see most clearly in Capote's response to Perry Smith, his imaginative breakthrough to others, while real on one level, has—and not surprisingly—been only a partial thing. While *In Cold Blood* is a sort of ultimate extension of that outward-turning that brought Capote his first imaginative liberation, it also remains deeply personal. It will be recalled that Capote said that liking Perry (and Dick) was the same as liking himself.

It is Capote's highly objective narrative technique that most clearly distinguishes *In Cold Blood* from his fiction and even—as many have remarked—from much journalism. Even this, however, is the completion of a trend that may be observed throughout his work. The early stories portray a world of abnormal, trapped individuals viewed as though from within that world itself: its rules are the only rules; its dreams are realities. There is little or no use of narrative technique to gain an effect of objectivity. In *Other Voices, Other Rooms* we see a similar world, still without clear or consistent distancing through narrative technique or tone; there is, however, a distinction made between the abnormal world and the outside world of society, and, more important, there is the beginning of a division between the central consciousness and this abnormal world through the use of a protagonist who comes from the outside, sees Skully's Landing as distinct from himself, and accepts it freely.

In his later work—as though Capote were coming to identify narrative distance with maturity—the narrative consciousness is more carefully defined and progressively withdrawn from the center of action, which is now dominated by a gently eccentric protagonist wandering through an increasingly realistic world. The first-person narrator of *The Grass Harp* is a boy similar to but slightly older than Joel, and the interest is split between him and his companions, especially the elderly heroine. In *Breakfast at Tiffany's* the narrator is a relatively mature young man more identifiable than ever with Truman Capote (though still ten years younger), and the emphasis has shifted almost completely from him to Holly Golightly. In *In Cold Blood* the narrator is in fact Mr. Capote, and he has virtually refined himself out of the book altogether.

Capote has done in his fiction what Billy Bob did in "Children on Their Birthdays," that first and most delightful expression of Capote's liberation. Having found a heroine who magically embodies the best, most private part of himself, he sadly but determinedly relinquishes her, allowing her to wander free and finally escape him by death. (It is in this story that Capote first employs a dramatized narrator, the young "Mr. C.," whose detachment from the events anticipates the move toward objectivity.) The same relinquishment can be seen taking place near the end of *The Grass Harp*, in a scene that exemplifies Capote's literary strategy more clearly than any other. Collin is seated in the rain-soaked tree house, waiting with Verena and the Judge to hear Dolly's decision about whether to marry: "My impatience equaled theirs, yet I felt exiled from the scene, again a spy peering from the attic, and my sympathies, curiously, were nowhere; or rather, everywhere: a tenderness for all three ran together like raindrops, I could not separate them, they expanded into a human oneness" (G 83). Objectivity of view blends with universality of sympathy: there could hardly be a better definition of Capote's aim in the nonfiction novel. (Self-effacing in one way, the stance is also godlike in its assumption of unlimited knowledge, power, and benevolence, and accords well with Capote's persistent drive toward a transcendental unity).

Collin's voluntary exile is attended with a strong reluctance to give up the narrower, more childlike identification with Dolly, and it is this reluctance that produces that nostalgic sadness which repeatedly appears as Capote's last word on experience, be it fictional or nonfictional. Standing among graves, listening to a grass harp or gazing at autumn Kansas wheat, he knows that growth is a series of deaths. In a recent interview, Capote gave this feeling a personal expression:

I was terribly bored with my own obsessions. I wanted to forget about my own navel. And now at last I've gotton rid of my own personality. I've gotten rid of the boy with the bangs. He's gone, just gone. I liked that boy. It took an act of will because it was easy to be that person—he was exotic and strange and eccentric. I liked the idea of that person, but he had to go.[16]

Perfect universal sympathy eluded Capote in *In Cold Blood* as surely as did perfect objectivity. Still, his account of the Clutter murders is deeply and broadly compassionate and thus marks a considerable advance along another of the lines Capote has been tracing in his career. Sympathy was almost completely absent in his earliest stories. When, in "Master Misery," he first began to treat his heroine sympathetically as a suffering dreamer, he also began to show a rather sinister tendency to despise everyone who did not share her dream—that is, most of the world. Spite against the townspeople is strong in *Other Voices, Other Rooms*, and the same tendency troubles us in "A Christmas Memory," where the two friends' distaste for the rest of the family seems not quite purified by their childish innocence. While the *Grass Harp* tree-dwellers' uprising against the Establishment is exhilarating, there is something unpleasantly narrow about it. Not only is Capote remote from these people so similar to the Herbert Clutters and the Alvin Deweys; he is positively antagonistic to them. A certain bitchiness in *Breakfast at Tiffany's* may be excused on the grounds that it fits the setting, but a reading of the nonfiction *The Muses Are Heard* suggests that it is still an essential part of Capote's equipment.

In Cold Blood, by bestowing its understanding in every quarter, emerges into a larger world. Here one feels that Capote attributes the sufferings of his victims not to stupid and malicious "other people" but to a more remote and mysterious principle—one closer to the source of genuine tragedy. The closing scene in Valley View Cemetery, while similar to the conclusion of *The Grass Harp*, resonates more widely and hence more deeply.

While Capote's vision of man's fate has grown larger and in that respect come closer to the stature of tragedy, it remains, even in *In Cold Blood*, essentially one of pathos. The tragic world view is an earth-centered one. But Capote's neoplatonists can be only exiles and victims in this world, for they have cast their lot in some other place. Even their power is eccentric, not geocentric. Speaking of the grotesque characters in the fiction of Capote, McCullers, and other Southern writers, Baldanza suggests that "on the philosophical level, the defects of the characters serve symbolically to represent the worthlessness of the material realm." [17] Capote's portrayal of Perry Smith has, finally, the same effect as does the scene in which neighbors burn a pile of the Clutters' belongings and one of the men muses, "How was it possible that such effort, such plain virtue, could overnight be reduced to this—smoke, thinning as it rose and was received by the big, annihilating sky?" (C 79). It is this strong current of evanescence tugging at a solid fabric of places, facts, and people that gives *In Cold Blood* its deepest intensity.

Dwight Macdonald has attacked *In Cold Blood* as nontragic and hence morally irresponsible and dramatically uninteresting.[18] Though the six major characters are real, he says, none of them

227

is a free agent in the central action and thus there is no significant conflict. We may, I think, agree with him on this last point without accepting his classification of the book as "prurient" in content and comparable in viewpoint to the sadomasochism of Alfred Hitchcock. On its deepest level *In Cold Blood* is not a tragic drama but a meditation on reality. Its immediate dramatic interest lies primarily in the sensational quality of the murders and the pursuit of the criminals, but Capote's approach to the events is not, as has been claimed, voyeuristic. In a *tour de force* deserving of much more respect than Macdonald accords it, Capote has transcended the *True Detective* genre story just as in "The Duke in His Domain" he transcended the *Photoplay*-type interview.

Truman Capote has not chosen to take the easy way. In the avowedly autobiographical *The Grass Harp*, Collin said, "I've read that past and future are a spiral, one coil containing the next and predicting its theme. Perhaps this is so; but my own life has seemed to me more a series of closed circles, rings that do not evolve with the freedom of a spiral: for me to get from one to the other has meant a leap, not a glide" (G 94). With intelligence and determination, Capote the artist has tried to grow up. Harper Lee says of him, "Truman is happy. But there's only one thing worse than promises unkept—that's promises kept. But not for T. He knows what he wants and he keeps himself straight. And if it's not the way he likes it, he'll arrange it so it is." [19] As she implies, Capote is usually the exception to the rule. By finding his own childhood under a tree of night and also in Perry Smith, he demonstrated that life moves in spirals, "one coil containing the next and predicting its theme"; but by finding Perry Smith in Kansas he made his life a straight, steadily advancing line.

The evolution of the nonfiction novel from a contradiction in terms to a tangible, salable, hardcover paradox was possible only because its creator had already made himself a living paradox. He is the dedicated artist who writes only for money; the man who can witness a friend's execution, mentally record it with cool precision, then cry for three days; the playboy who gives a party for a few "personal friends" and invites *Who's Who in America*; the eccentric youth who surprised the world into admiration. Recall the scene in *Breakfast at Tiffany's* where one of Holly Golightly's admirers asks the young narrator:

"So what do you think: is she or ain't she?"
"Ain't she what?"
"A phony."
"I wouldn't have thought so."
"You're wrong. She is a phony. But on the other hand you're right. She isn't a phony because she's a *real* phony" (*S* 181).

It takes one to know one.

2. PERSPECTIVE

While *In Cold Blood* was a tying together of many strands in Capote's career and hence a culmination of sorts, there are few American writers of his generation who show so much promise of varied and important work still to be done. His combination of technical virtuosity, extraordinary intelligence, and steadily broadening moral sensibility may yet produce literature of that genuine depth and maturity which has, it must be acknowledged, so far eluded him.[1] As Capote's own self-evaluation and relentless efforts at change attest, there was in all his work up to *In Cold Blood* a persistent, though varyingly manifested, narrowness of imaginative range. In 1958 Paul Levine observed, "Perhaps the most frequent criticism leveled at Capote's work is that he is limited in scope and remote from life."[2]

Critics have made various attempts to define the extremely personal quality of Capote's vision, seeing it most often as a limitation, but pointing out that at any rate it is shared in some degree by a number of contemporary writers—most of them Southern—the most obvious parallel being with Carson McCullers.[3] The work of these writers is often described as subjective, but the term (which can be applied to most modern fiction) only roughly defines Capote. With the failure of the old communal myths, literature, particularly in America with its

229

fluid social structure, began to evolve an amorphous personal mythology in which we have become increasingly aware of a circling back to the most primitive polarizations—the Oedipal pattern, for example, and that of death and rebirth.[4] In discussing Capote one must distinguish between subjective literature which, in tracing such patterns, conveys broad, mythic overtones and that which tends to remain narrowly personal.

John W. Aldridge has touched on this difference in applying to Capote, perhaps too comprehensively, a distinction between symbol and metaphor. He suggests that Capote's achievement, "for all its brilliance, is an achievement in the skilled use of metaphor rather than symbol," and is for this reason of smaller scope than, say, Conrad's *Victory*, Joyce's *Ulysses*, or Forster's *A Passage to India*.[5] Symbolism, Aldridge continues, places the work in "meaningful relation to recognizable life," whereas metaphor can only relate one part of the work to another, so that *Other Voices, Other Rooms* remains simply "the exquisitely written, metaphorically reinforced story of Joel Knox." [6]

Given a certain narrowness in his work, Capote's remarkable career nevertheless has, as I hope to show, largely corresponded to the "classic" pattern of American literature and has in fact gone through a transformation that reflects some usually divergent manifestations of it. Simply by being personal in orientation, by dealing with the isolated self, it immediately has much in common with *Moby Dick* and *The Sound and the Fury*. And the parallel extends to form, for Gothic was the American novel's earliest natural mode, as it was Capote's. (That within this mode symbolism has been the chief avenue to meaning gives point to Aldridge's critique.)

But the writer who seems closest to Capote is Henry James, who almost certainly influenced him strongly. In his *Paris Review* interview Capote acknowledged the stylistic influence of only one writer, and that rather slightingly: "I don't suddenly find another writer's style seeping out of my pen. Though once, during a lengthy spell of James, my own sentences *did* get awfully long." [7]

The exposure left its mark less in obvious stylistic similarity than in certain implicit attitudes toward the self and the writer's role and, in general, in an ever-growing emphasis on the self-effacing discipline of technique. *Other Voices, Other Rooms* marks the turning point in Capote's career, and the center of that book is Cousin Randolph, whom we have already seen to be linked to James through his quoting of the climactic lines from "The Middle Years." That story, like Capote's novel, is about accepting one's fate, a fate in both cases bound up with an *alter ego* with whom the main character gradually converges. In James the convergence is simply intellectual: Dencombe's coming to agreement about his own career with Dr. Hugh (you) in what can be read as a dialogue between the novelist and his wiser self. A clue to understanding Capote's ambivalence in, and about, his own novel may lie in the further observation that Dr. Hugh earned his wisdom by sacrificing his dependence on the mother-figure, a relinquishment that anticipates Dencombe's abandonment of the dream of a "second chance." Randolph, on the other hand, is not only the identity toward which Joel is moving but also the mother-figure *and* the dependent infant, which gives the novel a regressive quality absent in James's story.

If "The Middle Years" is about the artist's late-won maturity, that maturity is shown to be achieved only by desperate combat with the opposing tendency, so strong in James, toward passivity —a tendency he was to examine most harshly in "The Beast in the Jungle." As Leslie Fiedler puts it, "For all his subtlety and tact, James is basically, hopelessly innocent, an innocent voyeur, which is to say, a child." [8]

Randolph is a perverted Henry James.[9] His regression, as he himself admits, is so extreme as to invalidate his art: "I could scarcely be called an artist; not, that is, if you define *artist* as one who sees, takes and purely transmits: always for me there is the problem of distortion . . ." (*OV* 76). In Randolph, for the first time in Capote's fiction, the imprisoned child-self sees itself projected as *other* (already the beginning of a strategy of dissociation), and not only as other self but as *artist* self. The James influence here seems ambivalent, like the novel itself. *Other Voices, Other Rooms* embodies both acceptance and dissociation—the former in the explicit movement of the plot, the

231

latter in the very conception of Randolph and his world to serve as scapegoat for undesirable aspects of the self.

Capote has recently said, "*Other Voices, Other Rooms* was an attempt to exorcise demons: an unconscious, altogether intuitive attempt, for I was not aware, except for a few incidents and descriptions, of its being in any serious degree autobiographical. Regarding it now, I find such self-deception unpardonable." [10] As this indicates, Capote's artistic movement since *Other Voices, Other Rooms* has been, while always ambivalent, mostly in the direction of consciousness and control—and "exorcism" is the perfect word to describe it. Something else that was happening intuitively in this crucial novel was the discovery, in the person of Idabel, of one of the principal means of exorcism: the projection of part of the self into those feminine characters who would prove so much more viable than Randolph, largely because they were drawn from the "real" world.

In this development, dependent as it was on carefully controlled point of view, Capote's guide again was Henry James. *Daisy Miller*, in particular, with its careful distance between narrator and heroine, comes to mind as a prototype of such stories as "Children on Their Birthdays" and *Breakfast at Tiffany's*. This Jamesian subdivision of the self, eventually pushed to an extreme in the nonfiction novel, provided an acceptable dramatic structure for the essentially unitary Capote mythos, which has remained fundamentally unchanged: the suffering and limited defiance of the isolated self in a repressive and eventually destructive world.[11]

In turning away from the unconscious depths of the self as literary source, Capote has, for better or worse, emerged from the dark mine that has yielded up most of the great works of American fiction. Our major writers have, at their best, pushed forward in stubborn Faustian pursuit of a dream which repeatedly became a nightmare—have struggled to the death with the demons Capote sought to exorcise by delegating to his detached protagonists the pursuit of a symbolically diminished dream and the endurance of a nightmare domesticated to the near-clinical "mean reds" and ultimately to the literal imprison-

232

ment and execution of criminals by the state. Leslie Fiedler, in *Love and Death in the American Novel*, the most penetrating examination of American fiction since D. H. Lawrence's, charts a terrain much like that of Capote's work, particularly in its early phase: the failure of mature heterosexual love and consequent preoccupation with death and innocent homosexuality; the atmosphere of terror and loneliness; the threatening father, Oedipal guilt, and ambiguous woman-substitute; the flight in search of a sexless ideal; the dominance, usually veiled, of the ambivalent mother-figure. Capote's dark stories, written, as he acknowledges, under great neurotic "pressure," depict this inner landscape with precocious brilliance. But, paradoxically, it takes a writer with deep insight into the outer world of relationships to make effective symbolic use of "controlled regression" [12] into the psyche, and the young Capote seems instinctively to have known his strength lay elsewhere. When the terror of the depths is overwhelming, a frequent recourse is compulsively to grasp and order the visible texture of life, the things that *can* be seen and ordered. As Hilton Kramer points out, Capote's has always been "a gift for surfaces—of language, of feeling, of life itself." [13]

Fiedler insists on the writer's Faustian role (though admitting that none of our writers except possibly Melville have managed to sustain it), and in his discussion of one of the possible evasions, which he terms White Romanticism, comes particularly close to describing the Capote of the later phase, though he is not discussing him. [14] He is speaking of Sir Walter Scott's *Rob Roy* and how its title character, Scott's "surrogate for the primitive and the poetical," is at the end "dismissed to his Highland fastness, left to eke out his remaining days in a struggle for a lost cause, and to be no more a protector and a guide but only a bittersweet memory." [15] Fiedler adds, "It is his own youth which the bourgeois artist is dismissing."

It is the final tribute of the white Romantic to the world of untamed nature and the id, which he can bring himself neither to live by nor disown; and the Rob Roy-Robin Hood archetype projects this ambivalence. The bourgeois world could not afford to let so apt a symbol of its divided heart die out of the literature while that division lived on; and in America in particular it throve especially, both in the form Scott gave it and in the adaptation of James Fenimore Cooper.[16]

Capote delegated the primitive, Faustian role to his heroines and, in mid-twentieth century style, dismissed one of them, Holly Golightly, to deepest Africa. Ihab Hassan describes Holly as a "whimsical child of old Faust." [17] Miss Bobbit, who "loves" the devil, fits the role even more obviously.[18] The diminution of evil evident here is one of the hallmarks of White Romanticism. Others discussed by Fiedler (and evident in Capote) are the rejection of sexual passion and of tragedy, and the tendency to react to the unpleasantness of the world with nostalgia rather than rebellion.[19]

In a recent *Playboy* interview Capote boasted, "I've never been psychoanalyzed; I've never even consulted a psychiatrist. I now consider myself a mentally healthy person. I work out all my problems in my work." [20] In having used his writing as intuitive self-therapy, Capote is perhaps as closely bound to other American writers, past and present, as he is in any other respect, though few careers manifest the stages of a therapeutic process so clearly as his. The parallel with Whitman is striking, and particularly significant in view of the latter's archetypal position in American letters. A recent commentator describes Whitman's return to his childhood surroundings in terms that fit *Other Voices, Other Rooms*: "There, not unlike Marcel Proust (and there are many similarities between these two artists), Whitman conjured up his youth and its difficult relationships with the family and the external world. Like the boy-poet in 'Out of the Cradle Endlessly Rocking,' he faced the earliest trauma of loss— the death of the mother-child relationship—and, like his poetic counterpart, became 'extatic' with the advent of understanding." [21] That Capote was to follow James and Joyce in refining his authorial self out of existence should not obscure his resemblance to the Whitman who asserted, "I am there . . . I witness the corpse with its dabbled hair, I note where the pistol has fallen." Both writers were to seek growth through a willed expansion of the ego toward universal acceptance and love.

The issue of literary immaturity and growth has been placed in a broader context by James Baldwin in this most perceptive observation: "That the tensions of American life, as well as the possibilities, are tremendous is certainly not even a question. But these are dealt with in contemporary literature mainly compulsively; that is, the book is more likely to be a symptom of our tension than an examination of it." [22] *Tensions* and *possibilities*: the two poles of American literature, as of all American experience. It is also a good description of adolescence, and the quest for maturity characteristic of that age is evident in American writing today. Baldwin, discussing the phenomenon of expatriate writers, suggests a guidepost: "Europe has what we do not have yet, a sense of the mysterious and inexorable limits of life, a sense, in a word, of tragedy. And we have what they sorely need: a new sense of life's possibilities." [23]

While past American literature amply demonstrates that artistic power is not coextensive with mental health or "adjustment" in the popular sense, still we know that art is nourished by health and wisdom—and that the artist must finally accept responsibility, for himself and even for the "nightmare" world in which he may feel he lives.

There are, of course, numerous possibilities for evasion. A dominant motif in Capote's development, as in a number of recent books by other American writers, is the effort to escape from guilt; we know, too, that a too-facile clinging to innocence has been a major national flaw—the chief weakness of the American Adam.[24] The Oedipal innocence-guilt which produces a paralyzing ambivalence must be resolved, but this can be done only by accepting the guilt, the responsibility, of rebellion. Only thus do we enter the area of mature sexuality and of tragedy. While American literature has, at its best, endured the tension of this polarity, Capote has tended to follow the favorite American side-route, most broadly definable as Platonic or Transcendental, which attempts to resolve such dualities into placid, if not ecstatic, unities. Capote's accommodation to the "real world," so explicitly intended in, and even before, his nonfiction work, does not manifest the tense ambivalence that characterizes the "accommodation" to the prevalent culture attributed by Marcus

Klein to the best of our contemporary fiction.[25] To some extent, however, his work does fit Klein's description:

The goal is the elimination of the distance between self and society, the perfect union of self and society, but the issue of this novel is at best a lesson in the perpetual necessity of killing adjustments. What is at best to be achieved in this necessary marriage is a cautionary, tentative *accommodation*, and that is the method, in this world, of social engagement. The technical term for this mood is comedy. The hero exercises his wits and thereby lives with his dilemma, and managing to live within it he proposes the possibility of living.[26]

Comedy is, indeed, the mood of Capote's most satisfying work, and the above description fits Miss Bobbit and Holly Golightly quite well, with the important difference that they must finally be made to vanish by white magic, leaving only nostalgia. Why comedy should be the mode of Capote's post-liberation period is suggested by Hassan, who bases his comments on Freud's essays on "Humor" and "The Uncanny":

The uncanny, Freud believes, derives from an animistic conception of the universe occasioned by a narcissistic overestimation of the self. Freud also characterizes humor as a triumph of the pleasure principle, and of "narcissism, the ego's victorious assertion of its own invulnerability." His essays make it evident, however, that a humorous comment, while it begins by recognizing the threat of reality—and to that extent we are justified in seeing humor as a movement toward objectivity—ends by refusing to meet the threat. Humor, therefore, is like the uncanny in that both suggest a reactionary or "regressive" impulse toward the security of the narcissistic state.[27]

Again the ambivalence is clear, while below it is a familiar unifying theme—as Hassan goes on to say: "The bulk of Capote's work persuades us . . . that both humor and the supernatural are acts of the imagination intended to question our surface evaluations of reality, and indeed to affirm the counterreality of fantasy." [28]

Other Voices, Other Rooms and some of the early stories have the nightmare's haunting power, but also its evanescence.

Aside from the beautifully self-contained memoir "A Christmas Memory," Capote has never surpassed the "slight authentic music" [29] of the comic "Children on Their Birthdays." (Whatever may be said of comedy as a means of grasping reality, in the middle range of life where most of us live we know its pleasurable and liberating effect.) *The Grass Harp* has some of the same magic but the work is less well unified, as though Capote were trying to resolve too many conflicts, prove too many points. It is the work in which he deals most literally with the relinquishment of the dream world of childhood for the real world of maturity, but in juxtaposing the two it diminishes both, caricaturing society rather perversely (though at times amusingly) and exposing too harshly the dream world's components of willful childishness and abnormality, rather than setting it entirely apart in its own magic circle—the only place such a world can exist with dignity. *Breakfast at Tiffany's* is a much more successful imposition of magic-circle unity of frame and tone, and on much less congenial material. Clear evidence of Capote's growing mastery of style and narrative technique, it will, as Norman Mailer has said, probably be one of our enduring small masterpieces. "Among the Paths to Eden" is a modest but successful blend of fantasy with a more fully humane comic spirit.

In *Cold Blood* is, of course, a very special case. A major personal achievement and a remarkable literary *tour de force*, it is, I think, in itself finally a work of rather severely limited significance, one which I prefer to view not as a crowning artistic achievement but rather as an immensely enriching artistic *exercise* whose best fruits are hopefully yet to be seen. I am inclined to agree with Hilton Kramer in seeing as a crucial flaw the book's deliberate failure to be "what the language of fiction, the medium of a significant art, always is: the refraction of a serious moral imagination." [30] A moral view does come through, as I have attempted to show, but only, as it were, accidentally—much as Perry Smith's act of murder is presented as an accident, ultimately significant only as evidence of a pathetic world view. Evil again is exorcised, this time with the aid of psychiatry. Some would read the book as densely symbolic, but it is not a symbolic novel.[31] There is symbolism here, as there is sociology, law, and so on, but the symbols are in the *events*, and would be there if the account were found in *True Detective* or even if it had not been written at all.

The appearance of the "nonfiction novel" is a significant phenomenon on the American cultural scene, and Capote is undeniably a leader in a widespread movement, the scope of which we are still trying to measure. That radical changes are taking place in the literary situation is, though overstated by McLuhan, a patent fact. Capote's assertion that "journalism is really the most avant-garde form of writing existent today" [32] has been echoed by others. It has, furthermore, been supported in practice by a number of other writers, most notably Norman Mailer. The recent shift in the literary center of gravity has been perhaps best described by Norman Podhoretz:

I did not believe . . . that fiction was the only kind of writing which deserved to be called "creative," and I did not . . . believe that the novel was at the moment the most vital form that literature was taking in America. There were young novelists around I respected—Malamud, Bellow, Flannery O'Connor, Ellison, Donleavy, the Jones of *From Here to Eternity*, and especially Mailer —but the truth was that the American books of the postwar period which had mattered to me personally, and not to me alone either, in the large way that fiction and poetry once had mattered, were not novels . . . but works the trade quaintly called "nonfiction," as though they had only a negative existence: *The Liberal Imagination, The Origins of Totalitarianism, Notes of a Native Son*, and a host of still uncollected pieces. . . . Whether or not such writings merited the honorific "literature"—and I thought they did—they, and even lesser than they, had made an impact upon my mind, imagination, and soul far greater than anything I had experienced from reading even the best of the younger American novelists. . . . The center, I thought, had shifted to them.

But where exactly was that? I would not have been able to say. Vaguely it all came together in my mind as "society," in opposition to the privatized universe of most current American fiction, with its increasingly boring emphasis on love as the be-all and end-all of life, with its narcissism, its self-pitying tones, its constricted sense of human possibility, its unearned wisdoms, its trivial emotional dramas. "Society" was *out there*: it was where everything after all was really going on; it was where *history* was being made.[33]

When the proper terms are found to describe this flight from the "unreality" of fiction, of which Podhoretz acknowledges the (typically American) naiveté, Capote will no doubt be accorded an important role in it. But, taken as evidence of the artistic stature of nonfiction, *In Cold Blood* would seem to suggest a cautious approach.

Truman Capote's insistence on a literary second chance, if viewed once more in terms of James's "The Middle Years," can appear unrealistic, a naive refusal to accept what Baldwin called "the mysterious and inexorable limits of life, the sense of tragedy." Isn't there something stubbornly adolescent in this pursuit of what are generally agreed to be unattainable ideals? What can we make of this paradoxical mixture: the troubled young man trying to grow up; the intelligent, practical, aggressive man of affairs; the dreamer with his exaggerated sense of life's possibilities? If the pattern begins to sound familiar, we mustn't be too surprised. Perhaps, after all, we can understand why this writer, with all his obvious limitations, has spoken to us so powerfully. Only in America could Truman Capote have happened. We other Americans can only wish him well.

· NOTES ·

Chapter I

1. *Life*, February 18, 1966, p. 70.
2. *New Republic*, February 9, 1959, p. 28.
3. *The Selected Writings of Truman Capote* (New York: Random House, 1963), p. vii.
4. (Philadelphia: J. B. Lippincott Company, 1960), p. 154.
5. *Current Biography*, 1951, p. 92. Much of the information in this chapter is taken from this source.
6. *The Selected Writings*, p. 198.
7. *Current Biography*, p. 92.
8. Malcolm Cowley, ed., *Writers At Work: The Paris Review Interviews* (New York: The Viking Press, 1960), p. 293.
9. Interview in *The Delta Review*, November/December, 1966, p. 7.
10. Cowley, *op. cit.*, p. 287.

Chapter II

1. *The Selected Writings of Truman Capote* (New York: Random House, 1963). Quotations from this volume are identified in the text by *S* and the page number.
2. Malcolm Cowley, ed., *Writers At Work: The Paris Review Interviews* (New York: The Viking Press, 1960), p. 290.
3. *Current Biography*, 1951, p. 93.

Chapter III

1. Truman Capote, in conversation with William L. Nance, November 9, 1966.
2. Truman Capote, recorded interview with William L. Nance, November 10, 1966.
3. (New York: Signet Books, n.d.), p. 127. Quotations from this volume are identified in the text by *OV* and the page number.

4. Malcolm Cowley, ed., *Writers At Work: The Paris Review Interviews* (New York: The Viking Press, 1960), p. 290.

CHAPTER IV

1. *The Selected Writings of Truman Capote* (New York: Random House, 1963). Quotations from this volume are identified in the text by S and the page number.
2. Malcolm Cowley, ed., *Writers At Work: The Paris Review Interviews* (New York: The Viking Press, 1960), p. 290.
3. *"The Grass Harp" and "A Tree of Night" and Other Stories* (New York: Signet Books, 1961), p. 154.
4. *Ibid.*, p. 156.
5. *Ibid.*, p. 162.
6. *Theatre Arts*, January, 1955, p. 30.
7. Truman Capote, recorded interview with William L. Nance, November 10, 1966.

CHAPTER V

1. *"The Grass Harp" and "A Tree of Night" and Other Stories* (New York: Signet Books, 1961), p. 9. Quotations from this volume will be identified in the text by G and the page number.
2. Malcolm Cowley, ed., *Writers At Work: The Paris Review Interviews* (New York: The Viking Press, 1960), p. 297.
3. Truman Capote, recorded interview with William L. Nance, November 10, 1966.
4. This statement goes beyond the immediate need to protect the gentle Dolly from an unusually harsh reality. The belief that the world is bad and private worlds are the only answer is one that Capote's fiction has always supported. At the same time, he has in recent years made an increasingly strong effort to move away from this exclusivist position.

CHAPTER VI

1. *The Selected Writings of Truman Capote* (New York: Random House, 1963), p. 162. Quotations from this volume are identified in the text by S and the page number.

2. Truman Capote, recorded interview with William L. Nance, November 10, 1966.

CHAPTER VII

1. Malcolm Cowley, ed., *Writers At Work: The Paris Review Interviews* (New York: Viking Press, 1960), p. 290.
2. *Ibid.*
3. Irving Drutman, "Capote: End of the Affair," *New York Times Drama Review*, November 20, 1966, p. 3.
4. *Ibid.*
5. *Ibid.*
6. John S. Wilson, "Building a House of Flowers," *Theatre Arts*, January, 1955, pp. 30–31.
7. Drutman, *op. cit.*
8. Wilson, *op. cit.*, p. 31.
9. *Ibid.*, pp. 31, 91.
10. *Ibid.*, p. 91.
11. *Ibid.*
12. Drutman, *op. cit.*
13. Drutman, *op. cit.*
14. *Ibid.*
15. "Faulkner Dances," *Theatre Arts*, April, 1949, p. 49.
16. Wilson, *op. cit.*, p. 91.
17. *Ibid.*
18. Cowley, *op. cit.*, p. 294.
19. Drutman, *op. cit.*
20. *Ibid.*
21. Truman Capote, recorded interview with William L. Nance, November 10, 1966.
22. George Plimpton, "The Story Behind a Nonfiction Novel," *New York Times Book Review*, January 16, 1966, p. 2.
23. Cowley, *op. cit.*, p. 292.
24. Jane Howard, "How the 'Smart Rascal' Brought It Off," *Life*, February 18, 1966, pp. 75–76.
25. Plimpton, *op. cit.*, p. 2.
26. Howard, *op. cit.*, p. 76.
27. Truman Capote, in conversation with William L. Nance, November 9, 1966.
28. Norman Mailer, *Advertisements for Myself* (New York: G. P. Putnam's Sons, 1959), p. 465.
29. Barbara Long, "In Cold Comfort," *Esquire*, June, 1966, p. 173.
30. *Ibid.*
31. Cowley, *op. cit.*, p. 285.

32. Howard, *op. cit.*, p. 75.
33. See "Come With Mr. Capote to a Masked Ball," *Life*, December 9, 1966, p. 107.
34. Associated Press account, November, 1966.
35. "Come With Mr. Capote. . . ."
36. Jane Howard, "A Host With a Genius for Jarring Juxtapositions," *Life*, December 9, 1966, p. 117.
37. *Ibid.*
38. "Truman's Compote," *Time*, December 9, 1966, p. 90.
39. *Ibid.*
40. "A Nonfictional Visit With Truman Capote," *Life*, February 18, 1966, p. 22.
41. "Truman's Compote," p. 88.
42. Long, *op. cit.*, p. 127.
43. *Ibid.*, p. 124.
44. " 'In Cold Blood' . . . An American Tragedy," *Newsweek*, January 24, 1966, p. 63.
45. Long, *op. cit.*, p. 181.
46. *Ibid.*
47. *Ibid.*, p. 126.
48. " 'In Cold Blood' . . . An American Tragedy."
49. The phenomenon has become decidedly less rare in recent years. Styron's *The Confessions of Nat Turner* and Roth's *Portnoy's Complaint* are among the serious literary works that have recently brought their authors great wealth. In *Making It* (New York: Random House, 1968), Norman Podhoretz defends such blending of artistic and financial success.
50. Long, *op. cit.*, p. 173.
51. *Ibid.*, p. 176.
52. *Ibid.*, pp. 178, 179.
53. *Ibid.*, p. 181.

Chapter VIII

1. George Plimpton, "The Story Behind a Nonfiction Novel," *New York Times Book Review*, January 16, 1966, p. 2.
2. Haskel Frankel, "The Author," *Saturday Review*, January 22, 1966, p. 37.
3. Plimpton, *op. cit.*, p. 2.
4. Jonathan Baumbach, *The Landscape of Nightmare: Studies in the Contemporary Novel* (New York University Press, 1965), p. vii.
5. *Ibid.*, p. 35.
6. Quoted from an undated newspaper account.

7. Plimpton, *op. cit.*, p. 2.
8. *Ibid.*, p. 3.
9. Jane Howard, "How the 'Smart Rascal' Brought It Off," *Life*, February 18, 1966, p. 75.
10. Plimpton, *op. cit.*, p. 41.
11. Truman Capote, recorded interview with William L. Nance, November 10, 1966.
12. Plimpton, *op. cit.*, p. 3.
13. "Romance With Reality," *Newsweek*, February 5, 1962, p. 85.
14. Frankel, *op. cit.*, p. 37.
15. Malcolm Cowley, ed., *Writers At Work: The Paris Review Interviews* (New York: The Viking Press, 1960), p. 293.
16. Barbara Long, "In Cold Comfort," *Esquire*, June, 1966, p. 179.
17. " 'In Cold Blood' . . . An American Tragedy," *Newsweek*, January 24, 1966, p. 60.
18. Long, *op. cit.*, p. 178.
19. Plimpton, *op. cit.*, p. 3.
20. Howard, *op. cit.*, p. 70.
21. *In Cold Blood* (New York: Random House, 1965), p. 3. Quotations from this volume are identified in the text by C and the page number.
22. Howard, *op. cit.*, p. 70.
23. " 'In Cold Blood' . . . An American Tragedy," pp. 60–61.
24. Howard, *op. cit.*, p. 70.
25. " 'In Cold Blood' . . . An American Tragedy," p. 61.
26. "In a Novel Way," *Time*, October 8, 1965, p. 74.
27. Howard, *op. cit.*, p. 76.
28. " 'In Cold Blood' . . . An American Tragedy," p. 61.
29. *Ibid.*
30. "The Country Below the Surface," *Time*, January 21, 1966, p. 83.
31. Cowley, *op. cit.*, p. 286.
32. Howard, *op. cit.*, p. 70.
33. " 'In Cold Blood' . . . An American Tragedy," p. 61.
34. Plimpton, *op. cit.*, p. 3.
35. *Ibid.*
36. Long, *op. cit.*, p. 178.
37. Plimpton, *op. cit.*, p. 3.
38. Howard, *op. cit.*, p. 70.
39. *Ibid.*, p. 71.
40. *Ibid.*, pp. 70–71.
41. *Ibid.*, p. 71.
42. " 'In Cold Blood' . . . An American Tragedy," p. 61.
43. *Ibid.*
44. *Ibid.*

45. *London Observer*, quoted in *Kansas City Star*, March 17, 1966.
46. Frankel, *op. cit.*, p. 37.
47. Don Lee Keith, "Capote's Tiffany Touch," *The Delta Review*, November/December, 1966, p. 7.
48. Cowley, *op. cit.*, p. 291.
49. *Ibid.*
50. Plimpton, *op. cit.*, p. 42.
51. *Kansas City Times*, January 27, 1966, p. 8a.
52. Howard, *op. cit.*, p. 71.
53. Plimpton, *op. cit.*, p. 38.
54. *Ibid.*
55. Howard, *op. cit.*, p. 72.
56. Frankel, *op. cit.*, p. 37.
57. *Ibid.*
58. Keith, *op. cit.*, pp. 6, 7.
59. Howard, *op. cit.*, p. 72.
60. *Ibid.*
61. Keith, *op. cit.*, p. 7.
62. Howard, *op. cit.*, p. 70.
63. *Ibid.*
64. Plimpton, *op. cit.*, p. 38.
65. Long, *op. cit.*, p. 124.
66. Plimpton, *op. cit.*, pp. 2, 3.
67. Nance interview.
68. Plimpton, *op. cit.*, p. 38.
69. Nance interview.
70. Plimpton, *op. cit.*, p. 38.
71. *Ibid.*
72. Preface to *Roderick Hudson*. In R. P. Blackmur, ed., *The Art of the Novel* (New York: Charles Scribner's Sons, 1937), p. 5.
73. Plimpton, *op. cit.*, p. 39.
74. *Ibid.*, p. 38.
75. Nance interview.

CHAPTER IX

1. Truman Capote, recorded interview with William L. Nance, November 10, 1966.
2. Malcolm Cowley, ed., *Writers At Work: The Paris Review Interviews* (New York: The Viking Press, 1960), p. 293.
3. Dwight Macdonald, "Cosa Nostra," *Esquire*, April, 1966, pp. 44, 46.

4. Truman Capote, in conversation with William L. Nance, November 9, 1966.
5. Rebecca West, "A Grave and Reverend Book," *Harper's*, February, 1966, p. 108.
6. George Plimpton, "The Story Behind a Nonfiction Novel," *New York Times Book Review*, January 16, 1966, p. 39.
7. Truman Capote, in conversation with William L. Nance, November 9, 1966.
8. Nance interview.
9. *Ibid.* While the most striking resemblance is to Tico Feo, the guitar-playing wanderer imprisoned for knifing two men, the relationship goes much further, as suggested by Tico Feo's own resemblance to other Capote characters.
10. " 'In Cold Blood' . . . An American Tragedy," *Newsweek*, January 24, 1966, p. 63.
11. *Ibid.*
12. *Ibid.*
13. Plimpton, *op. cit.*, p. 41.
14. "In Cold Fact," *Esquire*, June, 1966, p. 171.
15. *Ibid.*, p. 170.
16. *Ibid.*, pp. 166, 167.
17. *Ibid.*, p. 167.
18. *Ibid.*, p. 171.
19. Nance interview.
20. *Ibid.*

CHAPTER X

1.

1. January 24, 1966, p. 62.
2. Truman Capote, in conversation with William L. Nance, November 9, 1966.
3. Truman Capote, recorded interview with William L. Nance, November 10, 1966.
4. *Ibid.*
5. *Ibid.*
6. *Ibid.*
7. *Ibid.*
8. *Ibid.*
9. *Ibid.*
10. *Georgia Review*, XII (1958), p. 151.
11. *Ibid.*, p. 164.
12. Nance interview.
13. *Ibid.*

14. *Ibid.*
15. *Ibid.*
16. *Newsweek*, January 24, 1966, pp. 62–63.
17. Baldanza, *op. cit.*, p. 154.
18. *Esquire*, April, 1966.
19. *Newsweek*, January 24, 1966, p. 63.

2.

1. Ihab Hassan expressed a similar expectation for Capote in *Radical Innocence: The Contemporary American Novel* (Princeton University Press, 1961), p. 258, citing "the growth of his vision and the evolution of his more dramatic style." As Robert K. Morris has observed, *In Cold Blood* was a remarkable, if oblique, fulfillment of the prophecy. See Morris' essay, "Capote's Imagery," in Irving Malin, ed., *Truman Capote's "In Cold Blood": A Critical Handbook* (Belmont, California: Wadsworth Publishing Company, 1968), p. 177.
2. "Truman Capote: The Revelation of the Broken Image," in Malin, *op. cit.*, p. 142.
3. See, for example, Louise Y. Gossett, *Violence in Recent Southern Fiction* (Durham: Duke University Press, 1965), and Mark Schorer, "Carson McCullers and Truman Capote," in *The World We Imagine* (New York: Farrar, Straus and Giroux, 1968), pp. 274–296.
4. As Leslie Fiedler has said, "The turning of the modern novel from mythology to psychology, from a body of communal story to the mind of the individual is an enterprise typical of our times. Indeed, only in the sub-mind of a dreaming man can we discover images common to everyone in our multifarious culture; and these images, though not traditional mythology, are myth in the profoundest sense of the word." *Love and Death in the American Novel* (New York: Stein and Day, 1966), p. 40.
5. *After the Lost Generation* (New York: The Noonday Press, 1958), pp. 216ff.
6. Hassan finds this stricture of Aldridge's too severe, seeing in it (mistakenly, I believe) a demand for greater literal realism. Nevertheless he is helpful in suggesting that "if the novel sometimes appears to be a 'concoction' rather than a 'synthesis' it is perhaps because the job of dramatic resolution is surrendered to ambience and verbal magic." Hassan, too, admits that "other novels seem to us greater." *Radical Innocence*, pp. 244–245.
7. *Writers at Work*, p. 293.

8. *Love and Death in the American Novel,* p. 344.
9. For this formulation I am indebted to Mr. E. S. Moffett.
10. Recent remarks made by Capote.
11. Earl Rovit, in his *Saul Bellow* (Minneapolis: University of Minnesota Press, 1967), pp. 23–24, discusses Bellow's use of Capote's habitual form, the "autobiographical tale narrated in retrospect," showing its close kinship to the essentially solipsistic journal form.
12. See Roy Harvey Pearce, "Robin Molineux on the Analyst's Couch: A Note on the Limits of Psychoanalytic Criticism," in Irving Malin, ed., *Psychoanalysis and American Fiction* (New York: E. P. Dutton & Co., 1965), p. 315.
13. "Real Gardens with Real Toads," *The New Leader,* January 31, 1966, p. 18.
14. Fiedler's glib discussion of Capote and his Southern contemporaries is one of the less satisfactory parts of his book.
15. Fiedler, *op. cit.,* p. 178.
16. *Ibid.,* pp. 178–179.
17. *Radical Innocence,* p. 253.
18. Even in this move Capote has the precedent not only of James but of Hawthorne (himself a considerable evader), for, as Fiedler recalls, our first Faust was the woman Hester Prynne (*op. cit.,* p. 442).
19. Fiedler, *op. cit.,* p. 163.
20. March, 1968, p. 53.
21. Edwin H. Miller, *Walt Whitman's Poetry: A Psychological Journey* (Boston: Houghton Mifflin Company, 1968), p. 14.
22. *Nobody Knows My Name* (New York: Dell Publishing Co., 1961), p. 22.
23. *Ibid.,* p. 23.
24. "Innocence," as applied to American literature, has inevitably become a highly ambiguous word. For example, Ihab Hassan chose the title *Radical Innocence* for his study of the contemporary American novel, applying the term to a composite character, some of whose qualities resemble the health and maturity of which I have spoken. More to the present point: it seems that in the recent trend toward "nonfiction" writing (to be discussed below), one of the deeper motives has been to evoke and dispel guilt—perhaps even the novelist's "guilt" at moving outside the traditional barriers. Along with *In Cold Blood,* Malamud's *The Fixer* and Styron's *The Confessions of Nat Turner* come to mind. Norman Podhoretz, a leading advocate of a broader interpretation of "literature," organized his autobiographi-

cal account, *Making It,* around his liberating renunciation of guilt at his own success in the literary world. The conclusions he comes to are reminiscent of the advice Holly Golightly gave her young writer friend. A germinal study of innocence in American literature is R. W. B. Lewis's *The American Adam: Innocence, Tragedy and Tradition in the Nineteenth Century* (The University of Chicago Press, 1955).

25. *After Alienation: American Novels in Mid-Century* (Cleveland: The World Publishing Company, 1964). Capote is not among the novelists chosen by Klein for extended discussion.
26. Klein, *op. cit.,* p. 30.
27. Hassan, *op. cit.,* p. 234.
28. *Ibid.,* p. 235.
29. The phrase is Leslie Fiedler's, *op. cit.,* p. 477.
30. Kramer, *op. cit.,* p. 18.
31. William Phillips refers to the delight which "most of the reviewers" seemed to take in the "moral symbolism" of *In Cold Blood*. See "But Is It Good for Literature?" in Malin, ed., *Truman Capote's "In Cold Blood": A Critical Handbook,* p. 104. Melvin J. Friedman seems to take for granted the book's symbolic character. He says, for example, "Several of the more inspired reviewers of *In Cold Blood* realized . . . that [Capote] was now entering a more authentically American tradition of story-telling than any revealed in his earlier work. . . . We can now begin using such literary catchphrases as 'Adamic myth' to explain Capote, just as we've used them up to now to explain the 'great tradition' in American fiction from Cooper to Hawthorne through William Styron." See "Towards an Aesthetic," also in the Malin handbook, p. 165. Friedman is thinking particularly of the parallel between Capote's killers and Huck Finn. Capote has a place in the American tradition, but not on these grounds.
32. *Playboy, op. cit.,* p. 56.
33. *Making It* (New York: Bantam Books, 1969), pp. 193–194. Robert Langbaum has helped to set the nonfiction trend in perspective: "Mr. Capote has pinpointed with his phrase, 'nonfiction novel,' a series of questions that have been going the rounds in literary discussions since World War II. With the decline of the novel since the war, critical and discursive writing has so often seemed bolder and more imaginative than fiction as to make us feel that the line between so-called creative and noncreative writing

is not so easily discernible as we used to think. The New Critics have also taught us since the war to give more weight to the actual structure of a work than to the circumstances that brought it into being. Once we look at structure, we find many nonfiction works as artful and sometimes more artful than many novels. Northrop Frye has, in his influential *Anatomy of Criticism*, gone so far as to apply the word *fiction* to any 'work of art in prose.' " See "Capote's Nonfiction Novel," in the Malin handbook, pp. 114–115.

INDEX

Abnormal(ity), 17, 41, 52, 94, 218-
220, 237
See also Grotesque(s)
Acceptance, 18, 110, 119, 123, 220,
223
fear as failure of, 22
in *Grass Harp,* 96-97, 102-103
as meaning of love, 17
See also Love
in *Other Voices, Other Rooms,* 17,
41, 43, 48, 50, 56, 58, 60, 62,
63
of reality, 38
Accommodation, social engagement
and, 235-236
Adamov, Josef, 139
Agee, James, 13
Aldridge, John W., 230
Alexander, Shana, 151
Alienation, 90, 156-157
"Among the Paths to Eden," 65, 83-
87, 104, 237
theme, characters, and symbolism,
83-87
Amory, Cleveland, 150, 151
Amy (in *Other Voices, Other
Rooms*), 43-44, 46, 47, 53, 55
Andrews, Lowell Lee, 184
Answered Prayers, 141
Appleseed (in "Jug of Silver"), 72,
82
Arlen, Harold, 75, 128, 129
As I Lay Dying (Faulkner), 130
Avery, William, 202
Awbrey, Stuart, 165

Bailey, Pearl, 128
Balanchine, George, 128
Baldanza, Frank, 221-222, 227
Baldwin, James, 235, 239
Baumbach, Jonathan, 155-156
"Beast in the Jungle, The" (James),
231
Beat the Devil (movie), 131-132
Beaton, Cecil, 149

Bell, Joe (in *Breakfast at Tiffany's*),
108, 110, 114, 116, 122
Belli, Ivor (in "Among the Paths to
Eden"), 83-87
Bellow, Saul, 157-158, 177, 238, 248
Berman, O. J. (in *Breakfast at Tiffany's*), 112, 114-115, 122
Bettis, Valerie, 130
Billy Bob (in "Children on Their
Birthdays"), 66, 67, 68, 69-
70, 71, 225
Black and White Masked Ball, 149-
152
Bobbit, Miss Lily Jane (in "Chil-
dren on Their Birthdays"),
65-71, 72, 73, 82, 94, 98,
110, 111, 113, 221, 223, 234
Brando, Marlon, 142-144, 151
Breakfast at Tiffany's, 9, 10, 12, 65,
83, 93, 107-124, 130, 140,
141, 145, 148, 153, 225, 227,
229, 232
movie version of, 132
theme, characters, and symbolism,
107-124, 237
Breen, Robert, 136, 137, 138-139
Brook, Peter, 128, 129
Brooklyn Heights, 145-149
Brooks, Richard, 132
Buddy (in "A Christmas Memory"),
78-83, 88
Buster, Reverend and Mrs. (in *Grass
Harp*), 93, 94, 101

Candle, Sheriff Junius (in *Grass
Harp*), 93
Capote, Truman
birth, childhood, parents, biographical data, 11-15, 40ff., 107,
145ff.
born Truman Streckfus Persons, 12
education, 13-14
physical description of, 10, 14-15
"Capote: End of the Affairs," 130
Cerf, Bennett, 152, 165

Change (growth), 60-62, 125-126, 143, 156, 217, 222, 228-239
See also Childhood (and maturity); Deceptiveness; specific works
Childhood (and maturity), 71ff., 97-106, 125, 126, 218ff., 231, 234ff.
in *Other Voices, Other Rooms*, 40-64
See also Change (growth); specific works
"Children on Their Birthdays," 65-72, 73, 88, 223, 224, 225, 232
theme, characters, and symbolism, 65-72
"Christmas Memory, A," 12, 41, 65, 78-83, 88, 107, 210, 223, 226-227
comedy in, 237
theme, characters, and symbolism, 78-83
TV production of, 132
Clare, Myrtle, 164
Cloud Hotel (in *Other Voices, Other Rooms*), 47-48, 49-50, 54, 55, 61, 63
Clutter, Bonnie, 170, 192, 201, 206
Clutter, Herbert, 170, 172, 191, 192, 200, 213-214, 227
Clutter, Kenyon, 170, 192
Clutter, Nancy, 168, 170ff., 179ff., 187-188, 192, 201, 203, 206, 208-209, 210, 224
Clutter murders, 159-185, 186-215, 226-228
See also *In Cold Blood;* specific family members by name
Collin, see Fenwick, Collin
Comedy (humor), 236-237
Cool, Judge Charlie (in *Grass Harp*), 93, 94-98, 100, 102-103, 106, 221
Cooper, James Fenimore, 234
Cooper, Rosa (in "Shut a Final Door"), 30, 31
Copland, Aaron, 127
County, Mr. and Mrs. (in *Grass Harp*), 99-100
Cox, Wally, 151
"Crazy," see Abnormal(ity); Grotesque(s)

Creek, Catherine (in *Grass Harp*), 89, 92, 94, 98-99, 105
Crime, 158ff.
See also *In Cold Blood;* Morality; Violence

Daisy Miller (James), 232
Dean, James, 144
Death, 26, 58, 59, 60, 61-62, 82-83, 106, 121, 123, 230, 233
Deceptiveness, 31, 51, 62-63
Destronelli, Mr. (in "Headless Hawk"), 24, 25, 27-28, 39
Dewey, Alvin, 164, 168, 171, 187, 190, 193, 202-203, 206-207, 208-209, 210, 213, 227
Dewey, Marie (Mrs. Alvin Dewey), 164, 189, 190, 191
"Diamond Guitar, A," 65, 73-75
theme, characters, and symbolism, 73-75
Disappearance (theme), 49, 58, 63
D.J. (in "Headless Hawk"), 23-29, 31, 33
Documentary novels, 177ff.
Dreams (dreamers; dreaming), 26, 31, 43, 48, 72, 78
in *Breakfast at Tiffany's*, 107, 124,
as characteristic motif, 17, 38, 74, 218-219, 225, 232, 237, 239
in "Children on Their Birthdays," 66
in *Grass Harp*, 88ff., 94ff., 102, 237
heroines-dreamers, 79, 83-87, 107-124, 222, 226
See also specific characters, works
in "Master Misery," 33-39, 226
Drutman, Irving, 130, 132
"Duke in His Domain, The," 142-144, 151
Dunphy, Jack, 135, 166

Eccentricity, see Abnormal(ity); Grotesque(s)
Esquire magazine, 212-215
Estelle (in "Master Misery"), 33, 35
Europe, Capote in, 126, 129, 133-140
Everyman Opera, Incorporated, 136, 138, 141
Ewalt, Nancy, 170
Exorcism, 232, 237

252

Father (and mother) figures, 40, 42, 44, 55ff., 219-220, 231, 233, 234
Faulkner, William, 12, 73, 130, 157, 230
  Sound and the Fury by, 230
Fenwick, Collin (in *Grass Harp*), 88-106, 107, 125, 126, 127, 225-226
Fiedler, Leslie, 231, 233-234, 247
Fox, Manny (in "Children on Their Birthdays"), 69
Frankel, Haskel, 161
Freedom, 27, 38, 39, 41, 63-64, 71, 96, 101, 110
Freud, Sigmund, essays on "Humor" and "The Uncanny" by, 236
Friedman, Melvin J., 249
Friendship, 29, 96-97, 149, 153, 164, 179, 224
  See also Acceptance: Love

Gish, Dorothy and Lillian, 126
Golightly, Doc (in *Breakfast at Tiffany's*), 116-117
Golightly, Holly (in *Breakfast at Tiffany's*), 12, 65, 83, 93, 104, 108-124, 224, 225, 229, 234
Graham, Kay, 150
Grass Harp, The, 9, 10, 22, 65, 83, 88-106, 125, 135
  stage version of, 127-128, 131
  theme, characters, and symbolism, 88-106, 21-, 225-226, 227, 228
Green, Logan, 201
Green Witch, 14
Greenwich High School, 13
Grotesque(s), 16, 18, 24, 44, 53
Growth, *see* Change (growth); Childhood (and maturity)
Guilt (and innocence), 26, 233, 235, 248
Guitars, 140
  See also "Diamond Guitar, A"

Haiti, 75-78, 128
Hassan, Ihab, 234, 236, 247, 248
"Headless Hawk, The," 16, 22, 30, 107, 148
  theme, characters and symbolism, 23-29

Henderson, Riley (in *Grass Harp*), 92-93, 95, 96, 98-99, 101-102, 105, 127
Hendricks, Larry, 184, 189
Heroines, 65ff., 83-87, 221, 222-224, 232, 234
  dreamer-heroines, 79, 83-87, 107-124
  See also specific characters, works
Hickock, Dick, 171-185, 186ff., 197, 198-215
  described; personality of, 198-200, 203, 206
  execution of, 201-203
  trial of, 200-201
Hitchcock, Alfred, 228
Holiday magazine, 155
Homer Honey (in *Grass Harp*), 100-101, 102
Homosexuality, 74-75, 233
"House of Flowers," 65, 75-78, 133
  as musical, 128-130
  theme, characters, and symbolism, 75-78
"House on the Heights, A," 145-149
Humor, *see* Comedy (humor)
Huston, John, 131-132

Identity, 41, 45, 48, 52, 53, 62, 63, 96-98, 123, 231
In Cold Blood, 9, 10, 11, 12, 17, 135, 150, 152, 155-185, 186-215, 217-219, 223, 224, 225, 225-228, 229
  accuracy, credibility, objectivity, 178-185, 215
  appraisal of, 237-239
  choice of subject; construction and style of, 155-185, 186ff., 210-215
Innocence (and guilt), 26, 233, 235, 248
Innocents, The (movie), 132
Irving (in "Shut a Final Door"), 30
"Ischia" (sketch), 133, 134-135

James, Henry, 79, 132, 182, 216, 230-232, 234, 239
Joel, *see* Knox, Joel Harrison
Johnson, June Bug, 70-71, 223
Jones, Dr. W. Mitchell, 195-196, 199
Journalism, 141ff., 155ff., 178, 217, 224, 238

Joyce, James, 183, 230, 234
"Jug of Silver," 72

Kazan, Elia, 143
Kay (in "Tree of Night"), 18-19, 20, 22, 23
Kennedy, Jackie, 150, 152, 165
Kidwell, Susan, 168, 170, 208-209, 224
Klein, Marcus, 235-236
Knapp, George, 146-147
Knox, Joel Harrison (in *Other Voices, Other Rooms*), 41-63, 71, 74, 88, 90, 93-94, 96, 99, 102, 103, 110, 113, 220-222, 230
Kramer, Hilton, 233

Landscape of Nightmare, The (Baumbach), 156
Lazarus, 18, 19
Lee, Edwin, 12
Lee, Harper, 11, 12, 70, 141, 162-163, 164, 165-166, 171, 219, 223, 224, 228
Lehrman, Leo, 149
Levine, Paul, 229
Life magazine, 135, 141, 149, 158, 166, 174
Little Sunshine (in *Other Voices, Other Rooms*), 47-48, 54, 58, 59-60, 63
Local Color, 133
Long, Barbara, 152, 177
Love, 23, 29, 30, 76, 233
 in *Breakfast at Tiffany's*, 116, 118-119, 123
 as central concern in Capote's work, 17, 22, 23, 224, 234, 238
 in *Grass Harp*, 95, 96-98, 102-104, 105
 in *Other Voices, Other Rooms*, 41, 46, 49, 50, 59, 62-63, 220-222
 See also Acceptance; Friendship; Sex (sexuality)
Love and Death in the American Novel (Fiedler), 233

McCain, James, 164
McCullers, Carson, 12, 221, 227, 229

Macdonald, Dwight, 188, 227-228
M'Naghten Rule, 195
Mademoiselle magazine, 14, 154
Mailer, Norman, 10, 141, 150, 177, 238
"Master Misery," 16, 90, 121, 128-129, 226
 theme, characters, and symbolism, 32-38, 39
Maturity, *see* Change (growth); Childhood (and maturity)
Meier, Wendle, 207, 213
Meier, Mrs. Wendle (Josephine; "Josie"), 207, 213
Melville, Herman, 233
 Moby Dick by, 230
Metaphors, symbolism and, 230
"Middle Years, The" (James), 216, 231, 239
Miller, Mrs. H. T. (in "Miriam"), 20-22, 23, 27
"Miriam," 14, 16, 22, 23, 27, 32, 219, 221
 theme, characters, and symbolism, 20-22, 39
Mitchell, Joseph, 177
Monroeville, Alabama, 12-13
Morality (moral viewpoint), 101, 117-124, 221, 227-228, 237
Morris, Robert K., 247
Mother (and father) figures, 40, 42, 44, 55ff., 219-220, 231, 233, 234
 See also specific characters, works
Movie adaptations, 131-132
"Murder Without Apparent Motive —A Study in Personality Disorganization (Satten)," 199
Muses Are Heard, The, 79, 132, 136-140, 144, 155, 161, 162, 169, 182, 227
Musical adaptations, 128-130, 133

Narcissism, 71, 236, 239
"New Orleans" (sketch), 133, 134
New Orleans, Louisiana, 12, 40, 61, 133, 134
New Republic magazine, 10
New York Times, 130, 155
New Yorker magazine, 14, 40, 124, 136, 142, 155, 162
Newsweek magazine, 152, 161, 162, 216

Nonfiction novel, the, 28, 83, 124, 126, 133, 155ff., 176ff., 186ff., 212, 216ff., 228ff., 238-239
Noon City (in *Other Voices, Other Rooms*), 41, 42, 51

Oedipal innocence-guilt, 230, 233, 235
Old Bonaparte (in "House of Flowers"), 77-78
"Old Mr. Busybody," 13
O'Meaghan, Mary (in "Among the Paths to Eden"), 83-87
Oreilly (in "Master Misery"), 34-35, 36-37
Orlov, 139-140
Other Voices, Other Rooms, 9, 12, 16, 17, 22, 28, 70, 71-72, 88, 90, 96, 97, 215, 216, 234
    theme, characters, and symbolism, 40-63, 71-72, 216, 219-223, 225, 226, 230-232, 236
Ottilie (in "House of Flowers"), 76-78

Paris Review interview, 22, 88, 135, 147, 161, 165, 169, 230
Phillips, William, 249
Platonism, 221-222, 223, 224, 227, 235
Plimpton, George, 160, 170, 180, 211-212
Podhoretz, Norman, 238-239, 243, 248-249
Poe, Edgar Allan, 12, 22, 140
Porgy and Bess, 79, 136-140, 169
Port-au-Prince, Haiti, 75-78
Porter, Katherine Anne, 12
Preacher Star (in "Children on Their Birthdays"), 66, 67, 68, 69-70
Proust, Marcel, 234

Quintero, José, 128

Radical Innocence: The Contemporary American Novel (Hassan), 247, 248
Random House, 14
Randolph (in *Other Voices, Other Rooms*), 43, 45-46, 50, 52-53, 55, 57, 58-59, 60-61, 62, 63,

71-72, 96, 97, 216, 220, 221, 231-232
Ranny, Walter (in "Shut a Final Door"), 29-32, 87
Reality, 71, 72, 88ff., 95ff., 178, 217, 222, 225, 228, 235, 238-239
    See also Dreams
Revercomb, A. F. (in "Master Misery"), 33-38, 39, 42
"Ride Through Spain, A" (sketch), 132, 133-134
Riordan, Maude (in *Grass Harp*), Ross, Lillian, 155, 177
Ritz, Dr. Morris (in *Grass Harp*), 91, 99
Rosalba Cat (in "Children on Their Birthdays"), 67, 68
Ross, Lillian, 155, 177
Rovit, Earl, 248
Royal Bonaparte (in "House of Flowers"), 76-78
Rupp, Bobby, 170, 179, 189, 190, 208
Russia, Capote in, 136-140, 141

Saint-Subber, Arnold, 128
Sansom, Edward R. (in *Other Voices, Other Rooms*), 41, 42, 46, 47, 49, 50, 53, 54, 55-56, 58, 61, 62, 63
Satten, Dr. Joseph, 181, 199-200
Saturday Review interview, 161
Sayonara (movie), 142
Schaeffer, Mr. (in "Diamond Guitar"), 73-75
Schorer, Mark, 11
Scott, Sir Walter, *Rob Roy* by, 233-234
Selected Writings, 11, 17, 133
Sex (sexuality), 32-33, 51-52, 56, 59, 68, 74, 97, 117-124, 157, 211, 220-221, 233, 234
    See also Homosexuality, Love; specific characters, works
Shapiro, Henry, 137-138
Shawn, William, 162
"Shut a Final Door," 16, 22, 107
    theme, characters, and symbolism, 29-32
Sister Ida (in *Grass Harp*), 100-102
Skully's Landing (in *Other Voices, Other Rooms*), 41ff., 63, 222, 225

Smith, Barbara, 197-198
Smith, Oliver, 145, 146
Smith, Perry, 171-185, 186ff., 189-215, 218-219
  background and family of, 196-198, 201
  Capote and, 14, 218-220, 221, 224, 227, 228
  described; character and personality of, 195-200, 203ff., 215
  trial and execution of, 200-203
Smith, Tex John, 196-197, 205
Spain, 133-134
Stimson, Anna (in "Shut a Final Door"), 29, 30-31, 32
Stoecklein, Alfred, 170
Streetcar Named Desire, A, 143
Styron, William, *Confessions of Nat Turner* by, 243, 248
Sylvia (in "Master Misery"), 33ff., 219, 221
Symbolism, 17, 28ff., 39, 63-64, 222, 227, 230, 232-234, 237-238
  metaphor and, 230
  See also specific kinds, works
Sympathy (tenderness), 103-104, 105, 226

Talbo, Dolly (in *Grass Harp*), 83, 88, 89-106, 109, 127, 210, 221-222, 226
Talbo, Verena (in *Grass Harp*), 89-106
Taormina, 135
Tate, Judge Roland, 194, 201, 208
"Tell-Tale Heart, The" (Poe), 12
Theatre (plays), Capote and, 126-133
Theatre Arts interview, 128, 131
Thompkins, Idabel (in *Other Voices, Other Rooms*), 11, 43, 47, 48, 50-58, 61, 63, 70, 72, 221, 223, 232
Thompson, Virgil, 128
Thoreau, Henry, 175, 221
Tico Feo (in "Diamond Guitar"), 73-75, 118
Time magazine, 151, 153, 165

To Kill a Mockingbird (Lee), 11, 141, 223
Tomato, Sally (in *Breakfast at Tiffany's*), 110-111, 120
Tompkins, Phillip K., 212-215
Tragedy (tragic view), sense of, 227, 234, 235, 239
  See also Death; Victims
Transcendentalism, 221-222, 235
Travelers (traveling), *see* Wanderers (travelers)
Trawler, Rusty (in *Breakfast at Tiffany's*), 113, 114, 117
"Tree of Night, A," 16, 17-19, 20, 22, 32, 133
  theme, characters, and symbolism, 17-19, 20, 22, 32
Tynan, Kenneth, 168

Valenzuela, Rudy, 164
Verbier, Switzerland, 135
Victims (victimization), 28, 38, 74, 96, 210, 218, 223, 227
Violence, 161ff., 203ff.

Wanderers (travelers), 65, 71, 93ff., 112, 123
  See also specific characters, works
Waters, Vincent (in "Headless Hawk"), 22, 23-29
Wells, Floyd, 172, 190
Welty, Eudora, 12
West, Duane, 213
West, Rebecca, 155, 177, 203
Whitman, Walt, 234
White Romanticism, 233-234
Wildwood, Mag (in *Breakfast at Tiffany's*), 113, 114, 117, 118
Willie-Jay, 198
Winn, Janet, 10
Wisteria, Miss (in *Other Voices, Other Rooms*), 56-57, 62, 66
Wolfe, Thomas, 13
Wood, Catherine, 14

Zoo ("Missouri Fever"; in *Other Voices, Other Rooms*), 44, 45, 47, 48-49, 51-52, 53-54, 59, 61, 63